Palestine in the World

SOAS Palestine Studies

This book series aims at promoting innovative research in the study of Palestine, Palestinians and the Israel Palestine conflict as a crucial component of Middle Eastern and world politics. The first ever Western academic series entirely dedicated to this topic, *SOAS Palestine Studies* draws from a variety of disciplinary fields, including history, politics, media, visual arts, social anthropology, and development studies. The series is published under the academic direction of the Centre for Palestine Studies (CPS) at the London Middle East Institute (LMEI) of SOAS, University of London.

Series Editor:
Dina Matar, PhD, Chair, Centre for Palestine Studies, and Reader in Political Communication, Centre for Global Media and Communications, SOAS
Adam Hanieh, PhD, Reader in Development Studies and Advisory Committee Member for Centre for Palestine Studies, SOAS

Board Advisor:
Hassan Hakimian, Director of the London Middle East Institute at SOAS

Current and Forthcoming Titles:

Palestine Ltd.: Neoliberalism and Nationalism in the Occupied Territory, Toufic Haddad

Palestinian Literature in Exile: Gender, Aesthetics and Resistance in the Short Story, Joseph R. Farag

Palestinian Citizens of Israel: Power, Resistance and the Struggle for Space, Sharri Plonski

Representing Palestine Media and Journalism in Australia Since World War I, Peter Manning

Folktales of Palestine: Cultural Identity, Memory and the Politics of Storytelling, Farah Aboubakr

Dialogue in Palestine: The People-to-People Diplomacy Programme and the Israeli-Palestinian Conflict, Nadia Naser-Najjab

Palestinian Youth Activism in the Internet Age: Social Media and Networks after the Arab Spring, Albana Dwonch

Palestinian National Movement in Lebanon, Erling Sogge

The Jewish Agency and Syria during the Arab Revolt: Secret Meetings and Negotiations, Mahmoud Muhareb

Palestine in the World: International Solidarity with the Palestinian Liberation Movement, Sorcha Thomson and Pelle Valentin Olsen

Palestine in the World

International Solidarity with the Palestinian Liberation Movement

Edited by
Sorcha Thomson and Pelle Valentin Olsen

BLOOMSBURY ACADEMIC
LONDON • NEW YORK • OXFORD • NEW DELHI • SYDNEY

I.B. TAURIS
Bloomsbury Publishing Plc
50 Bedford Square, London, WC1B 3DP, UK
1385 Broadway, New York, NY 10018, USA
29 Earlsfort Terrace, Dublin 2, Ireland

BLOOMSBURY, I.B. TAURIS and the I.B. Tauris logo are trademarks of
Bloomsbury Publishing Plc

First published in Great Britain 2023
Paperback edition first published 2024

Copyright © Sorcha Thomson and Pelle Valentin Olsen 2023

Sorcha Thomson and Pelle Valentin Olsen have asserted their right under the Copyright, Designs and Patents Act, 1988, to be identified as Editors of this work.

Cover image © Mohammed Chaba, 1978, Palestine Research Center, Archives of the Institute for Palestine Studies, Washington DC. Courtesy of The Palestine Poster Project Archives (PPPA).

All rights reserved. No part of this publication may be reproduced or transmitted in any form or by any means, electronic or mechanical, including photocopying, recording or any information storage or retrieval system, without prior permission in writing from the publishers.

Bloomsbury Publishing Plc does not have any control over, or responsibility for, any third-party websites referred to or in this book. All internet addresses given in this book were correct at the time of going to press. The author and publisher regret any inconvenience caused if addresses have changed or sites have ceased to exist but can accept no responsibility for any such changes.

A catalogue record for this book is available from the British Library.

A catalog record for this book is available from the Library of Congress.

ISBN: HB: 978-0-7556-4699-9
PB: 978-0-7556-4703-3
ePDF: 978-0-7556-4700-2
eBook: 978-0-7556-4701-9

Typeset by Newgen KnowledgeWorks Pvt. Ltd., Chennai, India

Series: SOAS Palestine Studies

To find out more about our authors and books visit www.bloomsbury.com and sign up for our newsletters.

Contents

List of Figures	vii
List of Contributors	viii
Acknowledgments	xi
Introduction: Palestine in the world *Sorcha Thomson and Pelle Valentin Olsen*	1

Part 1 Travelling Revolutionaries

1. 'Fight for everybody, everywhere'? Paul Robeson, Palestine and selective solidarity — 27
   Gabriel Polley

2. American activists' solidarity trips and interactions with Palestinians — 49
   Michael R. Fischbach

3. An archive of revolution retained in a filmmaker's memory: Masao Adachi and the Palestinian revolution — 69
   Dima Saqfalhait

Part 2 Connected Mobilizations

4. The other solidarity: Matzpen, the Mizrahi question and Palestine — 93
   Orit Bashkin

5. One struggle, many fronts: The National Union of Kuwaiti Students and Palestine — 117
   Kanwal Hameed

6. Palestine as rallying cry: The movement for migrant rights and the Question of Palestine in postcolonial France — 143
   Olivia C. Harrison

Part 3 Transnational Cultural Production

7 Presence and visibility in Cuban anticolonial solidarity: Palestine in OSPAAAL's photography and poster art   167
   Fernando Camacho Padilla and Jessica Stites Mor

8 Palestinian voices in the *Tricontinental*: Revolutionary journalism and the literary history of Palestine solidarity   197
   Anna Bernard

9 Black Panther Party: 'Intercommunalism' and global Palestine   221
   Elizabeth Bishop

Epilogue   247

Index   249

Figures

5.1	NUKS fifth annual conference in Kuwait, 1970	123
5.2	The liberatory framework proposed by the NUKS students in *al-Ittihad*, September 1970	128
5.3	The cover of *al-Ittihad* May 1971	133
6.1	Antiracist protest with Palestinian flags	147
6.2	Front page of *Fedaï*, no. 15 (23 February 1972)	154
7.1	*Tricontinental* magazine, no. 19–20 (1970), inside front cover	177
7.2	*Tricontinental* magazine, no. 31 (1971) pp. 117, 119	178
7.3	Book cover also used in poster art, *Palestine: Crisis and Liberation* (1970)	180
7.4	*Tricontinental* magazine, no. 3 (1967), p. 67	183
7.5	*Tricontinental* magazine, no. 9 (1968), p. 75	185

Contributors

Orit Bashkin is Professor of Modern Middle East History. She works on the intellectual, social and cultural history of the modern Middle East. She received her PhD from Princeton University, New Jersey (2004), writing a thesis on Iraqi intellectual history under the supervision of Professors Robert Tignor and Samah Selim. Since her graduation, she has been working as a professor in the Department of Near Eastern Languages and Civilizations at the University of Chicago, Illinois.

Anna Bernard is Reader in Comparative and English Literature at King's College, London. She is the author of *Rhetorics of Belonging: Nation, Narration, and Israel/Palestine* (2013) and *Decolonizing Literature* (forthcoming 2023) and coeditor of *Debating Orientalism* (2013) and *What Postcolonial Theory Doesn't Say* (2015). She is currently working on a book called *International Solidarity and Culture: Nicaragua, South Africa, Palestine, 1975–1990*.

Elizabeth Bishop is Associate Professor of History at Texas State University. Her work focuses on the history of the Middle East, the Postcolonial Arab World and the Global Cold War. She received her PhD from the University of Chicago, Illinois, and has published extensively on Palestine, Iraq and connections between the Soviet Union and the Arab World.

Michael R. Fischbach is Professor of History at Randolph-Macon College in Ashland, Virginia, where he has taught since 1992 after receiving his doctorate in modern Middle Eastern history from Georgetown University. More recently, Fischbach has researched how the Arab Israeli conflict caused divisions within the Black freedom movement and among left-wing white radicals in America during the 1960s and 1970s. His publications in this area include *Black Power and Palestine: Transnational Countries of Color* (2018) and *The Movement and the Middle East: How the Arab-Israeli Conflict Divided the American Left* (2019).

Kanwal Hameed received her PhD from the University of Exeter, UK, where she was a member of the Gulf Studies department and the European Centre for Palestine Studies. She works on modern histories of the Gulf. Her interests include critical histories, gender studies, education and academia beyond the university, and movements for social justice.

Olivia C. Harrison is Associate Professor of French and Comparative Literature at the University of Southern California. Her publications include *Transcolonial Maghreb: Imagining Palestine in the Era of Decolonization* (2016), *Souffles-Anfas: A Critical Anthology from the Moroccan Journal of Culture and Politics* (2016), and essays on Maghrebi literature, Beur and banlieue cultural production, and postcolonial theory. She is currently completing a monograph about the intersection of antiracism and Palestine solidarity movements in France and researching the recuperation of anticolonial and antiracist discourses by the nativist right in postcolonial France.

Jessica Stites Mor teaches in the history department at University of British Columbia, Okanagan, and serves as the editor-in-chief of the *Canadian Journal of Latin American and Caribbean Studies*. She is author of *Transition Cinema: Political Filmmaking and the Argentine Left since 1968* and *South-South Solidarity and the Latin American Left* and has published three edited volumes, *El Pasado que miramos* (*The Past We View*) with Claudia Feld, *Human Rights and Transnational Solidarity in Cold War Latin America*, and, most recently, *The Art of Solidarity* with art historian Maria del Carmen Suescun Pozas.

Pelle Valentin Olsen is a historian of the modern Middle East. He received his PhD from the University of Chicago, Illinois. His PhD dissertation examined the history of leisure, education, gender and sexuality in twentieth-century Iraq. In 2020–2, he was a postdoctoral fellow in the 'Entangled Histories of Palestine and Global New Left' research project at Roskilde University, Denmark. He is currently a Marie Curie Postdoctoral Fellow at the University of Oslo, Norway. His work has appeared in edited volumes as well as in *Journal of Middle East Women's Studies*, *Arab Studies Journal*, *Journal of Palestine Studies*, *Middle East Critique*, *Journal of Arabic Literature* and *Regards*.

Fernando Camacho Padilla teaches in the Department of Contemporary History at Universidad Autónoma de Madrid, Spain. He is author of *Suecia por Chile. Una historia visual del exilio y la solidaridad, 1970–1990* and *Una vida para Chile: la solidaridad y la comunidad Chilena en Suecia 1970–2010*. He has also published two edited volumes: *Miradas de Irán. Historia y cultura* (with Fernando Escribano Martín, Nadereh Farzamnia and José Luis Neila Hernández) and *Una vieja amistad. Cuatrocientos años de relaciones históricas y culturales entre Irán y el mundo hispánico* (with Fernando Escribano Martín).

Gabriel Polley completed his PhD in Palestine Studies at the European Centre for Palestine Studies, University of Exeter, UK, in 2020, under the supervision of Professor Ilan Pappé and Dr Nadia Naser-Najjab; his thesis explored the representation of Palestine in British travel literature during the late Ottoman era. He previously studied History of Art and Literature at the University of East Anglia, UK, and Palestine and Arabic Studies at Birzeit University, Palestine, and worked in the American School of Palestine in Ramallah, the occupied West Bank, in 2014–15. He was the recipient of the 2021 Ibrahim Dakkak Award for Outstanding Essay on Jerusalem. *Palestine in the Victorian Age: Colonial Encounters in the Holy Land*, his first book, is published in 2022. He currently works in London in the translation and international development sectors.

Mezna Qato is a historian of the modern Middle East, and in particular of education, migration, development, Palestinian refugee and exile communities, and theories of social, economic and political transformation amongst refugee and stateless communities. She is currently a Postdoctoral Fellow of the Margaret Anstee Centre at Newnham College at the University of Cambridge, UK. She was previously a Spencer Fellow at the National Academy of Education and Junior Research Fellow at King's College, Cambridge, UK. She is currently completing a book on education for the Palestinians.

Dima Saqfalhait is a Palestinian researcher. Dima has an MA in Global Cinemas from SOAS, University of London, UK, where she specialized in Japanese and Middle Eastern cinema. She supervises the Film Programme at the A. M. Qattan Foundation, Palestine, and teaches history of film at the Faculty of Art, Music and Design at Birzeit University, Palestine. Dima worked in several Palestinian and international film festivals and has written about film for different online platforms.

Sorcha Thomson is PhD Fellow at Roskilde University, Denmark, in the 'Entangled Histories of Palestine and the Global New Left' project. She researches the history of international solidarity with the Palestinian revolution in the 1960s and 1970s, specifically in the UK and Cuba. She holds an MPhil in Modern Middle Eastern Studies from the University of Oxford (2018), and her work has been published in *The Global South*, *Journal of Palestine Studies* and *Borderlines*. She is currently co-editing a book on revolutionary anti-colonial women of the twentieth century (Pluto Press, forthcoming 2023).

Acknowledgments

All books are the work of countless people, conversations and exchanges. Edited books in particular are always collaborative endeavours. *Palestine in the World* is no exception. This book was conceived in the context of the 'Entangled Histories of Palestine and the Global New Left' research project at Roskilde University. Led by Sune Haugbølle, the project analysed the Palestinian revolution (1965–82) in its encounters, exchanges and solidarities with New Left and Tricontinental activists and liberation movements. Over the course of three years and a pandemic, the project provided a space for conversations and workshops with scholars and activists, many of whom are now contributors to this book. Their work has illuminated the rich history of solidarity between the Palestinian movement and the world: how the Palestinians and their supporters creatively mobilised a global anticolonial movement, and how the Palestinian revolution inspired others in the struggle for liberation. We are proud to include their work here. Without the support and encouragement of Sune Haugbølle at the head of this project *Palestine in the World* would not exist. Special thanks are also due to those who contributed to the project in various ways, in particular the 'Entangled Histories of Palestine and the Global New Left' advisory board members: Joseph Prestel, Miriyam Aouragh and Toufoul Abou-Hodeib, as well as those who generously brought their expertise and insights in guidance, feedback and discussion: Maha Nassar, Dina Matar, Heba Taha and the editorial team at I.B Tauris, especially Yasmin Garcha and Sophie Rudland. Finally, we are grateful to Mezna Qato for writing an epilogue that thoughtfully and pertinently connects the commitments expressed in this book to the making of a just world.

Introduction: Palestine in the world

Sorcha Thomson and Pelle Valentin Olsen

On 2 September 1970, revolutionaries and activists from across the world gathered in Amman, Jordan, for the opening session of the Second World Conference on Palestine organized by the General Union of Palestinian Students (GUPS). During the five-day event, more than 200 participants from almost ninety organizations and liberation struggles across the world listened to speeches and engaged in a series of discussions with Palestinian students, the Palestine Liberation Organization (PLO) and Palestinian resistance organizations. The aim of the conference was to bring supportive international groups together at an important juncture of the Palestinian liberation struggle, to clarify the set of principles upon which the international solidarity movement should be based. The conference emphasized the necessity for its participants to meet and engage with Palestinians taking part in the revolutionary struggle in the Middle East, by visiting cadre bases, refugee camps, and social institutions including schools, vocational workshops, and medical clinics. Against the backdrop of Black September, the Jordanian authorities' crackdown on the Palestinian revolution's base in the country, the invitation of international delegates to the GUPS-organized conference signified the Palestinian movement's efforts to mobilize meaningful connections of solidarity among the networks of anti-imperialism at the outset of the 1970s. As participants returned to their home countries from the Amman conference – and several other conferences, symposia and meetings like it – they worked to build international solidarity with Palestine through acts of cultural and intellectual production, the foundation of institutions and committees, and the mobilization of political networks, carrying with them the principles and positions that the conference had promoted.[1]

The Amman meeting offers a glimpse into the multiple ways in which the Palestinian revolution (*al-Thawra al-Filastiniyya*) set out to establish its place in the world. The Palestinian revolutionary movement emerged from underground networks of student activists in the 1950s,[2] mostly living in exile since the onset of the Nakba (catastrophe) in 1947–8 during which Zionist forces displaced at least 750,000 Palestinians from their homes and occupied 78 per cent of the land of historic Palestine. Over the course of almost two decades of Palestinian political organizing, often bookmarked by Fatah's 1 January 1965 military communiqué declaring the beginning of armed struggle for the liberation of Palestine and ending with the departure of the Palestinian leadership from Beirut in 1982 following the Israeli invasion of Lebanon, the PLO became an umbrella organization for a national liberation movement. This movement was composed of ideologically diverse parties; unions of women, students, writers and workers; a vibrant sector of cultural production; and a range of services for the people. The aim of the movement was the liberation of Palestine through armed struggle and the return of the Palestinian people to the lands from which they were expelled.[3]

Central to the operation of the movement was an embrace of international solidarity as a principle and a practice through which the Palestinian people could build support for their struggle and change their relationship with the world, based on an understanding – in part inspired by the example of the Algerian national liberation movement (1954–62) – that in an anticolonial struggle, international solidarity provided moral and material sustenance to the movement that could alter the balance of power. As one of dozens of anticolonial national liberation movements shaping a Third World project for political and economic independence, and due to extensive outreach activities and organizational labour carried out by Palestinians, the movement won the support of progressive struggles across continents. In addition, by the mid-1970s, in the chambers of the United Nations, the PLO received the backing of a majority of states that passed resolutions declaring the movement as a leading front in the fight against colonialism and racism and calling for the self-determination of the Palestinian people.[4] How the movement changed its position on the international stage – from being viewed as a 'problem' of stateless refugees in need of humanitarian assistance to being recognized as a national movement with collective political rights – is a question that has inspired a recent body of work that seeks to uncover the global connections that the movement established in this era.

Among these works, Paul Thomas Chamberlin has stressed the diplomatic campaign carried out by the PLO and the state-driven forms of diplomacy and solidarity practiced by the Cold War powers.⁵ According to Chamberlin, after the 1967 Arab Israeli war, the PLO launched a diplomatic campaign, partly supported by the People's Republic of China (PRC), which aided its integration into socialist and national liberation networks across the Third World and beyond.⁶ In this historical context, he argues, the PLO and the Palestinian movement became a leading actor in a 'sprawling constellation of revolutionary networks'.⁷ Other works have complemented the focus on state actors, diplomacy and political history with the social history of the revolutionaries and solidarity activists – many of whom were students – who helped elevate Palestine to a global cause.⁸ Studies have shown how the movement engaged in the liberation struggle on many fronts, working to make itself visible through cultural and artistic activism with the participation of leftist writers, artists and filmmakers in collaboration with their Palestinian peers.⁹ Through this cultural activism, as Dina Matar has argued, the PLO emerged as a 'local, regional and global symbol' with a recognisable aesthetics of liberation.¹⁰

Many of these studies view solidarity with Palestine through a transnational lens to show how the movement imagined and made itself part of a global liberation struggle inside as well as beyond the Middle East.¹¹ Taking this transnational approach to Palestinian history shows that the national liberation movement was not only engaged in the building of a future Palestinian nation-state but also an important actor in a revolutionary terrain that sought to remake the rules and hierarchies upon which the international system was based. From this literature, it becomes clear that the ascendance of the Palestinian movement was intimately connected to the broader dynamics of the sixties and seventies, a period of worldwide transformation shaped by anticolonial struggle, student uprisings, worker revolts and antiracist internationalism.

A result of this literature has been a focus on the agency of Palestinians and their organizations in making their struggle resonate globally. This in turn has challenged the view that support for their struggle was primarily due to exogenous factors, the most prominent of those being the 1967 Arab Israeli war. Palestine was already an anti-imperial cause for nationalist, socialist and communist groups during the period of decolonization in the 1950s across most of the Arab world. However, the June 1967 war and its aftermath was crucial in convincing many leftists globally, and particularly in Europe and the United States, that Israel was a colonial and violent actor and that Palestine was paramount to the larger battle against colonialism, imperialism, capitalism and US hegemony. The 1967 war was also a turning point for Palestinian and Arab intellectuals and activists, who realized that the efforts of the Arab socialist regimes during the

1950s and 1960s had not created the changes necessary to liberate Palestine.[12] While not directly engaged in analyzing the global-historical significance of the 1967 war, the chapters in *Palestine in the World* complicate the role of 1967 as a universal watershed moment in the making of a global Palestinian cause. The chapters offer important additions to our knowledge of 1967 within a broader transnational perspective, by connecting it to longer processes of activism, cultural production and organizational labour that drew inspiration from the expertise and ideas of revolutionaries from different traditions of struggle. They also highlight alternative moments such as the 1956 Suez Crisis or the 1959 visit of Che Guevara to Gaza that contributed to the Palestinian movement's subsequent global resonance as an anticolonial struggle.

Palestine in the World takes this transnational approach as a starting point that places Palestine at the centre of the shared imagination of the movements that shaped this era, where it was viewed as a cause and a model struggle on par with those in Vietnam, Algeria, Cuba and South Africa, in a period when the anticolonial struggles of Africa, Asia and Latin America shaped the radical politics of the rest of the world.[13] Studies of the linkages that shaped this era have employed the terms the 'long 1960s' or the 'global sixties', to describe the (somewhat) politically coherent historical period that stretched from the mid-1950s to the mid-1970s, and to carve out an epistemological position in which transnational flows and networks of connectivity are understood as the basis for understanding (that period of) history.[14] Studies using this framework, motivated in part by the sixties' enduring place in the contemporary political imagination, have resulted in a shift away from viewing Paris, Prague or the civil rights movement in the United States as the epicentres of radical change in this period to instead highlight alternative nodes of radicalism in cities such as Beirut, Algiers and Cairo; in international exile and migrant communities; and in the 'small spaces' of resistance from prisons to refugee camps.[15] As the chapters in the collection show, the Palestinians were an integral part of this global landscape, viewed by a diverse revolutionary milieu as a movement at the forefront of anti-imperial struggle.

Yet the Palestinian revolution does not neatly fit into the periodization of the long or global 1960s. For some, the revolutionary movement entered into decline from the early or mid-seventies, while others argue that it achieved its landmark victories in the mid-seventies and continued until the evacuation of the PLO from Beirut in 1982. For Karma Nabulsi, debates about the revolution's precise endpoint distract from a more constructive discussion of its strengths and weaknesses and the potentially useful lessons that can be drawn from it.¹⁶ *Palestine in the World* features research on solidarity with the Palestinian movement that takes us from the late 1940s until the 1980s, travelling through the landmark events and sites of the 'global sixties' while charting changing forms of repression and internal fractures that were always present. The majority of the chapters deal with the practices and discourses of liberation that were most visible in the late 1960s and 1970s. However, they also locate these within a longer period, thereby highlighting alternative genealogies and timelines of the era. What is described by Palestinian historians as 'the golden age' of the resistance movement in the late 1960s and 1970s is brought into conversation with important prehistories and counter-histories, to demonstrate the significant changes that took place throughout this period and their alternative epicentres.¹⁷ In line with other work on the 1960s and 1970s that seeks to understand the period's relationship to the twenty-first-century condition, the collection views this history of international solidarity as part of a continuum, at once ruptured from and enabling of the struggles of our contemporary times.¹⁸

The main contribution of the collection is the positioning of solidarity as a central principle and practice that shaped the Palestinian revolution's place in the world. In addition to showcasing the multiple locations and ways in which the Palestinian revolution operated and received solidarity, the collection shows that international solidarity with Palestine existed on a spectrum of participation, commitment, belonging and identification to a constantly shifting global community. We believe that the example of the Palestinian liberation movement offers a model case of international solidarity, whose study can move us towards a more comprehensive understanding of solidarity as a concept and a practice relevant to both historical and contemporary anticolonial struggles, and allow for reflection on solidarity's meaning, efficacy and limits in shaping global movements.

By placing diverse scales, forms and timelines of solidarity side by side, the collection allows us to distinguish between different types of solidarity through case studies attentive to geographic and political differences. These cases show that solidarity looked different in the national and local contexts in which support for Palestine emerged. In Cuba and other socialist and revolutionary states, state-sponsored solidarity efforts created an infrastructure of internationalism through which Palestinian revolutionaries could communicate their aims and mobilize support. In these contexts, support for the PLO and the Palestinian revolution was seen as an extension of the state's wider engagement in the ideological battles of the period. In other places, solidarity was the domain of civil society, taking place among the networks of Black, migrant, socialist, women's and other forms of struggle that made up the multitudes of the New Left. While not attempting to examine the full planetary scale of support for Palestinian liberation, an endeavour beyond the scope of this collection's nine chapters, *Palestine in the World* features studies of solidarity with the Palestinian revolution from different parts of the world – including Cuba, the United States, Japan, Kuwait, Israel, Algeria, France and elsewhere. These locations are indicative of the networks of anticolonial and New Left mobilizations that sought to challenge imperial hegemony during the 1960s and 1970s. While attentive to the unique national contexts of each case, the chapters go beyond the nation state as the primary unit through which solidarity was expressed and organized, presenting different scales – including local, regional, 'transcolonial' and 'intercommunal' scales – through which differently situated solidarities operated and met in a transnational political culture.

As well as the distinction between different scales of solidarity, rather than existing as a stable and static state of mutual relations, the collection presents solidarity with Palestine as a dynamic practice reflecting the unique and shifting positions held by solidarity actors towards the Palestinian revolution. The ability of solidarity to take many different forms is emphasized by the interdisciplinary approach of the chapters, which include biography, literary studies, film studies as well as diplomatic and microhistories, and the engagement of archives in multiple languages and locations. The nine chapters that make up *Palestine in the World* collectively reflect on the archival challenges and possibilities affecting the retrieving and writing of Palestinian and anticolonial history. As Hana Sleiman reminds us, the archives of revolutionary and liberation movements, if they exist at all, are susceptible to theft, destruction and disappearance.[19] The PLO's Research Centre in Beirut, which contained private papers and PLO publications, as well as books, journals and other materials, was bombed, ransacked and looted by the invading Israeli army in 1982. Other central Palestinian archives have suffered a similar fate. The impressive range of sources analyzed in *Palestine in the World* does not attempt to replace what was lost, stolen and destroyed. The chapters draw on personal archives of activists, extant archives of local movements, memoirs, cinema, intelligence reports, various forms of print culture and the oral testimonies of historical actors. Collectively, the chapters examine different engagements *with* the Palestinian movement that are crucial for understanding its internationalization and global reach. By highlighting the entangled nature of these relations, *Palestine in the World* employs a 'multi-sided historiography that requires us to read into various archives but also to take the dialogical nature of intellectual production seriously'.[20] While Palestinian actors and voices are sometimes only retrievable in a mediated form in archives of liberation movements and solidarity groups in various parts of the world, when contextualized and read alongside Palestinian sources, such archives allow for a partial reconstruction of the entangled nature of the Palestinian struggle during this period.[21]

The outcome is a picture of Palestine's global resonance that goes beyond seeing 'the global' as the broad scale of planetary networks and ties. Instead, 'the global' is presented, by necessity, as constituted by the more hidden and less legible granular social and microhistories of those same connections. It is only with this scale, Mezna Qato argues, that it is possible to 'examine more closely conditions and contingencies in the history of popular mobilization and the everyday life of movement work … and unravel[s] the weaving of rhetorics of unity to find not only fissures and silences, but also the constitution of political discipline and cohesion in particular sites and communities'.[22] With its broad range of archival practices and close attention to the subjectivities and articulations of solidarity across various movements, groups and actors, *Palestine in the World* is a step towards filling some of the gaps in this history.

Typologies of solidarity

Each chapter in *Palestine in the World* offers new insights as to how solidarity with Palestine operated and what it meant. To explore and make legible these typologies of solidarity, the collection is organized into three parts, that each forefront different ways in which solidarity was organized, imagined and enacted: 'Travelling Revolutionaries', 'Connected Mobilizations', and 'Transnational Cultural Production'. These parts emerge from a review of the literature on the Palestinian revolution's internationalism and global connections and attempt to capture the characteristics that made the period an era of increased interconnection. Each part addresses one of the cross-border characteristics of the era: the increased opportunities for travel and mobility of political actors, the heightened mobilization of local movements in support of international causes and the emergence of a globalizing media landscape. Rather than separate our detailed case studies by region, scale, type of activity or the nature of the actors, organizing them within broader structural categories allows us to see connections of solidarity between places and peoples beyond the closed boundaries of identity or geography that can sometimes limit how we imagine solidarity to operate. These three parts are by no means exhaustive and, as many of the chapters show, constant crossovers existed between them. However, together, the parts make legible the intertwined intellectual, political and cultural currents that produced new formations of international politics in the years of the Palestinian revolution.

The first part, 'Travelling Revolutionaries', turns to the topic of the people – mostly young activists and political cadres – who became directly and symbolically attached to the Palestinian struggle through their cross-border journeys and activities. These travelling revolutionaries have mostly been studied as individual exceptional cases, from the perspective of other countries' national politics, or only as anecdotes in wider studies of regional political movements. The three chapters in this part approach the journeys of revolutionaries and activists to meet and join the Palestinian movement as part of the networks of movement that characterized the period. Gabriel Polley's chapter (Chapter 1) illustrates the neglected importance of the 1956 Suez Crisis on politically conscious people outside the Middle East. By looking at the life and travels of African American civil rights activist and singer Paul Robeson, Polley shows the extent to which perspectives changed in the early to late 1950s: from Black Jewish solidarities in the 1940s linked to support for Israel to a reassessment of this support in light of the dramatic events of 1956 and decolonization. Polley suggests an alternative genealogy of solidarity through an exploration of the individual political trajectory of Paul Robeson. The result is a historical understanding of solidarity as a practice made possible, and at times hindered, by various local communities with different stakes in the struggle over Palestine. Polley's chapter allows us to appreciate how different historical and personal circumstances create the conditions in which a person may choose and change the types of causes and principles to which they commit. Beyond the specific case of Robeson, Polley's chapter addresses the under-studied prehistory of solidarity with the Palestinian struggle among Black and communist activists in the United States, where support for Israel was a cause of the left and where Palestine had not yet been understood as linked to other anticolonial struggles.

Michael Fischbach (Chapter 2) also looks to radical struggles based in the United States that encountered the Palestinian revolution through the journeys of their protagonists. Fischbach's chapter shows how high-profile Black Power activists, left-wing writers, journalists and countercultural figures, of a later generation than Robeson, travelled to the Middle East on solidarity trips, to attend conferences and, in a few cases, to join the armed Palestinian fighters. His chapter demonstrates a different type of engagement with the Palestinian cause, in which activists travelled to the Middle East to meet with, learn from and in some cases become part of the movement at a time when few Americans knew much about the Palestinian cause. These activists expressed varying levels of commitment to the Palestinian cause – such as the 'LSD King' Timothy Leary who had a brief and rather inconsequential encounter with the PLO in Beirut – demonstrating the way in which Palestine became part of a broader global counterculture. Dima Saqfalhait's chapter (Chapter 3), on the other hand, shows us an example of an encounter that led to active participation in the movement and a lifelong commitment to the Palestinian cause. She takes us inside the Palestinian revolution by tracing the life of Japanese New Wave filmmaker Masao Adachi, uncovering the connections that existed between Japanese and Palestinian leftist groups, the role of Adachi's filmmaking in documenting and showcasing the everyday life of the revolution in Lebanon and the lasting impact of his solidarity with Palestine.

The chapters in this part demonstrate not just the ideas that travelled alongside individuals and movements but also the lasting effects of activists' knowledges, connections and symbolic capital in their political milieu and future lives. Read in the wider context of the period, these journeys illustrate the breaking down of territorial and social borders, through air travel, clandestine militant networks, training programs, delegations, diplomatic missions and other exchanges between national liberation movements, revolutionary regimes and progressive struggles. From these journeys emerged a generation of activists who clearly understood themselves as part of a global struggle.

The process of becoming part of this global struggle was never a straightforward process of encounter and adoption, and there were always contestations and negotiations within these encounters. The second part, 'Connected Mobilizations', focuses on differently situated mobilizations to show how people engaged in support for Palestine according to local, regional and global concerns and realities. The complex politics of situating the Palestinian people within a broader solidarity framework is addressed in Orit Bashkin's chapter (Chapter 4), which traces the origins and development of the 'Mizrahi' question as a means of building Jewish Palestinian solidarity relations inside of Israel. Examining the theoretical writings of a number of Mizrahi members of the radical Israeli Matzpen movement, Bashkin uncovers forgotten commonalities between Mizrahim and Palestinian revolutionaries as well as the significant labour that went into creating regional solidarities situated against capitalism and settler colonialism.

Studies of regional connections have shown how for students groups in Egypt, anti-Shah activists in Iran, intellectuals in Lebanon and literary writers of the Maghreb, the Palestinian cause connected domestic feelings of oppression to structures of power beyond the nation, acting as a catalyst for both mobilization and further radicalization of demands.[23] Taking up the regional politics of the transnational solidarity movement, Kanwal Hameed (Chapter 5) looks to the activities of the National Union of Kuwaiti Students (NUKS) in the 1970s to argue that mobilization with Palestine was connected to its place within the Arab anticolonial national struggle as well as, and primary to, its transnational positioning. She shows that the political and cultural work of anti-colonial Arab nationalist actors was not simply replaced by universalist Third World internationalism after 1967. Adding to the still largely invisible liberation geography of the Gulf, Hameed's dual orientation shows the limitations of the transnational framework by adding a new case – namely that of students in Kuwait – to our knowledge of Arab mobilization around the Palestinian cause.

Olivia C. Harrison (Chapter 6) presents the 'transcolonial' as the scale that shaped mobilizations with the Palestinian cause in France. Moving the focus away from the more well-known and celebrated French solidarity figures, such as Jean-Luc Godard and Jean Genet, she examines the politically more significant grassroots mobilizations of the often-anonymous Arab migrant workers and students responsible for the emergence of antiracist activism rooted in anticolonial solidarity with Palestinians. Tracing the history of the first autonomous migrant workers' movement in France, the Committees in Support of the Palestinian Revolution (CSRP), Harrison's chapter demonstrates that the movement for migrant rights in France emerged out of civil campaigns to support the Palestinian revolution. In France, Palestine also became a vehicle for a powerful critique of the French state and its colonial past and present. The encounters and collaborations between migrants living the realities of French colonial politics that emerge in Harrison's chapter provide us with an example of solidarity that is based firmly in everyday life and struggle rather than occasional commitment and identification.

The third part, 'Transnational Cultural Production', looks to the cultural and artistic forms of solidarity that emerged between the Palestinian revolution and its supporters. The circulation of anticolonial texts, sounds and images translated into multiple languages emerged as an international revolutionary canon, offering both shared strategy and theory understood as a weapon against colonial occupation and imperial aggression. The three chapters in this part examine the production and content of photography, magazines and radio to demonstrate the ways in which solidarity actors worked alongside Palestinian artists and institutions to represent and communicate their struggle to the world.

This part's first two chapters look to Cuba and the Tricontinental movement as a site and source of this transnational political culture. Jessica Stites Mor and Fernando Camacho Padilla (Chapter 7) show how, beginning with the visit of Ernesto 'Che' Guevara to Palestinian camps in Gaza in 1959, political contact between Cuban and Palestinian revolutionaries increased throughout the 1960s and made Palestine a key solidarity cause of Cuban foreign policy and diplomacy. The empirical richness of the chapter – drawing on conversations with Cuban state officials when the Cuban state archives remain largely closed on this topic and period – produces a new and detailed historical account of Cuban Palestinian relations. At the same time, by expanding on the cultural methods employed by Cuba to shape a narrative of the Palestinian struggle, Stites Mor and Camacho Padilla add to our understanding of solidarity as practiced by states and international organizations. Their chapter looks at how this was done in the photographic and artistic compositions of the Organization of Solidarity with the Peoples of Asia, Africa and Latin America (OSPAAAL), demonstrating the role of the image as a vehicle through which linguistically and geographically distant movements were communicated as part of a shared anti-imperial community.

The second chapter, by Anna Bernard (Chapter 8), also looks to the output of OSPAAAL, particularly its *Tricontinental* magazine and news bulletin. These publications articulated an explicitly Third Worldist, internationalist and revolutionary solidarity with national liberation struggles. In her analysis, Bernard shows how the publications offered a space for Palestinians to present their voices and promote their revolution to the Tricontinental audience. Although structured unevenly by gender, as she argues, these publications centred Palestinian solidarity and camaraderie based on shared political commitments, as opposed to the asymmetrical relations of solidarity that would come later, in which Palestinian suffering took precedence over Palestinian agency. In doing so, Bernard, in a style particularly attentive to literary forms, techniques and aesthetic practices, demonstrates the importance of literature as a site for the imagining and creation of international solidarity.

Finally, Elizabeth Bishop's chapter (Chapter 9) looks to the Black Panther Party (BPP), especially its international base in Algiers, and the connections with Fatah and other Palestinian groups in this Third World capital, in strengthening Black Palestinian solidarities. In Bishop's chapter, the placing of encounters and interactions together that otherwise might be considered inconsequential reveals a broader picture of interconnection often missing from approaches that remain inside national or regional boundaries. Using the concept of 'inter-communalism' to creatively explore the parallel histories of Fatah and the BPP in a number of cities, including Gaza, New York, Havana, Algiers and Oakland, Bishop sheds new light on solidarity at the intersection of the Afro-Arab world and its ability to shift between places in ways that often go unnoticed by dominant historical lenses.

From participation in a vibrant sphere of intellectual and cultural production, to the work of travelling revolutionaries as delegates, intermediaries and volunteers, and then to the connected mobilizations that took place in different corners of the world, in all of the chapters, solidarity emerges as a broad variety of practices. From the transnational discourse of tricontinentalism communicated in an image to the slower and more granular and everyday activities of solidarity that took place within local communities, solidarity with Palestine travelled between scales and registers, adopting unique characteristics along the way. Among the historical actors participating in the movement was a range of emotional, strategic and political relations to the Palestinian movement and its registries of anticolonial struggle. This is reflected in the different ways in which people enacted and articulated their support – from the embrace of revolutionary violence and a commitment to the taking up of arms, to organizing for labour rights and social justice and producing cultural and intellectual forms of identification. These different forms of solidarity intersected, overlapped and took shape within and beyond the major meeting places of the global sixties, from Havana, Paris, Algiers and Beirut to Tokyo, Kuwait City and Atlanta. Shared imaginations and material connections on different scales produced distinct trajectories of solidarity, yet in each case there existed a common belief that people were to some extent participating in a collective struggle.

At times, however, the collection looks critically at the fault lines of liberation and global cohesion, thereby showing that the era's 'constellation of revolutionary networks'[24] were sometimes less static than we assume today. The chapters in *Palestine in the World* bring attention to the role of internal disagreements, state surveillance, policing and persecution that made movement and collaboration across territorial and conceptual borders difficult and, at times, impossible. While those in solidarity with the Palestinian revolution agreed on many things, the question of solidarity could also exacerbate divisions and hierarchies of struggle. For example, Bashkin's chapter allows us to appreciate how the legitimate means and meanings of armed struggle and the question of violence became a point of stress and rupture. What these various types of solidarity show is that the ability of the Palestinian revolution to project its cause and win support around the world was never easy or even, and was always dealing with the contingencies of the interests and ideologies of the various state and non-state actors it engaged with.

Although a number of the chapters address the issue of gender, missing still is a full appreciation of the role of women, who featured less prominently in the official rhetoric and records of the movements in discussion, in the international struggle. The role of women and other silenced actors, behind the scenes and at the front, in constructing and organizing solidarities remains in need of further historical attention. The categories and archival methods suggested in this collection offer new avenues towards doing this important work by elevating the contributions of previously under-acknowledged actors. Also in need of further attention are the infrastructures and political economies of solidarity, including financial circulations, funding structures and the exchange of equipment and supplies, that often made possible the international connections revealed in the collection, yet whose details remain largely hidden.

Towards a global solidarity with Palestine

As well as enlarging our view of the different types and contingencies inherent to the practice of international solidarity, placing these types of solidarities side by side can illuminate a framework for understanding the changes that took place over the course of the 1960s and 1970s. Existing approaches to the theorization of solidarity can be thought of as belonging to two camps, essentialist and anti-essentialist, the latter shifting the focus away from the primacy of social identity in generating solidarity and towards shared relations to structures of power.[25] David Featherstone argues that solidarity of this kind is a transformative relation, which can involve the cementing of existing identities and power relations or the creation of new ones between places, activists and diverse social groups, and in doing so advance political horizons.[26] Only when viewed in this way can the inventiveness and agency of actors in making solidarities be appreciated. As the chapters in this collection show, those who built and sustained solidarity with the Palestinian revolution were not only those who had privileged access to international platforms and resources but also people who – in diverse registers, encounters and political imaginations – understood their lives and struggles as connected to a global movement. In this way, we can rethink what and who counts as doing solidarity and show solidarity itself as a political practice capable of intervening in the meaning of 'the global'.

At the same time, awareness of solidarity as something that is made by people highlights the uneven power relations and geographies through which solidarity emerges in the first place. In line with Featherstone's thinking, *Palestine in the World* recognizes solidarity as a historical phenomenon that shifted its parameters over time and drew on different traditions, reference points and positions to make Palestinian liberation an internationally recognized movement, yet that also witnessed disagreements and points of contention between differently situated groups. While acknowledging the scope for disagreement, one of the key strengths of international solidarity with the Palestinian revolution was the collective effort to challenge the colonial drive to continually present the colonized as invisible or inherently different and as such fit for domination.[27] In its multiple different expressions, solidarity with the Palestinian revolution was not defined by a single political act or actor but instead was a pillar and principle in a political culture exploring the variations of a globally resistant subjectivity relevant to the world of its existence.

Viewed in this way, the solidarity practices examined in *Palestine in the World* can be understood as operating within what Antonio Gramsci described as the 'war of position': the ongoing struggle over ideas and beliefs waged on the intellectual and cultural front against the hegemony of the dominant class (or their rule by the consent of the masses).[28] Sunaina Maira has used this framework to understand the role of the Boycott, Divestment and Sanction (BDS) movement, launched in 2005, through which the idea of Israel as a lone, democratic state in the Middle East besieged by Arab terrorists is contested with the idea of Israel as a settler-colonial state practicing a near sixty-year occupation over the Palestinian people and their land. In the absence of Gramsci's 'war of manoeuvre', or the armed struggle, she argues, this war of position – conducted through the building of solidarity alliances and challenging the splintering of Palestinian national struggle orchestrated by the Oslo paradigm – is an avenue through which Palestinian people and their anticolonial allies can make the case for Palestinian liberation today.[29]

Extending this framework to an earlier era of international solidarity with Palestine in the 1960s and 1970s evokes comparisons of two main differences: the primacy of the language of human rights and international law today in comparison to the revolutionary slogans, icons and theories that inspired support in the past and the difference between the institutional and geographic separation of Palestinian political life today in comparison to the earlier era when, in spite of internal ideological differences, the PLO offered a collective structure for Palestinian national liberation politics, with a range of institutions that mobilized Palestinian political life across the world. As Abdel Razzaq Takriti has argued, while BDS plays a crucial role in the global 'war of position' in which the Palestinian solidarity movement is engaged, it cannot replace representative national structures capable of implementing broader anticolonial strategies.[30]

At the same time, the comparison between *then* and *now* within this framework raises questions about the characterization of the 1960s and 1970s as an era during which armed struggle was the dominant mode of liberation and universally supported among the New Left, including the Arab New Left.[31] Armed struggle became a key meeting point and source of mobilization of solidarities between struggles, not just for Palestine. Yet, as several of the chapters show, the strategy of armed struggle created splits, disagreements and competing interpretations which never operated in isolation from a broader view of revolutionary political culture and thought. By reframing the period and going beyond a focus on the question of violence – a means of liberation which has increasingly been delegitimized and discursively linked to terrorism by state as well as non-state actors in the international sphere – *Palestine in the World* seeks to retrieve the full range of traditions and forms of anticolonial struggle and solidarity that came together during this period.

Rather than accept a complete rupture between then and now, as many of the chapters point out, at a moment when support for and in many cases even research on Palestine is under attack, looking to the past can offer important lessons for the present. Looking back to the transnational practices of solidarity with the Palestinian revolution that characterized the 1960s and 1970s highlights the important role that Palestinian activists, students, union members, parties and institutions played in mobilizing international support for their cause, through a collective framework of self-determination under the umbrella of a national liberation movement. The Palestinian revolution was not only engaged in a struggle for statehood and recognition of rights but also in a transnational effort to remake a world in flux. The failure of these movements to conjure a coherent and lasting alternative became evident as the counter-revolutions and internal ideological divisions of the 1970s and 1980s attacked and fractured their interconnectivity. However, as Nasser Abourahme points out, the ability to overthrow or create a stable state form is not the only yardstick by which we might measure the success of the Palestinian revolution. The Palestinian revolution, according to Abourahme, which was tied to the rise and waning of tricontinental Third Worldism, can also be read as a successful attempt to 'creatively make autonomous territory and declare communes' rather than merely 'the defeated end of a revolutionary historical arc'.[32]

Similarly, as many of the contributions to this collection make clear, the practices that those in solidarity with the Palestinian revolution were engaged in – their cultural innovations, their international journeys and the connections they built – produced traces that would outlive the end of the revolutionary era. Many of the people who were involved in international solidarity continued to work for the Palestinian cause, in a lifelong commitment to justice and equality. While many of the formal networks from the revolutionary era may have collapsed, the solidarities that were built have in many ways outlived the institutional infrastructures to which they were then tied. *Palestine in the World* hopes to illuminate this history of solidarity for a new generation seeking to learn from the earlier era, because even if some of the frameworks and boundaries of anticolonial politics have changed, the desire for liberation has not retreated.

Notes

1. Sorcha Thomson, Pelle Valentin Olsen, and Sune Haugbolle, 'Palestine Solidarity Conferences in the Global Sixties', *Journal of Palestine Studies* 51, no. 1 (2022): 27–49.
2. Mjriam Abu Samra, 'The Palestinian Student Movement 1948–1982: A Study of Popular Organisation and Transnational Mobilisation', PhD dissertation, University of Oxford, 2020; Mjriam Abu Samra and Loubna Qutami, 'Alterity across Generations: A Comparative Analysis of the 1950s Jeel al-Thawra and the 2006 Palestinian Youth Movement', *Revue des mondes musulmans et de la Méditerranée*, no. 147 (October 2020): 3–15; Yoav Di-Capua, 'Palestine Comes to Paris: The Global Sixties and the Making of a Universal Cause', *Journal of Palestine Studies* 50, no. 1 (2021): 19–50.
3. For an overview of the history of the Palestinian revolution, see Karma Nabulsi and Abdel Razzaq Takriti, *The Palestinian Revolution*, 2018. Available online: http://learnpalestine.politics.ox.ac.uk/. (accessed 5 October 2021)
4. Noura Erakat, *Justice for Some: Law and the Question of Palestine* (Palo Alto: Stanford University Press, 2019).
5. Paul Thomas Chamberlin, *The Global Offensive: The United States, the Palestine Liberation Organization, and the Making of the Post-Cold War Order* (Oxford: Oxford University Press, 2012).
6. Ibid., 20–2; Paul Thomas Chamberlin, 'The Struggle against Oppression Everywhere: The Global Politics of Palestinian Liberation', *Middle Eastern Studies* 47, no. 1 (2011): 38. For recent works addressing the earlier history of Third World connections and solidarities, see, for example, Michele Louro, Carolien Stolte, Heather Streets-Salter, and Sana Tannoury-Karam, eds, *The League Against Imperialism: Lives and Afterlives* (Leiden: Leiden University Press, 2020);

Christopher J. Lee, eds, *Making a World after Empire: The Bandung Moment and Its Political Afterlives* (Athens: Ohio University Press, 2010); Su Lin Lewis and Carolien Stolte, 'Other Bandungs: Afro-Asian Internationalism in the Early Cold War', *Journal of World History* 30, no. 1–2 (2019): 1–19.

7 Chamberlin, *The Global Offensive*, 14.

8 Sune Haugbolle and Pelle Valentin Olsen, 'The Emergence of Palestine as a Global Cause', *Middle East Critique* (forthcoming 2022); Samra, 'The Palestinian Student Movement 1948–1982'; Di-Capua, 'Palestine Comes to Paris'.

9 Jessica Stites Mor, 'The Question of Palestine in the Argentine Political Imaginary: Anti-Imperialist Thought from Cold War to Neoliberal Order', *Journal of Iberian and Latin American Research* 20, no. 2 (2014): 186; Dina Matar, 'PLO Cultural Activism: Mediating Liberation Aesthetics in Revolutionary Contexts', *Comparative Studies of South Asia, Africa and the Middle East* 38, no. 2 (2018): 354–64; Zeina Maasri, *Cosmopolitan Radicalism: The Visual Politics of Beirut's Global Sixties* (Cambridge: Cambridge University Press, 2020); Kristine Khouri and Rasha Salti, *Past Disquiet: Artists, International Solidarity, and Museums in Exile* (Chicago: University of Chicago Press, 2018); Nadia Yaqub, *Palestinian Cinema in the Days of Revolution* (Austin: University of Texas Press, 2018); Khadija Habashneh, *Fursan al-Sinima: Sirat Wahdat Aflam Filastin* (Amman: al-Ahliyya, 2020); Shahab Ahmad, 'The Poetics of Solidarity: Palestine in Modern Urdu Poetry', *Alif: Journal of Comparative Poetics* 18 (1998): 29–64.

10 Matar, 'PLO Cultural Activism', 354–64.

11 See, for example, Maha Nassar, '"My Struggle Embraces Every Struggle": Palestinians in Israel and Solidarity with Afro-Asian Liberation Movements', *Arab Studies Journal* 22, no. 1 (2014): 74–101; Michael R. Fischbach, *Black Power and Palestine: Transnational Countries of Color* (Palo Alto: Stanford University Press, 2018); Michael R. Fischbach, *The Movement and the Middle East: How the Arab-Israeli Conflict Divided the American Left* (Palo Alto: Stanford University Press, 2019); Joseph Ben Prestel, 'Heidelberg, Beirut, und die "Dritte Welt": Palästinensische Gruppen in der Bundesrepublik Deutschland (1956–1972)', Zeithistorische Forschungen/*Studies in Contemporary History* 3 (2019): 442–66.

12 Yezid Sayigh, *Armed Struggle and the Search for State: The Palestinian National Movement, 1949–1993* (Oxford: Oxford University Press, 1999); Rashid Khalidi, *The Iron Cage: The Story of the Palestinian Struggle for Statehood* (London: Oneworld Publications, 2007); Helena Cobban, *The Palestinian Liberation Organisation: People, Power and Politics* (Cambridge: Cambridge University Press, 1984); Rosemary Sayigh, *The Palestinians: From Peasants to Revolutionaries* (London: Zed Books, 1979); Walid Kazziha, *Revolutionary Transformation in the Arab World: Habash and His Comrades from Nationalism to Marxism* (London: C. Knight, 1975).

13 Cynthia Young, *Soul Power: Culture, Radicalism, and the Making of a U.S Third World Left* (Durham: Duke University Press, 2006); Christopher Kalter, *The Discovery of the Third World: Decolonization and the Rise of the New Left in France, C1950–1976* (Cambridge: Cambridge University Press, 2016); Richard Wolin, *The Wind from the East: French Intellectuals, the Cultural Revolution and the Legacy of the 1960s* (Princeton: Princeton University Press, 2012); Samantha Christiansen and Zachary A. Scarlett, *The Third World in the Global 1960s* (New York: Berghahn Books, 2013); Quinn Slobodian, *Foreign Front: Third World Politics in Sixties West Germany* (Durham: Duke University Press, 2012).

14 Chen Jian, Martin Klimke, Masha Kirasirova, Mary Nolan, Marilyn Young, and Joanna Waley-Cohen, eds, *The Routledge Handbook of the Global Sixties: Between Protest and Nation-Building* (London: Routledge, 2018); Yoav di-Capua, 'The Slow Revolution: May 1968 in the Arab World', *American Historical Review* 123, no. 3 (2018): 733–8.

15 See, for example, Zeina Maasri, Cathy Bergen, and Francesca Burke, eds, *Transnational Solidarity: Anticolonialism in the Global Sixties* (Manchester: Manchester University Press, 2022); Maasri, *Cosmopolitan Radicalism*; Jeffrey Byrne, *Mecca of Revolution: Algeria, Decolonization, and the Third World Order* (Oxford: Oxford University Press, 2016); Nasser Abourahme, ' "Nothing to Lose but Our Tents": The Camp, the Revolution, the Novel', *Journal of Palestine Studies* 48, no. 1 (2018): 33–52; Nahla Abdo, *Captive Revolution: Palestinian Women's Struggle Within the Israeli Prison System* (London: Pluto Press, 2014).

16 Karma Nabulsi, 'Lament for the Revolution', *London Review of Books* 32, no. 20–1, October 2010.

17 Samra, 'The Palestinian Student Movement 1948–1982', 30.

18 Angela Davis, 'Steve Biko Memorial Lecture', Transnational Solidarity, University of South Africa (UNISA), April 2021. Available online: https://www.us-africabridgeb uilding.org/essays/angela-davis-steve-biko-memorial/ (accessed 2 March 2022).

19 Hana Sleiman, 'The Paper Trail of a Liberation Movement', *Arab Studies Journal* 24, no. 1 (Spring 2016): 42–67.

20 Haugbolle and Olsen, 'The Emergence of Palestine'.

21 Thomson, Olsen, and Haugbolle, 'Palestine Solidarity Conferences in the Global Sixties', 29.

22 Mezna Qato, 'Forms of Retrieval: Social Scale, Citation, and the Archive of the Palestinian Left', *International Journal of Middle East Studies* 51, no. 2 (2019): 312. See also Sune Haugbolle, 'Entanglement, Global History, and the Arab Left', *International Journal of Middle East Studies* 51, no. 2 (2019): 301–4.

23 Reem Abou-El-Fadl, 'Building Egypt's Afro-Asian Hub: Infrastructures of Solidarity and the 1957 Cairo Conference', *Journal of World History* 30:1–2 (2019): 157–92; Olivia C. Harrison, *Transcolonial Maghreb: Imagining Palestine in the Era of*

Decolonization (Palo Alto: Stanford University Press, 2015); Fadi A. Bardawil, *Revolution and Disenchantment: Arab Marxism and the Binds of Emancipation* (Durham: Duke University Press, 2020); Naghmeh Sohrabi, 'Remembering the Palestine Group: Global Activism, Friendship, and the Iranian Revolution', *International Journal of Middle East Studies* 51, no. 2 (2019): 281–300.

24 Chamberlin, *The Global Offensive*, 14.
25 Tommie Shelbie, *We Who Are Dark: The Philosophical Foundations of Black Solidarity* (Cambridge, MA: Harvard University Press, 2005), 12.
26 David Featherstone, *Solidarity: Hidden Histories and Geographies of Internationalism* (London: Zed Books, 2012), 18–19.
27 Partha Chatterjee, 'The Colonial State', in *The Nation and Its Fragments: Colonial and Postcolonial Histories*, ed. Partha Chatterjee, 14–34. (New Jersey: Princeton University Press, 1993).
28 Antonio Gramsci, *Selections from the Prison Notebooks* (New York: International Publishers, 1971).
29 Sunaina Maira, *Boycott! The Academy and Justice for Palestine* (Berkeley: University of California Press, 2018). See also Kareem Estefan, Carin Kuoni, and Laura Raichovich, eds, *Assuming Boycott: Resistance, Agency and Cultural Production* (New York: Or Books, 2017).
30 Abdel Razzaq Takriti, 'Before BDS: Lineages of Boycott in Palestine', *Radical History Review* 134 (2019): 58. Available online: https://doi-org.ep.fjernadgang.kb.dk/10.1215/01636545-7323408.
31   Laure Guirguis, ed., *The Arab Lefts: Histories and Legacies, 1950s-1970s* (Edinburgh: Edinburgh University Press, 2020).
32 Nasser Abourahme, 'Revolution after Revolution: The Commune as Line of Flight in Palestinian Anticolonialism', *Critical Times* 4, no. 3 (2021): 445.

Bibliography

Abdo, Nahla. *Captive Revolution: Palestinian Women's Struggle within the Israeli Prison System*. London: Pluto Press, 2014.

Abou-El-Fadl, Reem. 'Building Egypt's Afro-Asian Hub: Infrastructures of Solidarity and the 1957 Cairo Conference', *Journal of World History* 30, no. 1–2 (2019): 157–92.

Abourahme, Nasser. ' "Nothing to Lose but Our Tents": The Camp, the Revolution, the Novel'. *Journal of Palestine Studies* 48, no. 1 (2018): 33–52.

Abourahme, Nasser. 'Revolution after Revolution: The Commune as Line of Flight in Palestinian Anticolonialism'. *Critical Times* 4, no. 3 (2021): 445–75.

Abu Samra, Mjriam. 'The Palestinian Student Movement 1948–1982: A Study of Popular Organisation and Transnational Mobilisation', PhD dissertation, University of Oxford, 2020.

Abu Samra, Mjriam, and Loubna Qutami. 'Alterity across Generations: A Comparative Analysis of the 1950s Jeel al-Thawra and the 2006 Palestinian Youth Movement', *Revue des mondes musulmans et de la Méditerranée* no. 147 (October 2020): 3–15.

Ahmad, Shahab. 'The Poetics of Solidarity: Palestine in Modern Urdu Poetry'. *Alif: Journal of Comparative Poetics* 18 (1998): 29–64.

Bardawil, Fadi. *Revolution and Disenchantment: Arab Marxism and the Binds of Emancipation*. Duke: Duke University Press, 2020.

Ben Prestel, Joseph. 'Heidelberg, Beirut, und die "Dritte Welt": Palästinensische Gruppen in der Bundesrepublik Deutschland (1956–1972)'. Zeithistorische Forschungen/*Studies in Contemporary History* 3 (2019): 442–66.

Byrne, Jeffrey. *Mecca of Revolution: Algeria, Decolonization, and the Third World Order*. Oxford: Oxford University Press, 2016.

Chamberlin, Paul Thomas. *The Global Offensive: The United States, the Palestine Liberation Organization, and the Making of the Post-Cold War Order*. Oxford: Oxford University Press, 2012.

Chamberlin, Paul Thomas. 'The Struggle against Oppression Everywhere: The Global Politics of Palestinian Liberation', *Middle Eastern Studies* 47, no. 1 (2011): 25–41.

Chatterjee, Partha. 'The Colonial State', in *The Nation and Its Fragments: Colonial and Postcolonial Histories*, edited by Partha Chatterjee, 14–34. New Jersey: Princeton University Press, 1993.

Christiansen, Samantha, and Zachary A. Scarlett. *The Third World in the Global 1960s*. New York: Berghahn Books, 2013.

Cobban, Helena. *The Palestinian Liberation Organisation: People, Power and Politics*. Cambridge: Cambridge University Press, 1984.

Davis, Angela. 'Steve Biko Memorial Lecture', Transnational Solidarity, University of South Africa (UNISA), April 2021. Available online: https://www.us-africabridgeb uilding.org/essays/angela-davis-steve-biko-memorial/ (accessed 2 March 2022).

Di-Capua, Yoav. 'Palestine Comes to Paris: The Global Sixties and the Making of a Universal Cause'. *Journal of Palestine Studies* 50, no. 1 (2021): 19–50.

Di-Capua, Yoav. 'The Slow Revolution: May 1968 in the Arab World'. *American Historical Review* 123, no. 3 (2018): 733–8.

Erakat, Noura. *Justice for Some: Law and the Question of Palestine*. Palo Alto: Stanford University Press, 2019.

Estefan, Kareem, Carin Kuoni, and Laura Raichovich, eds. *Assuming Boycott: Resistance, Agency and Cultural Production*. New York: Or Books, 2017.

Featherstone, David. *Solidarity: Hidden Histories and Geographies of Internationalism*. London: Zed Books, 2012.

Fischbach, R. Michael. *Black Power and Palestine: Transnational Countries of Color*. Palo Alto: Stanford University Press, 2018.

Fischbach, R. Michael. *The Movement and the Middle East: How the Arab-Israeli Conflict Divided the American Left*. Stanford: Stanford University Press, 2019.

Gramsci, Antonio. *Selections from the Prison Notebooks*. New York: International Publishers, 1971.

Guirguis, Laure. ed. *The Arab Lefts: Histories and Legacies, 1950s-1970s*. Edinburgh: Edinburgh University Press, 2020.

Habashneh, Khadija. *Fursan al-Sinima: Sirat Wahdat Aflam Filastin*. Amman: al-Ahliyya, 2020.

Haddad, Toufic. *Palestine Ltd.: Neoliberalism and Nationalism in the Occupied Territory*. London: I.B. Tauris, 2018.

Harrison, Olivia. C. 'Consuming Palestine: Anticapitalism and anticolonialism in Jean-Luc Godard's Ici et ailleurs', *Studies in French Cinema* 183 (2018): 178–91.

Harrison, Olivia C. *Transcolonial Maghreb: Imagining Palestine in the Era of Decolonization*. Palo Alto: Stanford University Press, 2015.

Haugbolle, Sune. 'Entanglement, Global History, and the Arab Left', *International Journal of Middle East Studies* 51, no. 2 (2019): 301–4.

Haugbolle, Sune, and Pelle Valentin Olsen. 'The Emergence of Palestine as a Global Cause'. *Middle East Critique* (forthcoming 2022).

Jian, Chen, Martin Klimke, Masha Kirasirova, Mary Nolan, Marilyn Young, and Joanna Waley-Cohen, eds *The Routledge Handbook of the Global Sixties: Between Protest and Nation-Building*. Milton Park: Routledge. 2018.

Kalter, Christopher. *The Discovery of the Third World: Decolonization and the Rise of the New Left in France, C1950–1976*. Cambridge: Cambridge University Press.

Kazziha, Walid. *Revolutionary Transformation in the Arab World: Habash and His Comrades from Nationalism to Marxism*. London: C. Knight, 1975.

Khalidi, Rashid. *The Iron Cage: The Story of the Palestinian Struggle for Statehood*. London: Oneworld Publications, 2007.

Khalili, Laleh. *Heroes and Martyrs of Palestine: The Politics of National Commemoration*. Cambridge: Cambridge University Press, 2007.

Khouri, Krtisitne, and Rasha Salti. *Past Disquiet: Artists, International Solidarity, and Museums in Exile*. Chicago: University of Chicago Press, 2018.

Lee, Christopher J. *Making a World after Empire: The Bandung Moment and Its Political Afterlives*. Athens: Ohio University Press, 2010.

Lewis, Su Lin, and Carolien Stolte. 'Other Bandungs: Afro-Asian Internationalism in the Early Cold War'. *Journal of World History* 30, no. 1–2 (2019): 1–19.

Louro, Michele, Carolien Stolte, Heather Streets-Salter, and Sana Tannoury-Karam, eds *The League Against Imperialism: Lives and Afterlives*. Leiden: Leiden University Press, 2020.

Maasri, Zeina. *Cosmopolitan Radicalism: The Visual Politics of Beirut's Global Sixties*. Cambridge: Cambridge University Press, 2020.

Maasri, Zeina, Cathy Bergen, and Francesca Burke, eds. *Transnational Solidarity: Anticolonialism in the Global Sixties*. Manchester: Manchester University Press, 2022.

Maina, Sunaina. *Boycott! The Academy and Justice for Palestine.* Berkeley: University of California Press, 2018.

Matar, Dina. 'PLO Cultural Activism: Mediating Liberation Aesthetics in Revolutionary Contexts'. *Comparative Studies of South Asia, Africa and the Middle East* 38, no. 2 (2018): 354–64.

Nabulsi, Karma. 'Lament for the Revolution', *London Review of Books* 32, no. 20 (October 2010).

Nabulsi, Karma, and Abdel Razzaq Takriti. *The Palestinian Revolution*, 2018. Available online: http://learnpalestine.politics.ox.ac.uk/ (accessd 5 October 2021)

Nassar, Maha. '"My Struggle Embraces Every Struggle": Palestinians in Israel and Solidarity with Afro-Asian Liberation Movements'. *Arab Studies Journal* 22, no. 1 (2014): 74–101.

Qato, Mezna. 'Forms of Retrieval: Social Scale, Citation, and the Archive of the Palestinian Left', *International Journal of Middle East Studies* 51, no. 2 (2019): 312–5.

Sayigh, Rosemary. *The Palestinians: From Peasants to Revolutionaries.* London: Zed Books, 1979.

Sayigh, Yezid. *Armed Struggle and the Search for State: The Palestinian National Movement, 1949–1993.* Oxford: Oxford University Press, 1999.

Shelbie, Tommie. *We Who Are Dark: The Philosophical Foundations of Black Solidarity.* Massachusetts: Harvard University Press, 2005.

Sleiman, Hana. 'The Paper Trail of a Liberation Movement'. *Arab Studies Journal* 24, no. 1 (Spring 2016): 42–67.

Slobodian, Quinn. *Foreign Front: Third World Politics in Sixties West Germany.* Durham, NC: Duke University Press, 2012.

Sohrabi, Naghmeh. 'Remembering the Palestine Group: Global Activism, Friendship, and the Iranian Revolution'. *International Journal of Middle East Studies* 51, no. 2 (2019): 281–300.

Stites Mor, Jessica. 'The Question of Palestine in the Argentine Political Imaginary: Anti-Imperialist Thought from Cold War to Neoliberal Order'. *Journal of Iberian and Latin American Research* 20, no. 2 (2014): 183–97.

Tabar, Linda. 'From Third World internationalism to "the internationals": The transformation of solidarity with Palestine'. *Third World Quarterly* 38, no. 2 (2017): 414–35.

Takriti, Abdel Razzaq. 'Before BDS: Lineages of Boycott in Palestine'. *Radical History Review* 2019, no. 134 (2019): 58–95.

Thomson, Sorcha, Pelle Valentin Olsen, and Sune Haugbolle. 'Palestine Solidarity Conferences in the Global Sixties'. *Journal of Palestine Studies* 51, no. 1 (2022): 27–49.

Tzu-Chun, Judy. *Radicals on the Road: Internationalism, Orientalism, and Feminism during the Vietnam Era.* New York. Cornell University Press, 2013.

Yaqub, Nadia. *Palestinian Cinema in the Days of Revolution.* Austin: University of Texas Press, 2018.

Young, Cynthia. *Soul Power: Culture, Radicalism, and the Making of a U.S Third World Left*. Durham: Duke University Press, 2006.

Wolin, Richard. *The Wind from the East: French Intellectuals, the Cultural Revolution and the Legacy of the 1960s*. Princeton: Princeton University Press, 2012.

Zolov, Eric. 'La Tricontinental y El Mensaje Del Che Guevara. Encrucijadas de Una Nueva Izquierda'. *Latin American & Caribbean Studies* 6, no. 9 (2016): 1–13.

Part 1
Travelling Revolutionaries

1

'Fight for everybody, everywhere'? Paul Robeson, Palestine and selective solidarity

Gabriel Polley

'"Mazeltov" to Israel'

This chapter explores the attitudes of the African American actor, singer and left-wing and civil rights campaigner Paul Robeson towards the Palestine Question.[1] Despite his passionate denunciations of colonialism and settler colonialism elsewhere, Robeson repeatedly made statements strongly supportive of Zionism and even performed at a celebratory rally on the day of Israel's establishment. Subsequent changes in his position in the 1950s, however, powerfully illustrate how, from the end of the Second World War to the 1950s, leftist and radical Black opinion on Israel could change drastically. This chapter includes a short examination of Robeson's life and how he practiced internationalist solidarity; a review of his public pronouncements on Palestine, taken largely from previously unanalyzed primary sources, particularly the leftist and Black press; and a consideration of Robeson's views in the context of the Communist Party of the USA's (CPUSA's) positions.

On the evening of Saturday, 15 May 1948, hours after the Zionist movement declared the State of Israel's independence, 40,000 people assembled at New York's Polo Grounds in Upper Manhattan to celebrate the occasion. The event was held under the auspices of the American Committee of Jewish Writers, Artists and Scientists, a pro-Soviet group active during the Second World War (Albert Einstein was its honorary president).[2] Palestinians had been undergoing ethnic cleansing perpetrated by Zionist paramilitary groups since the United Nations (UN) vote on Palestine's partition on 29 November 1947;[3] nevertheless, the crowd in New York gathered – in the cheery headline of the *Daily Worker* (*DW*), the newspaper of the CPUSA – to 'say "Mazeltov" [congratulations] to Israel'.

As one speaker at the rally stated, the rally's purpose was also to congratulate those Americans who had supported Israel's establishment.[4] The event was the apogee of a hard-fought campaign, during which Zionists intensely lobbied President Truman to back the creation of a Jewish state in Palestine and supplied this cause with donations and illegally smuggled arms to be used against the Palestinians.[5] The speakers at the Polo Grounds vocally supported Israel's war effort, demanding the US government 'stop payments of oil royalties to the Arab nations' and charged the Arab states with 'outright acts of aggression before the bar of the United Nations'. The antifascist rallying cry of the Spanish Civil War, '*No Pasaran*', echoed against the Palestinians.[6]

Notably, most of the speakers at the rally were left wing, even socialist, indicating the extent to which support for Israel was a cause of the left at the time. Several were under investigation by the infamous House Un-American Activities Committee (HUAC) for alleged communist connections. There was Bartley Crum, not only a California-born lawyer known as 'Comrade Crum' for his leftist inclinations, but also a pro-Zionist member of the Anglo-American Committee of Inquiry advising Truman on Palestine,[7] and the leftist Idaho congressmen Glen Taylor, who ran for vice-president on the Progressive Party's 1948 ticket. In his speech, the playwright Arthur Miller proclaimed that the establishment of Israel had 'redeemed our honour in the eyes of the world'. From Israel itself was Ya'akov Riftin, part of Israel's first UN delegation, subsequently a member of the Knesset for the left-Zionist faction Mapam.[8]

Of all the speakers at the pro-Israel gala on the day of the Palestinian Nakba, the one whose attendance is most striking is the Black American actor, singer and tireless civil rights and socialist campaigner Paul Robeson. In the bass baritone that earned him worldwide fame, the fifty-year-old led the crowd in a rendition of *HaTikvah*, the new Israeli anthem. Robeson stated, 'This day, the founding of the Jewish State in Palestine, gives hope to the Negro peoples all over the world.'[9]

Robeson's appearance was symptomatic of the mid-twentieth century when left-wing sympathies lay firmly with Zionism, and his participation in the gala should be seen in this context. Yet Robeson's case deserves to be considered in its own right because of his particular concern with the oppression faced and struggles waged by colonized peoples of colour globally. It is difficult to square Robeson's pro-Israel position with his passionate denunciations of other examples of settler colonialism. For example, in an October 1947 column in the radical African American newspaper the *People's Voice*, Robeson lambasted the situation: 'In East, Central and South Africa, [and] French North Africa', where 'a small minority of foreign settlers and commercial interests have usurped the land and complete political control, converting the native inhabitants into a landless peasantry.'[10] In British-occupied Palestine, too, the colonial practices of a small minority of Jewish settlers had converted many of the native inhabitants into landless peasants, a process which reached a tragic magnitude in 1948.

The participation of Robeson's discursive linking of Israel with Black struggle, not only in the United States where he led the American Crusade against Lynching (ACAL), but also in the liberation struggles of colonized Africans, also contrasts dramatically with the positions of later Black radicals. As Michael Fischbach writes of 1960s Black Power activists, 'Stemming from their internationalist anti-imperialism, black militants latched on to the Palestinian cause as another liberation struggle waged by a people of color deserving their support. They saw themselves and the Palestinians as kindred peoples of color waging a revolution against a global system of oppression.'[11] While it is unfair to directly contrast Robeson with the Black radicals a generation (or two) his junior, the question of what circumstances led him to take a position diametrically opposed to those later radicals is illustrative of the changes that took place between these generations regarding solidarity with the Palestinians.

This chapter considers what led Robeson to perform for the Israeli cause on the evening of 15 May 1948. Why did a man who described his political philosophy as 'fight for everybody, everywhere',[12] fail to extend this solidarity to the Palestinians in their hour of greatest suffering? This question asked of a man once, as the pioneering Black sociologist and activist W. E. B. Du Bois put it – 'the best known American on earth, to the largest number of human beings',[13] and a personal friend of towering anticolonial figures including Jawaharlal Nehru and Kwame Nkrumah – is fascinating in its own right. However, through Robeson's personal involvement with Palestine, broader trends emerge regarding the left's shifting understandings under the influence of decolonization struggles of the global South and the competing ties of affinity of African Americans with Israel and with the Palestinians. This chapter presents a short examination of Robeson's life, before moving to a review of his public pronouncements on Palestine, an exploration of his views in the context of the CPUSA's positions on Palestine and finally a consideration of what caused his view of Israel to begin to shift.

A life in solidarity

Robeson does not today enjoy the same canonization as other Black civil rights campaigners of the mid-twentieth century, partly because, as an unapologetic advocate of socialism during the Cold War, and a close associate (though never a member) of the CPUSA, the US government did everything in its power to silence Robeson. He saw American racism as inextricably bound up with capitalism and imperialism, a claim which still makes liberal arbiters of acceptability uncomfortable. It is thus useful here to provide a brief account of Robeson's life and internationalist outlook.[14]

Paul Leroy Robeson was born in Princeton, New Jersey, in 1898, the fifth and youngest child of a Presbyterian preacher (and formerly enslaved escapee) father and a teacher mother. Educated at Rutgers College, New Jersey, and Columbia University's law school, Robeson began acting professionally in 1922 and singing in 1925. During his artistic career, he recorded over 450 songs; before 1947, by which time he was frustrated with the typecast and racially stereotyped roles he was offered, he starred in ten films and many plays and musicals. Robeson moved to London in the late 1920s with his wife Eslanda Cordozo Goode, remaining there until the late 1930s. Largely shunning elite concert halls, he earned the adoration of working-class audiences. He met the leaders of anticolonial liberation movements, made the first of several visits to the Soviet Union, which he praised for its apparent absence of racism in 1934, and in 1937 travelled to Republican Spain to sing for the antifascist fighters.

Robeson returned to the United States in 1940, now perhaps the country's premier entertainment figure. He vigorously supported the Allies against Nazi Germany but also founded the Council on African Affairs, campaigning for African decolonization. After the Second World War, he became a prominent voice critiquing imperialist ventures of the United States abroad and Jim Crow racism at home. Under increasing Federal Bureau of Investigation (FBI) surveillance for closeness to the Soviet Union and the CPUSA, Robeson's passport was rescinded by the US State Department in August 1950, on the excuse that his travel would be 'contrary to the best interests of the United States', and was blacklisted by the entertainment industry. After a worldwide campaign in his support, he was finally allowed to travel again and tour internationally in 1958. In 1961, however, he suffered a nervous breakdown in Moscow, and after two years of depression and mentally damaging 'treatment' in Europe, he returned to the United States to live a reclusive life. He died at the age of seventy-seven in 1976.

Robeson had an instinctive ability to empathize with people whom he recognized as in struggle against the same oppressive structures from which African Americans also suffered. Like the Black radicals who later viewed themselves and Palestinians as 'kindred peoples of color',[15] Robeson saw himself as part of a global oppressed community. Robeson's capacity for empathy is illustrated by his and his wife's trip to Egypt during filming for the 1937 film *Jericho*. Robeson began learning Arabic to communicate with ordinary Egyptians; his polyglottic achievement (he studied over twenty languages, including several African tongues, Hebrew, Hindi, Mandarin Chinese, Russian and Yiddish) is evidence of his respect for other cultures. Britain had withdrawn most of its troops in 1936, leaving Egypt and Sudan (itself subjected to Egyptian rule) nominally independent under the pro-British monarchy, and Cordoza Goode, Robeson's wife, voiced their feeling of being among kin and remarked it was 'great fun to see an enormously rich country like this, where the coloured folks are the bosses'.[16] Yet Robeson's feeling of kinship with Egyptian Arabs evidently did not extend to Palestinians a decade later.

Robeson's writings and speeches of the 1940s engage with almost the full breadth of the anticolonial and socialistic struggles of the time, among which he clearly numbered the Zionist enterprise in Palestine. Robeson sometimes drew unorthodox connections between struggles. For example, he spoke at a New York rally on 5 April 1948 (well into the period of Zionist military operations and refugee flight in Palestine) in support of the Chinese Communist Party during the Chinese Civil War. After singing 'several Jewish and Chinese songs', Robeson proclaimed that the cause of the Chinese communists was 'the same thing Mrs. Ingram is saying to America from Georgia and what Jewish mothers are crying in agony from Palestine'.[17] In her recent work on British radical solidarity for anticolonial movements, Priyamvada Gopal identifies 'a pedagogical process … [of] "reverse tutelage," in which metropolitan dissidents came to learn something from their anticolonial interlocutors and the movements they represented'.[18] Robeson's approach connected international struggles with the neo-imperial domination of US capitalism. Robeson also saw the injustice meted out against national liberation movements as a potential precursor of violence against US workers, especially African Americans. As Robeson said to a Jewish audience in late 1945, after denouncing 'the British bombing and strafing of Indonesians and the Jews in Tel-Aviv (*sic*)', 'What's happening abroad can happen in the United States.'[19]

These attitudes should be borne in mind during the following discussion of Robeson's views. He held a view, then widespread, of the Zionist movement as a heroic liberation movement opposing the forces of imperialism. This enabled the mischaracterization of the Zionist cause in Palestine as, in Kaplan's locution, 'one among a number of progressive movements for liberation and social justice',[20] leaving little room for solidarity with the Palestinians.

Robeson and Palestine

Robeson's affinity with the Jewish people, often expressed through his music, has already been noted.[21] While this feeling certainly influenced his support for Zionism, his comments specifically on the Palestine Question reveal a distinct historical context. Robeson's earliest statements on Palestine appeared in the press in the mid-1930s. In early 1935, Robeson took a rather mystical view of Palestine as part of an Oriental source of knowledge and rebirth, alternative to European cultural hegemony. Imploring Black cultural producers to 'recognize our cultural affinity with the East', he continued, 'Instead of coming to the Sorbonne and Oxford, I would like to see students of culture go to Palestine and Pekin [Beijing] … I would like to watch the flowering of their inherent qualities under sympathetic influences there.'[22] More concretely, Robeson stated to a US Jewish newspaper that he was interested in visiting Palestine and had begun learning Hebrew and making recordings of Hebrew ('Palestinian') songs. Complaining that 'the Negro in America despises his culture', Robeson asserted that 'you had the same thing in the early days of Zionism. If only we could have the same self-respect of the real Jew, who is proud of his culture.'[23] Robeson straightforwardly accepted Zionism as a model for Black national consciousness, similar to other Black radicals such as Marcus Garvey.[24]

During the Second World War, Robeson's participation in antifascist organizing in the United States brought him into contact with leading American Zionists. For example, Robeson performed to around 50,000 at the Polo Grounds in July 1943, welcoming the Soviet delegation of the Jewish Anti-Fascist Committee, which included the dramatist Solomon Mikhoels and poet Itzik Feffer, with whom Robeson formed close bonds. Among the speakers at the welcome were the prominent Zionist campaigner Stephen Wise and member of the World Zionist Organization executive Nahum Goldmann. Linking the fight against Nazism with Zionist efforts in Palestine, Goldmann announced that he spoke at the rally 'because I am a Zionist'.[25]

After the war's end, liberal pro-Zionist Americans returned the solidarity by supporting the African American struggle. Robeson's coalition building at this time did much to cement the alliance between Black civil rights campaigners and liberal Jews in particular, later drawn upon by Martin Luther King, until the emergence of more radical Black groups whose hostility towards such liberals partly sprang from their opposing analysis on Palestine, especially after 1967.[26] In the 1940s, prominent supporters of Zionism like Crum were involved in Robeson's ACAL.[27] Another speaker at the 1948 Polo Grounds rally called in October 1946 for increased Jewish participation in the ACAL, but also for Black support of Zionism, claiming that 'the Jews of Palestine are being lynched on a more ferocious scale than Negroes have ever known'.[28] This was a period in which tensions were escalating between Zionist militant groups and both the Palestinians and the British authorities, epitomized by the bombing of the British administrative headquarters in Jerusalem's King David Hotel on 22 July 1946 by the right-wing Zionist militia the Irgun, killing ninety-one Arab, British and Jewish civil servants.

Interviewed in early 1946, Robeson stated that he had 'thought a lot about the Jewish problem', concluding that he could 'see no justification today for not allowing them to go to Palestine'. On Arab Jewish relations, Robeson stated, 'I can see only advancement for the Arabs, and betterment of their lot through the development of Jewish Palestine – a labor Palestine.' Given his own continuous espousing of a solidarity with the oppressed which crossed all borders, it was ironic that Robeson 'dismissed … with a wave of his hand' the interviewer's opposing of Zionism to 'an internationalism which will do away with all homelands', describing such a position as 'purely academic'. Robeson still interpreted Zionism through the lens of Black national consciousness, arguing that 'assimilation is impossible', and likening his own identification with Africa to Zionist Jews' identification with Palestine.[29] While seeking the elimination of racial injustice everywhere, Robeson had internalized Zionism's narrative that Jews could only escape racism in a national homeland, without comprehending the implications of this for the indigenous people residing in the territory selected as that homeland.

In the last weeks of the mandate, when Zionist forces had already begun the capture of Palestinian villages and expulsion of their inhabitants,[30] Robeson made a drastic, though unfulfilled, pledge. In March 1948, Robeson asserted to an interviewer that 'if an all-out war was declared in the Holy Land he would immediately go to Palestine to sing for Jewish troops as he did for Loyalists [i.e. Republicans] during the Spanish civil war'.[31] Once 'all-out war' between Zionist settlers, Arab armies and Palestinian irregulars had begun, Robeson continued his supportive pronouncements on the new Israeli state, while campaigning for the CPUSA-backed Progressive Party candidate Henry Wallace in the November presidential election.[32] Wallace accused Truman of allowing 'unnecessary, shameful mass murder in Palestine', and condemned his '"do nothing" policy … while Mr. [British foreign secretary Ernest] Bevin arms the Arab feudal lords so they can continue the work of Adolf Hitler'.[33] At a Wallace campaign event in August, Robeson praised the Haganah, the largest body in the Zionist movement's armed forces, for having 'fought courageously for their homeland' and demanded Truman 'to lift the embargo against arms so that the Jewish people can defend themselves against the Arabs'. He reprised the familiar refrain that the victory of Zionism was 'a question of the oppressed people all over the world – the Jewish people, the Negro people'.[34]

In February 1949, in the left-wing British newspaper *Reynold's News*, Robeson reflected the prevalent view among American progressives that Truman had not given Israel sufficient support because of Arab oil, describing himself as 'a friend of Israel, not of the oil interests'.[35] This prognosis was based on a common misconception of the positions of the Arab states where US 'oil interests' were located. In fact, as Finkelstein points out, 'Most Arab leaders were prepared to acquiesce in Palestine's division'. US policy was, in 1948, not primarily driven by the unfounded fears of the domestic oil lobby and supposed intransigence of 'Arab feudal lords'.[36]

By 1949, the Western left began to realize that the picture was more complex than Jewish workers fighting imperialist-backed Arab reaction, that the Zionist movement had been guilty of serious crimes and that Palestinian civilians had been made homeless or killed. For instance, the *DW* reported in July and November 1948 on the Deir Yassin massacre of 9 April when at least ninety-three civilians were killed at the Jerusalem-area village, describing it as a 'pogrom' which 'helped embitter and fill with fear hundreds of thousands of Palestine Arabs'.[37] Indicative of the left's continuing support for Israel, however, the massacre was lamented as 'very damaging to the Jewish cause' and explained as the responsibility of the Irgun alone, not part of Zionism's systemic drive to occupy the largest area of land with the fewest possible Palestinians.[38]

The first note of moderation in Robeson's public statements on Palestine came in an address at a London anti-apartheid meeting on 29 March 1949. Deploring white settlers' efforts to foment division between Africans and Indians in South Africa, Robeson stated that such a 'fratricidal clash' could 'have the same tragic consequences … as the Arab-Jewish conflicts had for the people of Palestine or Hindu-Moslem antagonisms for the people of India'.[39] Robeson's acknowledgement, though brief, of the 'tragic consequences' accompanying Israel's establishment, contrasted with his earlier unambiguous support for Zionism. Nevertheless, at a large concert in Los Angeles in October 1949, he sang 'A marching song of Israel's Hagannah [*sic*] in Hebrew', which was 'thunderously applauded by the many Jews present'.[40]

Robeson would have performed in Israel had he been able to travel there. When his passport was confiscated in August 1950, Robeson was scheduled for a world tour involving sixteen concerts in Israel.[41] Five passport-less years later, Robeson revealed that during his effective imprisonment in the United States, he was again invited to perform in Israel.[42] At his appearance in front of the HUAC in June 1956, in a statement he was not permitted to read, he again noted that he hoped to tour in Israel.[43] Detectable in the travel destinations he had wanted to name – Britain, Western Europe, Australia and Israel – is Robeson's desire to demonstrate that providing him with a passport would not be contrary to US interests, as all these countries were Western allies. Israel, despite its labour Zionist-run governments, was not a Soviet-allied socialist state but quickly positioned itself in the Western Bloc.

There can be little doubt that, had he been able to travel, Robeson would have fulfilled his long-held dream of performing in Palestine/Israel. However, the world would change before his passport was returned. Now, though, we turn to the context of the American left.

The Palestine Question and the CPUSA

While Robeson's support for Israel can be viewed within a tradition of Black enthusiasm for Zionism as a model African Americans could emulate,[44] it can also be framed within the context of the US left. Sections of Western societies were deeply shocked by revelations of Jewish suffering in Nazi-occupied Europe, leaving the door open to strong sympathy and support for the Zionist movement and Israel. For leftists, this was especially pronounced. Associating opposition to Zionism with reaction and even fascism, progressives also projected their own idealism onto the new Israeli state – the 'labor Palestine' which Robeson had envisaged.

It might be assumed that Robeson's and the CPUSA's positive appraisals of Zionism after 1945 were a result of a widespread revulsion towards the Holocaust. However, as Novick has shown, until the 1970s the Holocaust had 'nowhere near the centrality in consciousness' it later gained.[45] Articulating the Jewish people's plight was, to a significant extent, the specific prerogative of the left, setting the likes of Robeson and the CPUSA apart from the political mainstream as they attempted to highlight an issue not on most Americans' agenda. Further, support for Zionism was far from the only possible reaction from those sincerely deploring the Nazis' persecution of European Jews;

Einstein, for instance, remained highly sceptical of Zionism after the Holocaust. Other factors explaining Robeson's position should thus be sought.

Given Robeson's close association with the CPUSA, it is worth investigating how the Party approached events in Palestine. Before the Second World War, the CPUSA maintained a sceptical, even hostile, position towards Zionism. For instance Paul Novick, editor of the CPUSA's Yiddish-language paper *Morgen Freiheit*, in 1938, stridently asserted that 'the slogan that Palestine is the only place for Jewish refugees has no basis in fact'; castigated 'those Zionists favoring partition, like the leader of the Labor Zionists, Ben-Gurion', for desiring 'the "transfer" (banishment, in simple language) of the 300,000 Arabs now living in the coastal regions'; and called for a binational solution – that is, an Arab Jewish state.[46]

However, this position drastically shifted towards a total acceptance of Zionism's premises. This shift originated in Moscow where, as for all the world's Soviet-affiliated communist parties, the important policies of the CPUSA were determined. The Communist Party of the Soviet Union had strongly opposed Zionism throughout the 1920s and 1930s, attacking the settlement enterprise in Palestine as occurring in conjunction with British imperialism. With the Nazis' attack on the Soviet Union in June 1941, the Soviet position abruptly changed, ceasing its anti-British and anti-Zionist stances. This continued with the Soviet UN vote for Palestine's partition in November 1947, diplomatic recognition of Israel three days after its establishment and the Eastern Bloc's arms supply to Zionist forces through Czechoslovakia.[47]

Following the war, the CPUSA initially occupied an ambiguous position: while officially advocating binationalism, its leadership and membership were increasingly sympathetic to Zionism. For instance, an October 1946 statement of the Party's candidate (publicly endorsed by Robeson) in the elections for New York state comptroller proclaimed, 'There are Jews who want to go to Palestine. We believe that they should be allowed to do so. Imperialism has closed the gates and keeps them closed. The gates will not be closed if they shout "Open the gates!" long enough.' The statement continued that this fight was 'an integral part of the struggle for freedom and independence of Palestine'.[48]

The CPUSA bitterly attacked the US government's perceived opposition to the establishment of a Jewish state, and continuing trade with Arab states. This narrative influenced Robeson's solidarity with the Zionist movement; if US imperialism opposed Jewish aspirations in Palestine, then Zionists and African Americans possessed a common enemy in the Truman administration. The CPUSA line, reflected in the *DW*'s reporting, often bore little resemblance to reality. When a truce between Israel and the Arab states (but not Palestinians) was announced in June 1948, the paper thundered that 'the so-called "truce" in Palestine is of small use to the embattled new state of Israel' and again called for Washington's supply of Israel with arms, or be 'convicted – once again – of siding with reaction and war'.[49] As the *DW*'s headline stated, it was indeed a 'Phony "Truce"' but not in the way the author intended – Zionist militias used the four-week period to capture tens of Palestinian villages, expel their inhabitants and raze their homes.[50]

The settlers' fight in Palestine, in the eyes of Western leftists a struggle for survival against Anglo-American imperialism and reactionary Arab monarchies, exerted a powerful pull for Black radicals. Not confined to pro-Moscow communists, it included the Trinidadian Trotskyist C. L. R. James, who wrote in 1947 of the Haganah that 'the world revolution manifests itself not in the Red Army but in Palestine'. As Robeson often did, he drew comparisons between Zionist efforts against the British and anticolonial struggles 'in Indonesia, in Indo-China, in India, China and Burma'.[51]

Du Bois, a close associate of Robeson and another Black figure affiliated with the CPUSA, also viewed Zionism as an anti-imperialist liberation movement.[52] In a 1948 article saturated with Orientalist discourse, Du Bois described Palestine as 'sparsely inhabited' and its indigenous Arab population as characterized by 'widespread ignorance, poverty and disease and a fanatic belief in the Mohammedan religion' and a backward society which 'makes effective use of democratic methods difficult'. '[As] Americans ought to know', he argued, 'the question of possession of a land is in the long run the question of the use to which it is put.'[53] The positive appeal to American beneficiaries of Native Americans' dispossession, to support the Zionist settler project precisely because of its similar features, reads awkwardly not least because Du Bois, Robeson and other Black progressives were struggling against the structural racism emanating from the settler-colonial origins of the United States.

Like Robeson, Du Bois provided Zionism with a progressive slant, stating that 'young and forward thinking' Jewish settlers were building 'by democratic methods … a new and peculiarly fateful modern state'. This claim resembled that of left-Zionist settlers in Palestine, represented by the pro-Soviet Mapam, that the concentration of Jewish workers in Palestine would allow the development of a socialist society. Furthermore, Du Bois continued, this would be 'for the advantage, not simply of the Jews, but of the Arabs'.[54] For Du Bois to make this claim in the very year of Palestinian dispossession indicates the chasm between the nature of the events then taking place and Western left and Black radicals' understanding of the situation. The next few years, marked by decolonial upheavals and an emerging pattern of imperial intervention in the Middle East, would change this state of affairs.

Changing perspectives and the Suez Crisis

While Robeson expressed his wish to visit Israel throughout the earlier 1950s, he was also exposed to voices challenging the narrative he had believed so strongly. The international communist movement, which had loudly trumpeted its backing for Israel in 1948, began to experience a disillusionment in these years. This had very little to do with Israel's responsibility for Palestinian suffering, which remained effectively absent from the left's awareness, but rather owed to the Israeli government's failure to align with the Soviet camp as a token of gratitude for the Eastern Bloc's vital support in 1948. Instead, Israel allied itself with the capitalist West, and David Ben Gurion's government was castigated in the *DW* as having 'sold itself hand and foot to Washington's anti-Soviet war plotters'. A *DW* editorial in February 1952 noted that Israel had blocked discussion of Tunisia's independence at the UN and lamented that such positions against the emerging decolonizing world 'endanger[ed] the peace, independence and very existence of Israel'.[55]

Such feelings – justified, perhaps, from the communist perspective, though missing the mark by overlooking the Palestinian refugee crisis – were unfortunately combined with the ugly anti-Semitism of the late Stalin era, a period Brossat and Klineberg assert was characterized by 'a reactionary policy which broke fundamentally with the programme of the October Revolution'.[56] In November 1952, fourteen high-ranking members of the Communist Party of Czechoslovakia, including its general secretary Rudolf Slánský, were charged on Moscow's orders with high treason. Ten of the accused were Jewish, and among the fabricated charges was that they were Israel's secret agents aiming to undermine the Eastern Bloc from within. After an eight-day show trial, Slánský and ten others were hanged. The CPUSA, including Jewish members, willingly overlooked the blatant falsifications. Louis Harap, the editor of the CPUSA's Jewish affairs magazine *Jewish Life*, parroted the Stalinist narrative that Slánský and his co-defendants 'were ideologically hostile to socialism and the Soviet Union, namely Trotskyites, Slovak and Jewish nationalists (Zionists), that is, people who place the interests of the dominant capitalist elements above those of the working class'.[57]

Robeson could not have been unaware of these events and the changing discourse on Israel which gripped the US left's attention; whether he believed the outrageous claims amid a travesty of justice is another question. He saw firsthand that life in the Soviet Union was far from perfect when he visited in 1949. His Jewish pianist was denied a visa; more tragically, his wartime friend Mikhoels had been brutally killed probably on Stalin's orders in early 1948, and Feffer was imprisoned, brought to Robeson's hotel room and only able to communicate through hand signals and written notes as the room was bugged (Feffer was executed three years later). Robeson symbolically expressed his solidarity with Soviet Jews (and a critique of the Soviet authorities), performing the Yiddish resistance song of the Warsaw Ghetto, *Zog Nit Kaynmal*, to a Moscow concert hall. Returning to the United States, he continued to publicly defend the Soviet Union as a paradise for its minorities.[58]

A more sincere critique of Israel came from a source closer to Robeson. In October 1952, Robeson had a final meeting with his friend Einstein in Princeton. Explaining why he had rejected the offer of the ceremonial role of Israel's presidency then recently made to him by the Israeli government, Einstein told Robeson that he had been in favour of a binational Arab Jewish state, rather than the kind of state Israel had turned out to be.[59] While he recognized Israel's value as a haven for Jews, he also reflected that were he Israel's president, he 'would have to say to the Israeli people things they would not like to hear'.[60]

But it was ultimately the process of decolonization, during which the struggles of the Arab world were framed in a new and progressive light, which had the biggest impact on Robeson's understanding of Israel. In April 1955, Robeson sent his greetings to the Afro-Asian Conference at Bandung, Indonesia, hailing it as a sign of 'the power and the determination of the peoples of these two great continents to decide their own destiny'.[61] Yet Bandung issued a resolution declaring 'support for the rights of the Arab people of Palestine and … the implementation of the United Nations resolutions on Palestine and … the peaceful settlement of the Palestine question'.[62] While Robeson had viewed Zionism as akin to African and Asian liberation movements, Bandung underlined the newly decolonizing world's identification with the Arab cause. This owed largely to Egypt's Arab nationalist president Gamal Abdel Nasser. While the elites of the declining empires compared him to Hitler, Abdel Nasser was seen very differently by the African and Arab masses emerging from, or still fighting against, colonization.[63] Before the Palestine Liberation Organization (PLO) emerged as a politically independent body in the late 1960s, Abdel Nasser was also the most prominent figure giving voice to Arab demands vis-à-vis Palestine. His resolution at Bandung called for the creation of an Arab Palestinian state and the right of return for hundreds of thousands of refugees to their former homes in Israel as per UN Resolution 194. As Nahed Samour notes, Bandung's 'tensions and contradictions' meant the conference was 'almost inconsequential' in practical terms regarding Palestine.[64] But for a Western left which recently gave Israel almost entirely uncritical support during 1948, and which had virtually ignored the plight of Palestinian refugees, the new framing of the Palestinian cause heralded the start of profound changes of perspective.

In late October 1956 came the Suez Crisis and Britain, France and Israel's attack on Abdel Nasser's Egypt; Israel would remain in occupation of the Gaza Strip and Sinai until March 1957. While Israel, according to the beliefs of radicals like Robeson, had been established through a heroic struggle *against* imperialism, it had now allied itself with two imperial powers against an independent African country that was a light to the global South.

This turn of events, and the strong Soviet backing for Egypt, was a dramatic moment for the Western left. Following the Soviet position on the conflict, the CPUSA was quick to make stringent criticisms of Israel's behaviour, something not welcomed by all quarters of the Party's membership and erstwhile sympathisers. A heated exchange continued for months in the *DW*'s letters pages. One disgruntled reader wrote in labelling Abdel Nasser 'a fascist dictator' and blaming the Soviet standpoint against Israel on 'the ages [*sic*] old sickness called anti-Semitism'.[65] Another, signing themselves 'A Jewish Communist', wrote to emphasize 'what the Israeli people feel and need – the right to self-determination and peaceful borders'.[66] On the other side, the most powerful critique of Israel came from Ben Davis, a prominent Black CPUSA leader and a close friend of Robeson.[67] Writing in early March 1957, as Israeli troops finally left Gaza, Davis noted that 'Negroes are anything but neutral in this matter. I believe that they are mostly pro-Egyptian and that they're right, and that they're pro-Egyptian in the sense that they're anti-colonial, not anti-Semitic'.[68]

The Suez Crisis thus created significant divisions where previously there had been effective alliances. Among the body of Jewish progressives, and between Jewish liberals and sections of Black America, there were two camps. One steadfastly refused to make any criticism of Israel and hence accepted Israel's and the imperialist powers' narrative of Abdel Nasser as a fascist who had to be stopped. The other, while not questioning the necessity of Israel's existence or Jewish settlers' actions in 1948, now raised serious questions about Israel's subsequent behaviour towards the Arabs, the likes of which had not been heard on the left since communists' anti-Zionist rhetoric dwindled in the early 1940s.

This division was not yet terminal; after Israel had withdrawn from the Arab territory it briefly occupied, the two camps could return to their cooperation on the domestic issue of the African American struggle, for a while. Yet the seed of leftists' and Black radicals' post-1967 break with Zionism and solidarity with the Arab, later specifically the Palestinian, cause had been planted.

Against this background, Robeson made another statement in November 1956, drastically different in tone from his earlier pronouncements on Israel. Robeson's anger and disappointment with the behaviour of a state the cause of which he had long and passionately espoused is palpable, demonstrating how his intuitive sense of internationalist solidarity had now turned him against Israel:

> I would interpret this [the invasion of Egypt] as a complete attack on the basic concept of Bandung.
>
> The nations are saying that 'we (the strongest western nations) do not accept the fact that colored peoples of the world – Africa, Asia and so forth – have any right to their independence'.
>
> Anytime we feel they don't accept the fact, we'll step in and take it back.

Robeson continued that if Israel, Britain and France could rob Egypt of its independence, colonial powers would be emboldened to 'wrest [independence] from the Indians' and roll back the self-governance measures in Gold Coast (later Ghana) and Nigeria which were leading to independence. He warned that 'the colored nations can have no future at all if this can stand'.[69]

The positions of Davis and Robeson in 1956, like the CPUSA's stridently pro-Israel line in 1948, might be thought to derive from loyalty to Moscow; it was, after all, the Soviet Union's staunch support for Egypt that had brought the Suez Crisis to a rapid finish.[70] But Robeson, at least, was unafraid to voice criticisms of Moscow when its policies ran contrary to his affinity with the Jewish people. In January 1959, he once again sang in Moscow in Yiddish, interpreted by Jews in the audience as a sign of solidarity with their community in defiance of the Soviet government's attempts to repress their identity.[71] Yet Robeson's continued solidarity with Jews did not, after the Suez Crisis, translate into open support for Israel, and once he could again travel freely, he never fulfilled his earlier wish to perform there. His final condemnation of Israel and solidarity with Egypt forms a striking contrast with the support which some mainstream African American leaders of the civil rights movement maintained for Israel over a decade later, despite its crushing defeat of the Arab states and military occupation of the Palestinian territories beginning in 1967.[72]

Conclusion

While throwing himself into progressive causes including the civil rights struggle, support for decolonization and espousal of socialism as a cure for the world's ills in the late 1940s, Paul Robeson simultaneously made repeated statements on the Palestine Question that unambiguously placed him on the pro-Zionist and pro-Israel side. Even as Palestinian dispossession and suffering reached a grim apogee, Robeson's mantra of 'fight for everybody, everywhere' did not resound on Palestinians' behalf, drowned out as it was by his effusive praise of the Haganah on US stages before audiences of tens of thousands.

Robeson's abrupt volte face when Israel invaded Egypt indicates that the beginnings of the radical Black identification with the Arab cause, commonly dated to the mid-1960s, can in fact be significantly backdated to 1956.[73] Support for Egypt over Suez, following Soviet foreign policy, does not necessarily indicate an awareness of Palestinians' suffering and solidarity with their cause. Yet the transformation from Robeson literally singing the praises of the Zionist forces in 1948 to the blistering anger at Israel's colonial behaviour palpable in his words of November 1956 indicates the door was slowly being opened for the Western left's subsequent pro-Arab sentiments.

Robeson lived through later key moments of the Middle East conflict, including the 1967 Six-Day War which precipitated a break in Soviet Israeli relations, and the emergence of a prominent and articulate voice for the Palestinians, the PLO. The significance of the latter cannot be overstated. Jack O'Dell, a Black CPUSA member in the 1940s and 1950s and later outspoken supporter of Palestine, noted that leftists who supported Israel's creation in 1948 'knew nothing of the Palestinians'.[74] Perhaps the PLO's outstanding success was that from the late 1960s onwards, its range of tactics, from armed struggle to diplomacy to building coalitions of solidarity, ensured *everyone* knew *something* about the Palestinians. The PLO enabled Palestinians to put forward their perspective, giving Black radicals a reason to rethink the narrative they had hitherto received, through means such as the pamphlets and solidarity delegations to refugee camps, as recounted in Michael Fischbach's chapter in this volume (Chapter 2).

Due to Robeson's later seclusion, we may never know what he thought of the radical left's reorientation towards the Palestinian cause, the appearance of a Black solidarity with Palestine and the shattering of the bond between liberal Jews and radical African Americans partly as a result. But there is no doubt that even as subsequent generations of radicals drew inspiration from Robeson as a trailblazing fighter for justice, they began also to passionately voice their support for Palestinian rights.

Notes

1. The author would like to extend his appreciation to Colter Louwerse and Nadia Naser-Najjab for their constructive commentary on early drafts of this article, the editors of this volume for their subsequent feedback, Nadine Aranki for her support and Tayo Aluko for providing the impetus for this article's writing.
2. 'As the Sun Rises in Palestine…', *Daily Worker*, 14 May 1948, 12.
3. Ilan Pappé, *The Ethnic Cleansing of Palestine* (London: Oneworld Publications, 2006).
4. '40,000 Say "Mazeltov" to Israel at Rally Here', *Daily Worker*, 17 May 1948, 5, 7.
5. Dov Waxman, *Trouble in the Tribe: The American Jewish Conflict over Israel* (Princeton: Princeton University Press, 2016), 34.
6. '40,000 Say "Mazeltov" to Israel at Rally Here.'
7. Amy Kaplan, *Our American Israel: The Story of an Entangled Alliance* (Cambridge, MA: Harvard University Press, 2018), 15.
8. "Wallace Hails Polo Grounds Palestine Rally," *Daily Worker*, 14 May 1948, 3; '40,000 Say 'Mazeltov' to Israel at Rally Here'.
9. '40,000 Say 'Mazeltov' to Israel at Rally Here'.
10. Paul Robeson, 'Plain Talk: From B'way to South Africa', *People's Voice*, 11 October 1947, 14.
11. Michael R. Fischbach, *Black Power and Palestine: Transnational Countries of Color* (Palo Alto: Stanford University Press, 2019), 3.
12. Philip. S. Foner ed., *Paul Robeson Speaks: Writings, Speeches, Interviews 1918–1974* (New York: Citadel Press, 1978), 183.
13. Paul Robeson, *Here I Stand* (Boston: Beacon Press, [1958] 1988), x.
14. For an authoritative account, see Martin Bauml Duberman, *Paul Robeson: A Biography* (New York: Ballantine Books, 1990).
15. Fischbach, *Black Power and Palestine*, 3.
16. Duberman, *Paul Robeson*, 199; Paul Robeson, Jr, *The Undiscovered Paul Robeson: An Artist's Journey, 1898–1939* (New York: John Wiley, 2001), 282.
17. John Hudson Jones, 'Garment Workers Chase Spies for Chiang at China Rally Here', *Daily Worker*, 6 April 1948, 5. Rosa Lee Ingram, a Black woman who was sentenced to death in January 1948 with two of her sons after a violent and abusive white sharecropper was killed in their self-defence, was at the centre of a huge campaign, eventually securing their reprieve and release; Dayo F. Gore, *Radicalism at the Crossroads: African American Women Activists in the Cold War* (New York: New York University Press, 2011), 74–99.

18 Priyamvada Gopal, *Insurgent Empire: Anticolonial Resistance and British Dissent* (London: Verso, 2019), 24.
19 'General Motors; Jewish, Indonesian Repression, Blasted by Paul Robeson', *People's Voice*, 1 December 1945, 1.
20 Kaplan, *Our American Israel*, 39.
21 Jonathan Karp, 'Performing Black-Jewish Symbiosis: The "Hassidic Chant" of Paul Robeson', *American Jewish History* 91, no. 1 (2003).
22 'Robeson Will Continue His Career in Europe', *Afro-American*, 23 February 1935, 9.
23 'Paul Robeson Begins Study of Hebrew', *Jewish Advocate*, 29 November 1935, 1.
24 Robert Weisbord and Richard Kazarian, Jr, '"That Marvellous Movement": Early Black Views of Zionism', in *Persistent Prejudice: Perspectives on Anti-Semitism*, ed. Herbert Hirsch and Jack D. Spiro (Fairfax: George Mason University Press, 1988), 118–22.
25 Michael Singer, 'The Greatest Demonstration of Jewish Unity for Victory', *Daily Worker*, 10 July 1943, 4.
26 For this alliance and its later demise, see Fischbach, *Black Power and Palestine*, 31–5.
27 Duberman, *Paul Robeson*, 306.
28 Arthur D. Kahn, 'A Jewish Vet Speaks to Negroes', *People's Voice*, 5 October 1946, 17.
29 "Paul Robeson: Firm Zionist," *Jewish Advocate*, 18 April 1946, 13.
30 Pappé, *The Ethnic Cleansing of Palestine*, 72–86.
31 Foner, *Paul Robeson Speaks*, 183.
32 Duberman, *Paul Robeson*, 324. Wallace had been vice-president under Roosevelt from 1940 to 1945 but was sacked from the US government by Truman for his conciliatory position towards the Soviets.
33 'Record Harlem Rally Hears Wallace', *Daily Worker*, 16 February 1948, 2. Jordan's King Abdullah was a particular bogeyman of the left, notwithstanding his backstage deals with the Zionist leadership.
34 Mary Faulkner, 'On a Tour of Four Homes with Robeson', *Sunday Worker*, 15 August 1948, 14, 13.
35 Foner, *Paul Robeson Speaks*, 193.
36 Norman G. Finkelstein, *Knowing Too Much: Why the American Jewish Romance with Israel is Coming to an End* (New York: OR Books, 2012), 55.
37 A. B. Magil, 'The Irgunists Unmasked Themselves at Tel Aviv', *Daily Worker*, 12 July 1948, 7. For the Deir Yassin massacre, see Pappé, *The Ethnic Cleansing of Palestine*, 90–1.
38 'Magil Calls Irgun Chief Disloyal to Israel', *Daily Worker*, 30 November 1948, 5.
39 Foner, *Paul Robeson Speaks*, 196. Robeson's reference here to 'the people of Palestine' was probably meant to include Jewish settlers in addition to the indigenous population.
40 ANP, 'Robeson Sings in Peace to Capacity L.A. Crowd', *Afro-American*, 15 October 1949, 8. This enthusiastic reaction resulted partly from the events in Peekskill,

New York, on 27 August 1949, when a racist riot broke out before Robeson was due to perform. Partly from fear of similar disorder, partly because of antipathy to Robeson (one white councillor stated that he was 'inclined to be down there [at Robeson's concert] throwing rocks myself'), the LA city council deployed 2,200 police and told the city's residents to stay away. Ultimately, 15,000 people attended the concert, which was peaceful. ANP, "Robeson Sings in Peace to Capacity L.A. Crowd"; Duberman *Paul Robeson*, 376-7.

41 'DuBois Gets Permit to Go Abroad', *Afro-American*, 19 August 1950, 15.
42 'Robeson's Passport Bid Bitterly Fought', *Afro-American*, 13 August 1955, 5.
43 Foner, *Paul Robeson Speaks*, 435.
44 Weisbord and Kazarian, Jr, 'That Marvellous Movement', 127.
45 Peter Novick, *The Holocaust in American Life* (Boston: Houghton Mifflin Company, 2000), 19.
46 Paul Novick, 'Turmoil in Palestine', *Sunday Worker*, 6 November 1938, 5.
47 Avi Shlaim, *The Iron Wall: Israel and the Arab World* (London: Penguin Books, 2000), 35.
48 'Our Candidates Say': *Daily Worker*, 31 October 1946, 5.
49 'The Phony "Truce" Tactic', *Daily Worker*, 3 June 1948, 1.
50 Pappé, *The Ethnic Cleansing of Palestine*, 148-56.
51 C. L. R. James and Raya Dunayevskaya, *The Invading Socialist Society* (1947).
52 Alex Lubin, *Geographies of Liberation: The Making of an Afro-Arab Political Imaginary* (Chapel Hill: University of North Carolina Press, 2014), 105-6.
53 W. E. B. Du Bois, 'The Ethics of the Problem of Palestine' (1948), 1.
54 Ibid., 3-5.
55 "The USSR and Israel," *Daily Worker*, 18 February 1952, 5.
56 Alain Brossat and Sylvia Klineberg, *Revolutionary Yiddishland: A History of Jewish Radicalism* (London: Verso, [1983] 2016), 235.
57 Louis Harap, 'The Truth about the Prague Trial (VII): The Crime, the Methods, the Motives', *Daily Worker*, 4 February 1953, 4.
58 Duberman *Paul Robeson*, 352-4. I am indebted to Tayo Aluko for his emphasis on these events.
59 Fred Jerome and Rodger Taylor, *Einstein on Race and Racism* (New Brunswick: Rutgers University Press, 2005), 124.
60 Alice Calaprice ed., *The Ultimate Quotable Einstein* (Princeton: Princeton University Press, 2011), 225.
61 Duberman *Paul Robeson*, 431.
62 Joel Beinin, *Was the Red Flag Flying There? Marxist Politics and the Arab-Israeli Conflict in Egypt and Israel, 1948-1965* (Berkley: University of California Press, 1990), 153.

63 Saïd K. Aburish, *Nasser: The Last Arab. A Biography* (New York: Thomas Dunne Books, 2004), 111, 313.
64 Nahed Samour, 'Palestine at Bandung: The Longwinded Start of a Reimagined International Law', in *Bandung, Global History, and International Law: Critical Pasts and Pending Futures*, ed. Luis Eslava, Michael Fakhri and Vasuki Nesiah (Cambridge: Cambridge University Press, 2017), 595.
65 Reader, 'Israel Was Right in Egypt Attack', *Daily Worker*, 25 November 1956, 6.
66 A Jewish Communist, 'Israel Also Asks Peaceful Parleys', *Daily Worker*, 31 December 1956, 4.
67 Gerald Horne, *Black Liberation/Red Scare: Ben Davis and the Communist Party* (Newark: University of Delaware Press, 1994), 283–4.
68 Benjamin J. Davis, 'Negro-Jewish Relations', *Daily Worker*, 8 March 1957, 4.
69 'Robeson Still Fighting Personal, World Battles', *Afro-American*, 17 November 1956, 13.
70 Shlaim, *The Iron Wall*, 181–2.
71 Ben Ami [Arie L. Eliav], *Between Hammer and Sickle* (Philadelphia: The Jewish Publication Society of America, 1967), 40–5.
72 Fischbach, *Black Power and Palestine*, 51–70.
73 Surprisingly, two recent studies of Black Palestinian and Black Arab solidarity barely mention the Suez Crisis. See Lubin, *Geographies of Liberation*, 118; Fischbach, *Black Power and Palestine*, 1, 15, 25.
74 Fischbach, *Black Power and Palestine*, 203.

Bibliography

Aburish, Saïd K. *Nasser: The Last Arab. A Biography*. New York: Thomas Dunne Books, 2004.

Beinin, Joel. *Was the Red Flag Flying There? Marxist Politics and the Arab-Israeli Conflict in Egypt and Israel, 1948–1965*. Berkley: University of California Press, 1990.

Ben Ami [Arie L. Eliav]. *Between Hammer and Sickle*. Philadelphia: Jewish Publication Society of America, 1967.

Brossat, Alain, and Sylvia Klineberg. *Revolutionary Yiddishland: A History of Jewish Radicalism*. London: Verso, [1983] 2016.

Calaprice, Alice ed. *The Ultimate Quotable Einstein*. Princeton: Princeton University Press, 2011.

Duberman, Martin Bauml. *Paul Robeson: A Biography*. New York: Ballantine Books, 1990.

Du Bois, W. E. B. 'The Ethics of the Problem of Palestine', in W. E. B. Du Bois Papers, Special Collections and University Archives, University of Massachusetts Amherst

Libraries, 1948. Available online: https://credo.library.umass.edu/view/full/mums 312-b209-i090 (accessed 15 November 2021).

Finkelstein, Norman G. *Knowing Too Much: Why the American Jewish Romance with Israel Is Coming to an End*. New York: OR Books, 2012.

Fischbach, Michael R. *Black Power and Palestine: Transnational Countries of Color*. Palo Alto: Stanford University Press, 2019.

Foner, Philip. S. ed. *Paul Robeson Speaks: Writings, Speeches, Interviews 1918–1974*. New York: Citadel Press, 1978.

Gopal, Priyamvada. *Insurgent Empire: Anticolonial Resistance and British Dissent*. London: Verso, 2019.

Gore, Dayo F. *Radicalism at the Crossroads: African American Women Activists in the Cold War*. New York: New York University Press, 2011.

Horne, Gerald. *Black Liberation/Red Scare: Ben Davis and the Communist Party*. Newark: University of Delaware Press, 1994.

James, C. L. R., and Raya Dunayevskaya. *The Invading Socialist Society* (1947). Available online: https://www.marxists.org/archive/james-clr/works/1947/invading/ch01.htm (accessed 15 November 2021).

Jerome, Fred, and Rodger Taylor. *Einstein on Race and Racism*. New Brunswick: Rutgers University Press, 2005.

Kaplan, Amy. *Our American Israel: The Story of an Entangled Alliance*. Cambridge, MA: Harvard University Press, 2018.

Karp, Jonathan. 'Performing Black-Jewish Symbiosis: The "Hassidic Chant" of Paul Robeson', *American Jewish History* 91, no. 1 (2003): 53–81.

Lubin, Alex. *Geographies of Liberation: The Making of an Afro-Arab Political Imaginary*. Chapel Hill: University of North Carolina Press, 2014.

Novick, Peter. *The Holocaust in American Life*. Boston: Houghton Mifflin Company, 2000.

Pappé, Ilan. *The Ethnic Cleansing of Palestine*. London: Oneworld Publications, 2006.

Robeson, Paul. *Here I Stand*. Boston: Beacon Press, [1958] 1988.

Robeson, Paul, Jr *The Undiscovered Paul Robeson: An Artist's Journey, 1898–1939*. New York: John Wiley, 2001.

Samour, Nahed. 'Palestine at Bandung: The Longwinded Start of a Reimagined International Law', in *Bandung, Global History, and International Law: Critical Pasts and Pending Futures*, edited by Luis Eslava, Michael Fakhri and Vasuki Nesiah, 595–615. Cambridge: Cambridge University Press, 2017.

Shlaim, Avi. *The Iron Wall: Israel and the Arab World*. London: Penguin Books, 2000.

Waxman, Dov. *Trouble in the Tribe: The American Jewish Conflict over Israel*. Princeton: Princeton University Press, 2016.

Weisbord, Robert, and Richard Kazarian, Jr '"That Marvellous Movement": Early Black Views of Zionism', in *Persistent Prejudice: Perspectives on Anti-Semitism*, edited by Herbert Hirsch and Jack D. Spiro, 109–32. Fairfax: George Mason University Press, 1988.

2

American activists' solidarity trips and interactions with Palestinians

Michael R. Fischbach

Like other nationalities, Americans travelled to the Middle East and North Africa to meet with Palestinians in the late 1960s and early 1970s. As part of their revolutionary internationalism, they made solidarity trips, attended official conferences and on a few occasions even became involved with armed Palestinian fighters. Each in their own way contributed to the growth of pro-Palestinian solidarity activism waged by progressive Americans at a time when few Americans knew much about the Palestinians and fewer still (even within the left) sympathized with them.[1]

Several famous pro-Palestinian Americans made such trips, including high-profile Black Power activists. Malcolm X made a two-day visit to Egyptian-controlled Gaza from 4 to 6 September 1964 during his lengthy stay in Cairo. Back in the Egyptian capital, he then attended a 15 September press conference held by Ahmad Shuqayri, chair of the newly established Palestine Liberation Organization (PLO), and two days later he published a strong statement about Zionism and the Palestinians in the *Egyptian Gazette*, an English-language newspaper.[2] Stokely Carmichael, former chair of the Student Nonviolent Coordinating Committee (SNCC) and another noted pro-Palestinian Black Power activist, travelled to North Africa and the Middle East in 1967. After arriving in Syria on 19 September Carmichael visited Palestinian refugee camps and apparently pledged that American Blacks would provide military support to the Arabs in their struggle against Israel.[3] The Black Panther Party (BPP) was also strongly supportive of the Palestinians, and when BPP minister of information Eldridge Cleaver fled the United States to escape prosecution, he took up residence in Algiers in July 1969 where he was befriended by officials from the Palestinian revolutionary group Fatah. On 27 December 1969 he even met Yasser Arafat, chair of both Fatah and the PLO. Finally, the famous boxer and outspoken Black Power activist Muhammad Ali took time from an international trip to fly to Beirut on 2 March 1974. Accompanied by Palestinian fighters he visited two refugee camps in southern Lebanon where he stated, 'In my name, and in the name of all Muslims in America, I declare support for the Palestinian struggle to liberate their homeland and oust the Zionist invaders.'[4]

Other Americans also met up with the Palestinians, including ordinary activists, young journalists writing for left-wing and countercultural publications and countercultural figures. Less famous Black activists such as those who attended a Palestine National Council meeting in Jordan in 1970 also contributed to the growing web of connections between American activists and Palestinians, as did white progressives who met with the Palestinians. Among these were a group of mostly white left-wing journalists who travelled through Lebanon, Syria and Jordan in 1970 and whose trip was cut short by the bloody Jordanian Palestinian fighting during Black September. Even the LSD king, Timothy Leary, travelled to the Middle East to visit the Palestinians. Finally, a few Americans became directly involved with the Palestinians in their armed struggle. The most famous was the Nicaraguan American militant, Patrick Argüello, who, in an attempted airplane hijacking with Leila Khaled in 1970, was killed. Others were less famous, including three men who trained with a refugee camp militia in Lebanon. While their trips were generally less publicized by the media, archival research and interviews can help resurrect these more obscure encounters and illustrate the scope of American solidarity with the Palestinian struggle during the global 1960s.

By plumbing various archives in the United States, conducting interviews, and collecting personal documents and obtaining declassified American intelligence documents, we can reconstruct some of these trips, which shed valuable light on the history of American solidarity activities on behalf of and in collaboration with the Palestinian resistance movement during a turbulent period of global history.

The American left and solidarity with the Palestinians during the global 1960s

The left in the United States first took real note of the Palestinian cause in mid-1967, in the wake of the June War that saw Israel defeat several Arab armies and occupy the West Bank and Gaza. This was a time when Palestinian guerrilla groups like Fatah and the Popular Front for the Liberation of Palestine (PFLP) escalated attacks on Israeli targets, and the PLO as a whole began a global public relations offensive to win support.[5] Black New Left groups like SNCC and the BPP were quick to champion the Palestinians as a kindred people of colour struggling, as they themselves were, against US-backed imperialism and oppression. White activists in Old Left Marxist parties like the Socialist Workers Party (SWP), the Workers World Party, the Progressive Labor Party and the Communist Party USA similarly supported the Palestinians starting in 1967 although the communists were bitterly divided when it came to denouncing Israel. On the other hand, the Socialist Party of America was staunchly pro-Israeli.[6]

Among whites within the youthful New Left, however, there was more dissension about what stance to adopt regarding Israel. The largest and most famous New Left group was the Students for a Democratic Society (SDS). As early as mid-1967, just after the war, some SDS activists urged the group to express its solidarity with the Palestinians forcefully and received some pushback in the process. One reason for this was that like the Old Left, the New Left contained a disproportionately large number of Jewish activists. Yet unlike the strict orthodoxy imposed on its members by Old Left parties, Jews in the New Left were free to express a variety of opinions about the Middle East. As a result, while some young Jews were strongly supportive of the Palestinians and harshly criticized Israel, others could not bring themselves to adopt such positions. In fact, it would not be until early 1969 that the SDS leadership came down firmly on the side of the Palestinians, notably through its national publications like *New Left Notes*.[7]

For their part, some Palestinians in the 1960s tried to cultivate left-wing American support for their struggle against Israel. The Arab League had established the Arab Information Office (AIO) in New York in 1955 to present Arab perspectives to journalists and other opinion makers in the United States; AIO branches soon were opened in other cities. The major force leading this public relations effort was the Palestinian Syrian intellectual Fayez Sayegh. Similar agencies that were specifically Palestinian also opened up in New York thereafter, including the Palestine Arab Refugee Office and the Palestine Arab Delegation. Soon after its establishment, the PLO set up an office in New York in 1965.

Yet it was not until the very late 1960s that Palestinian officials in AIO and PLO offices in the United States really exerted efforts to reach progressive young Americans and even then they were not particularly effective.[8] Where Palestinian publicity efforts to reach left-wing Americans were more successful was through

English-language pamphlets issued by groups like Fatah, the PLO and others that ended up in the hands of activists in the United States. Significant among these was *Do You Know? Twenty Basic Questions About the Palestine Problem*, written in 1965 for the PLO by Sayegh, upon which SNCC drew when it issued the first major pro-Palestinian, anti-Israeli statement coming from the New Left in America in August 1967.[9] Moreover, the BPP's newspaper, *The Black Panther*, sometimes reprinted Fatah statements verbatim.[10]

'How could I have been fooled so long': Journalists, activists and Palestinians

Beyond all this what really seemed to cement ties of solidarity between Palestinian and American activists, however, were trips the latter made to the Middle East. For example, in April 1970, a Black activist and member of the SWP in Harlem who espoused pro-Palestinian sentiments, Paul Boutelle, was contacted by Randa Khalidi al-Fattal of the AIO in New York: 'Would he be interested in traveling to the Middle East as part of a delegation of black American activists and meet with Palestinians?' American intelligence quickly learned about the planned trip, even before it took place.[11] In August of that year, Boutelle and five other men and women ended up traveling to Lebanon, Syria and Jordan. With al-Fattal serving as their guide, the Americans met with Palestinians in various locales, including refugee camps and guerrilla encampments.[12]

In Amman, the group attended the meeting of Palestine National Council, the PLO's 'parliament', which took place from 27 to 29 August 1970. While there, the group met with Arafat, and a photo of Boutelle and the others shaking hands with Arafat was featured on the front page of *Fatah*, the group's newspaper. Headed by Arafat, Fatah was the largest of the Palestinian guerrilla organizations that made up the PLO. The paper also ran a quotation from one of the group, who said, 'It is better to die as men than die as slaves.' 'Our revolution is exactly like the Palestinian revolution', the person continued, 'and it is a drop of blood, a drop of sweat, and a drop of ink that will accept nothing except the liberation of everyone.'[13]

The trip deepened Boutelle's commitment to the Palestinian cause. Back in the United States he formed a group called the Committee of Black Americans for Truth about the Middle East that placed an advertisement in a November 1970 issue of the *New York Times* titled 'An Appeal by Black Americans against United States Support of the Zionist Government of Israel'.[14] A total of fifty-seven persons signed the statement.

Other young Americans travelled to meet with Palestinians in mid-1970 as well, including some eager young activists and journalists; Nick Medvecky was one of them. The previous year the student-journalist who also had been involved with the SWP had secured an invitation from none other than Arafat himself to tour Lebanon, Syria and Jordan as a guest of Fatah. Paying for his airfare with advances for stories he would write after he returned, Medvecky flew to Beirut in late August 1969. He met with a Fatah official at the Strand Hotel and then visited several Palestinian refugee camps in the city. Medvecky visited the camps dressed as a Palestinian, his face covered with a *kufiyya* headscarf, to hide from Lebanese soldiers stationed at the camp entrances. He left Lebanon for Syria on 28 August 1969 and from there entered Jordan carrying a letter of introduction from Kamal Adwan, a leading spokesperson for Fatah from the group's central information office. Medvecky visited various locations in Jordan, including refugee camps and a Fatah military camp in the mountains outside Amman, and also conducted an interview with Arafat.[15]

Medvecky wrote news dispatches that he sent to the Liberation News Service in the United States. He freely admitted the challenge of witnessing the Arab Israeli conflict up close for the first time: 'My greatest problem is in seeing so much & having so little time to write and rest. I'll try to be as prompt as possible,' Medvecky wrote to the editors. He later sent a dispatch noting, 'I can't overstate the amount of misery and degradation these people [Palestinians] continue to live under. I also can't overstate the extent these people are rallying behind and joining Al Fatah.'[16]

The following year, Medvecky returned to the Middle East in the company of sixteen other activists and journalists. The genesis of the trip lay with a Middle East study group in Boston made up of members of the Committee of Returned Volunteers, which was made up of former volunteers with the Peace Corps and other such organizations. The seventeen individuals represented various Black, underground and left-wing papers and news services, including *Rat: Subterranean News*, *Liberated Guardian*, *Fifth Estate*, *Sun-Dance*, the *Metro*, *Inner City Voice*, *Muhammad Speaks*, the *Baltimore African-American*, *The Great Speckled Bird*, Liberation News Service and the Afro-World News Associates. They planned to fly to Beirut and then travel overland through Syria to Jordan and attend the Second World Conference on Palestine in Amman from 2 to 6 September 1970. While in the Middle East, the group members were to be hosted by the General Union of Palestinian Students (GUPS).

In late August 1970, the group flew to Beirut. They spent about one week in Lebanon, visiting Palestinian refugee camps, a Palestine Red Crescent

Society hospital and Ba'labakk.[17] Shortly before their scheduled departure to Jordan, Fatah officials met with the group. The Palestinians had learned that some in the group intended on traveling to Israel and reportedly 'freaked out'.[18] American intelligence was monitoring the trip. Through its Operation MH/CHAOS program, the Central Intelligence Agency (CIA) was investigating any possible foreign connections with American antiwar and other protest groups and monitoring Americans' travel abroad. The CIA received information – presumably from someone within the group – that at the meeting Peewee 'Rufus' Griffin had called Medvecky a 'Zionist pig'. Medvecky told the Fatah officials that group members were journalists who should be able to report from both Arab countries and Israel. The result was that the group expelled him and travelled onward.[19]

Medvecky stayed in Beirut. Through the good offices of an American journalist living in Beirut, Marc Schleifer, he met officials from other Palestinian factions; it would not be the last time that Schleifer interacted with Americans in the Middle East that summer of 1970. The Popular Front for the Liberation of Palestine-General Command (PFLP-GC), headed by Ahmad Jibril, eventually agreed to work with Medvecky. The PFLP-GC gave him lodging, a car and driver as well as an English-speaking interpreter. He spent his time traveling throughout Lebanon, Syria and Jordan in the company of PFLP-GC fighters, sometimes carrying weapons like them.[20]

Minus Medvecky, the rest of the group travelled onwards to Jordan. They first spent one week at an international student work camp in southern Jordan working on building projects for Palestinians including one that became a camp for members of the *Ashbal* (Arabic: lion cubs), an armed Fatah youth brigade. After visiting the ruins of Petra, some toured a Fatah medical clinic in Shawbak. Jeanne Townes remembered that the Palestinians offered to let the Americans practice shooting AK-47 assault rifles.[21] After a week, three members of the group remained to work at the clinic, mostly sorting medicine; the others returned to Amman.[22] There they attended the Second World Conference on Palestine. Over 1,000 delegates from around the world were at the gathering amid rising tension and firefights between Palestinian guerrillas and Jordanian soldiers.

Journalists sent reports back to newspapers and press agencies in the United States detailing their travels. Orville 'Chris' Robinson and Roger Tauss managed to type up a story titled 'Palestine: They Say There Is No Resistance' and send copies to the *Liberation News Service*, the *Philadelphia Free Press* and the *Liberated Guardian*. The two finished the dispatch on 4 September 1970 and hailed the Palestinians as the 'vanguard struggle against Western imperialism in the Middle East'.²³ Separately, Medvecky also reported back to the radical press. In a dispatch from Damascus dated 12 September 1970, he described how he and his PFLP-GC guide managed to leave Jordan and enter Syria just four days before the Black September fighting broke out.²⁴

The trip was eye-opening for many. Susie Teller later recalled, 'At the time there was no question that I was pro-Israeli. I thought planting trees in Israel was a wonderful idea.' Yet in an article she wrote shortly after returning, she exclaimed, 'I've been misled. I've been taken advantage of.'²⁵ Georgia Mattison recalled, 'I came back with a great appreciation for the Palestinian point of view and how wrenching it was for them, or anybody, to be thrown out of their land.'²⁶ Finally, Gene Guerrero also was impacted by his experience. 'Over and over again', he wrote shortly after returning to Atlanta, 'while I was there I wondered how I could have been fooled so long. The issue is so simple. A nation of people – brutally expelled from their land by an outside power.'²⁷ Six weeks after returning, several enthusiastic tour members decided to form the Middle East Research and Information Project (MERIP) and produce a publication to focus on American policy in the Middle East. The group is still in existence today.

'The struggle is international': Americans in the Palestinian resistance

A small number of Americans did more than just visit with Palestinians; they worked with the resistance. In a June 1970 document, the Federal Bureau of Investigation (FBI) reported that an American citizen who was detained in May 1969 claimed that he had been recruited and trained by Fatah for 'sabotage' operations in Israel. Both the FBI and the CIA investigated possible Palestinian activity in the United States by monitoring left-wing Americans and those that maintained connections with Palestinians specifically. The FBI document claimed that the person was not only a 'suspected intelligence provocateur' but also noted that 'there are definite indications' that he in fact had travelled to Lebanon, Syria and Jordan shortly before he was detained, and he had met with agents from Fatah and Egyptian intelligence. The FBI did not say where the person was detained, or by whom, but did report that he carried two pistols in addition to bombs concealed in soap and shaving cream.²⁸

More press and FBI reports emerged in 1969 and 1970 about Fatah allegedly recruiting American radicals, yet there remained a question mark over whether there was truth to these rumours. On 4 September 1970, while the American tour group was still in the region, the NBC-TV 'Nightly News' broadcasted a report from journalist Marc Schleifer in Beirut.[29] His footage showed three white Americans, whom he described as New Leftists, training in a Palestinian refugee camp in Beirut as part of a militia organized in the camp not by Fatah but the Popular Democratic Front for the Liberation of Palestine (PDFLP). The men gave their names as 'George', from Boston, and 'Bobby' and 'Huey', from Oakland. All three had their faces covered with *kufiyya* headscarves to obscure their identity. Schleifer's footage showed the men training with the militia although not actually carrying any weapons. Schleifer also interviewed them:

Schleifer: These Americans train each day with the militia in this camp, armed Palestinian civilians who support the guerrillas and defend the camps. They keep their faces covered with Arab headdress in order to preserve anonymity and avoid what they describe as the possibility of reprisals from the CIA and pro-Zionist groups like the Jewish Defense League. And they study the tactical and military problems of revolution in the underdeveloped world, what they call the Third World. The three Americans are active in the New Left. George, where are you from in the States?

George: Well, I'm from Boston, and Bobby and Huey are from Oakland.

Schleifer: And what brought you here into the ranks of the Popular Democratic Front?

George: Well, we figure that any national liberation struggle in the world is really important, and it's important to aid it not only morally and by words but materially. So we came here to materially aid the revolutionary struggle.

Schleifer: Do you intend to go back to the United States?

George: I intend to go back to the United States eventually, with the revolution.

Huey: We came here because the struggle is international – like the Democratic Front says, it's 'alami [Arabic: international] – of the world, and whether we fight in Oakland, Chicago, New York, or in Jordan, Lebanon, or Palestine, it's the same struggle.

Bobby: We're here primarily to express the American movement's solidarity and support of the Palestinian liberation struggle, and to pick up whatever skills are necessary for liberation and struggles in America.

The two aliases 'Bobby and Huey' were clearly adopted from the BPP's two founders, Bobby Seale and Huey Newton. Like other left-wing Americans, these activists in the camp felt that their support for the Black freedom struggle at home in America and for the Palestinians in the Middle East were part of the same global movement against racialized imperialism. As 'Huey' expressed in the interview, the men viewed the struggle as international and were looking to the PDFLP for training and skills to take back to the United States.

Finally, the historical record long has been clear about one US citizen who is known to have trained with Palestinian guerrillas, carried weapons and ended up dying on one of their most famous armed operations – Patrick Argüello. Patricio José Argüello Ryan was born in San Francisco to a Nicaraguan father and an American mother. He later returned to Nicaragua and became involved in the revolutionary Sandinista National Liberation Front (FSLN). The FSLN, like other revolutionary organizations, collaborated with Palestinian guerrillas and wanted to train its fighters in their camps. As part of this, the FSLN dispatched Argüello to Jordan to undergo training at the hands of the PDFLP from April to June 1970. Argüello then travelled to Europe and contacted the PFLP. The PFLP agreed to work with him and recruited him for one of the group's most dramatic actions.

On 6 September 1970, Argüello joined up with the famous PFLP militant Leila Khaled in a bid to hijack an Israeli airliner flying from Amsterdam to New York and divert it to a desert airfield in Jordan as part of a mass, coordinated hijacking. However, they were foiled in their attempt: the pilot put the plane in a steep dive, knocking them off their feet, whereupon they were attacked by passengers and armed Israeli sky marshals. The latter shot and killed Argüello; Khaled was captured. She was turned over to British authorities in London where the plane made an emergency landing. Argüello's mother, Catalina 'Kathleen' Ryan, acknowledged Patrick's commitment to the Palestinians in a statement she issued in October 1970: 'My husband and I deny that we are ashamed of Pat. We are proud that he felt so deeply about the Palestinians that he was prepared to die for them.'[30]

'Grooving with the guerillas [sic]': Timothy Leary and Fatah

The same month that Catalina 'Kathleen' Ryan issued her statement a well-known countercultural figure tried to contact Palestinians from Fatah. On 24 October 1970, an American man and several companions boarded a plane in

Algiers. After a circuitous route that took them first to Tunisia, Libya and finally Egypt, the group spent the night at the Umar al-Khayyam Hotel in Cairo before continuing onwards to Beirut the next day. Upon arrival, the man presented immigration officers with an American passport, number A1837171, bearing the name William John McNellis. His customs and currency declaration form indicated that he was bringing $300 in cash and $120 in traveler's cheques into Lebanon.[31] The man and his entourage were admitted without incident, after which they ensconced themselves in the famous St. Georges Hotel along the seaside cornice in West Beirut.

What Lebanese officials did not realize was that 'McNellis' was none other than Timothy Leary – escaped convict, hero to the American counterculture and the world's most high-profile advocate of the drug LSD. In a press conference held after their arrival, the Americans stated that they had come to meet with Fatah guerrillas in Jordan. What was Timothy Leary doing in Beirut, and why was America's foremost advocate of psychedelic drug use trying to meet with Fatah?

In the late 1960s, Leary was arrested on several occasions for possession of marijuana, and in January 1970, he was sentenced to ten years imprisonment in the United States. On 12 September 1970, operatives from the radical Weather Underground Organization (WUO) helped him escape from a prison near San Louis Obispo, California. Whether or not the pro-Palestinian WUO influenced him in this direction is not clear, but in a manifesto that Leary published in the underground press within a week of his breakout he connected his cause with that of the Palestinians – a perhaps unintentional indication of where he was headed:

> Listen. There is no choice left but to defend life by all and every means possible against the genocidal machine ... If you fail to see that we are the victims – defendants of genocidal war you will not understand the rage of the blacks, the fierceness of the browns, the holy fanaticism of the Palestinians, the righteous mania of the Weathermen, and the pervasive resentment of the young.[32]

The WUO eventually helped the disguised fugitive obtain a false passport in Chicago, after which Leary and his wife, Rosemary Woodruff Leary, fled to Algeria to take up residence with fellow fugitive Eldridge Cleaver, head of the BPP's international section that had been established a year earlier in Algiers. The Algerian government assumed that Cleaver was hosting a fellow Black American and, on 21 October 1970, an article appeared in an official government newspaper stating that the government had granted asylum to a Black American psychologist and his wife so that they could work with the Panthers.[33] The Algerians were not amused when they eventually discovered that Leary was not in fact a Black radical but rather a prominent countercultural advocate of drugs. Once again, the CIA was active in following Leary's travels.[34]

When the American press learned of Leary's presence in the country, Algerian officials became even more annoyed with Cleaver and concerned about their image – a puritanical revolutionary country hosting such a controversial character. By that time, several other Americans had arrived to be with Leary and Cleaver, including two people associated with the Yippies, Jonah Raskin and Anita Hoffman, as well as the WUO's Brian Flanagan and the younger sister of leading WUO figure Bernardine Dohrn, Jennifer Dohrn.

Everyone involved in the situation had a different agenda. Leary was seeking shelter in a country that would not extradite him while claiming to team up with Cleaver and the Panthers in an effort to merge the political and countercultural revolutions as the Yippies had been trying to do. The volatile Cleaver, who later turned against Leary, wanted to lead a group of American expatriate revolutionaries. The Algerians were balancing their commitment to Cleaver and the Panthers' cause with their frustration about finding out through the press who Leary was and what he stood for. In a bid to get Leary out of the country for a while to avoid further media scrutiny, Cleaver and the Algerians decided to send him to Beirut, thence overland through Syria to Amman to meet with Palestinians from Fatah and visit their training camps. Cleaver hoped that by visiting Palestinian revolutionaries, Leary could come back to Algeria with 'a little Third World legitimacy … Third World credentials' and 'prove his revolutionary zeal' by meeting with the guerrillas.[35] Cleaver decided that Leary would be accompanied on his trip to Beirut by three other Americans: BPP Field Marshal Donald 'D.C.' Cox, another fugitive living with Cleaver in Algeria; Martin Kenner, a lawyer who did fundraising for the Black Panthers; and Jennifer Dohrn.[36]

When they arrived in Beirut on 25 October, however, no Fatah representatives were awaiting the Americans at the airport. Complicating matters was the fact that a journalist recognized Leary on the flight to Beirut, and the group was anxious to avoid further media detection while determining what to do next. Their taxi driver took them to the St. Georges Hotel, which, unbeknownst to them, was in fact one of the main places in Beirut where journalists congregated. Leary and his entourage were soon surrounded by inquiring reporters. Leary remained holed up in Suite 203 of the hotel, while Cox went out the next day to try to find the local Fatah office and see what was going on.

Marc Schleifer inadvertently became part of the action once again. By chance, he was one of the journalists at the hotel. He recognized Leary's travel companion Martin Kenner, and together they came up with a plan. Schleifer left the hotel and brought back his Black American wife, Aliah. The two of them went up to the suite housing Leary and his compatriots, telling the other curious journalists that Aliah was a relative of Cox, the only Black member of the group. In return for agreeing to grant him an exclusive interview when Leary arrived in Syria, Schleifer devised a plan to stage a press conference on the night of 26 October as a diversion while simultaneously sneaking Leary out of the hotel. Thereafter, Schleifer would use his contacts to drive Leary to Damascus. At a press conference held by the other three members of the group, Cox denied that Leary was with them and told reporters, 'We are in the process of going to either Damascus, Syria, or Amman, Jordan' and 'We have come to learn about the Palestinian struggle, and to inform them of our own struggle in the United States.' He also claimed that the trip had been arranged by Cleaver and coordinated with Fatah.[37]

The plan went awry, however, when Leary was recognized while trying to rush out of the lobby. Schleifer eventually told Leary that it was impossible to continue with his plans to travel to Jordan via Syria and recommended that he call Cleaver in Algiers and decide what else to do. For its part, the Lebanese government, now aware of Leary's presence, was not going to allow him to cross the border into Syria anyway. Leary's entourage announced to the mob of journalists that they would hold another press conference in the morning.

Schleifer still wanted his journalistic scoop, however. After midnight, he and his crew interviewed the group in Leary's suite and a few hours later accompanied them to the Beirut airport so that the Americans could leave the country without holding the promised press conference (they first paid the hotel bill, about $385.00). He was not alone; also escorting Leary's entourage was a Lebanese police vehicle, raising the question of whether Leary was being deported. The Lebanese Public Security Department later said that Leary's departure was 'not considered expulsion in its precise meaning but by way of advice only'. They had told Leary that his continued, very public presence in Lebanon would work to the detriment of US-Lebanese relations.[38] The group caught a flight to Cairo several hours later, just three days after they had departed the same airport on their ill-fated trip to Beirut.

Regardless of what had been arranged in Algiers, Fatah activists in the Middle East were caught unawares. Given the media storm in Beirut, Fatah officials in Beirut as well as in Jordan soon found out about Leary. Staff at Fatah's information office in Beirut denied that they had invited Leary and his companions, or indeed that they had any ties with him. In an apparent nod to Cleaver, they did acknowledge that Fatah had ties with the BPP, 'which joins with the Palestinian revolution in its struggle with American imperialism'. Fatah officials in Amman also denied that they had invited Leary but indicated that if he were to come to Jordan, they would be happy to meet with him in Jarash, not in battle-scarred Amman, from which the Jordanian army had expelled Palestinian fighters just weeks earlier during the bitter Black September fighting.[39]

After Leary and his wife returned to Cairo, he mailed a postcard to his children in California that read, in part, 'Tripping around the Middle East, grooving with the guerillas …[*sic*].'[40] They left Cairo on 29 October 1970 and arrived back in Algiers the next day. After their own return from Algeria, Dohrn and Kenner held a press conference in New York on 11 November 1970 at which Dohrn stated that their trip to Algeria and Lebanon had been to 'bring revolutionary greetings' to Palestinian guerrillas. The two also played a tape-recorded message from Leary. It was the end of a bizarre incident, in which an LSD advocate and the Palestinian issue briefly came together, although neither came away transformed from the experience.

Conclusion

What is significant about American New Left and Black Power solidarity trips to the Middle East during the 1960s and early 1970s is not only that they took place but also that they seem to have transformed the lives of most who made the journeys. Some already supported the Palestinians and sought to share such sentiments directly with them. Others, like Argüello and the three men involved with a PDFLP militia in Beirut, joined up with Palestinian fighters to learn concrete skills. Still others, like those who attended the Second World Conference on Palestine, felt that much of what their elders and teachers had taught them about America and the world had been wrong; the Vietnam War had shown them that. Some therefore wanted to learn the facts about the Palestinians and the Arab Israeli conflict on their own terms, from direct travel and experiences in the Middle East. For some of these young Americans and others, actually being with Palestinians in the Middle East helped propel them onward to a life of activism and involvement with the Palestinian cause thereafter, laying the foundations for future Palestine solidarity activities in the decades thereafter. As noted, MERIP grew directly from the large group trip in 1970. Organizations that emerged later in the 1970s, like the Palestine Solidarity Committee and the Palestine Human Rights Committee, included activists who similarly had been impacted by travel to the region. Also in the 1970s, Marxists like those in the New Communist Movement and socialists like those in the New American Movement, continued the 1960s tradition of solidarity with the Palestinians.

Yet at the same time it is important to note that the American left was far from united about what stance to adopt toward Israel and the Palestinians during the 1960s.[41] The sometimes-bitter strife about the Middle East affected progressive American Jews in particular. While some Jewish activists strongly aligned themselves with the Palestinians, others found that the pro-Israeli beliefs they had grown up with led them to take other positions and even make their own solidarity trips to Israel. Other left-wing Jews abandoned the left altogether, including those who drifted into the Neoconservative Movement beginning in the 1970s.

Nonetheless, twenty-first-century American solidarity with the Palestinians has grown and can look back to the global 1960s for its origins. Support for the Palestinian people has moved permanently into the progressive mainstream in the years since, as witnessed by the creation of campus groups like Students for Justice in Palestine in 1993 and the growing support for the Palestinians expressed by Black Lives Matter activists starting in 2016. Pro-Palestinian sentiments even have emerged publicly within the ranks of the Democratic Party, notably among left-wing members of Congress like those associated with the Democratic Socialists of America. 1960s-era Palestinian solidarity actions like those of Americans who travelled to the Middle East indeed laid the seeds of permanent connections between both Black and white American progressives and modern-day Palestinian activists.

Notes

1. For more information, see the author's books *Black Power and Palestine: Transnational Countries of Color* (Palo Alto: Stanford University Press, 2018) and *The Movement and the Middle East: How the Arab-Israeli Conflict Divided the American Left* (Palo Alto: Stanford University Press, 2019).
2. Malcolm X, 'Zionist Logic', *Egyptian Gazette*, 17 September 1964.
3. Robert G. Weisbord, *Bittersweet Encounter: The Afro-Americans and the American Jews* (Westport: Negro Universities Press, 1970), 101.
4. 'Ali Belts Zionism', *Jewish Telegraphic Agency*, 8 March 1974.
5. For more on the Global 1960s, see Chen Jian, Martin Klimke, Masha Kirasirova, Mary Nolan, Marilyn Young, and Joanna Waley-Cohen, eds, *The Routledge Handbook of the Global Sixties: Between Protest and Nation-Building* (Milton Park, UK: Routledge, 2018); Anne Garland Mahler, *From the Tricontinental to the Global South: Race, Radicalism, and Transnational Solidarity* (Durham, NC: Duke University Press, 2018); and Karen Dubinsky, Katherine Krull, Susan Lord, Sean Mills, and Scott Rutherford, eds, *New World Coming: The Sixties and the Shaping of Global Consciousness* (Auburn, ME: Between the Lines, 2009). For how the Middle East and the Palestinians fit into the Global 1960s, see Paul Thomas Chamberlin, *The Global Offensive: The United States, the Palestine Liberation Organization, and the Making of the Post-Cold War Order* (Oxford: Oxford University Press, 2012); Cyrus Schayegh and Yoav Di-Capua, 'Roundtable: Why Decolonization?' *International Journal of Middle East Studies* 52, no. 1 (2020): 137–45; and the other contributions to the roundtable in that same issue of the *International Journal of Middle East Studies*, including Jeffrey James Byrne, 'Finding the Middle East of the Insurgent Global South' (146–9).
6. See Fischbach, *The Movement and the Middle East*, for more details.
7. Ibid.
8. Michael R. Fischbach, 'Palestinian Offices in the United States: Microcosms of the Palestinian Experience', *Journal of Palestine Studies* 48, no. 1 (Autumn 2018): 104–18.
9. See Fischbach, *Black Power and Palestine*, 39.
10. For example, see Al-Fateh, 'To Our African Brothers', *The Black Panther*, 11 October 1969.
11. Federal Bureau of Investigation (FBI), 'The Fedayeen Impact: Middle East and United States' (June 1970); declassified document available online: https://www.governmentattic.org/2docs/FBI_Monograph_Fedayeen_Impact_1970.pdf, 43 (accessed 16 March 2021).
12. Kwame Somburu (formerly, Paul Boutelle), telephone interview with the author, 19 October 2010; Randa Khalidi al-Fattal, interview with the author, Beirut, 24 June 2012.

13 'Mumaththil Harakat Tahrir al-Sud: La Budda an Najatami` fi Filastin al-Hurra' [Representative of the Liberation Movement of Blacks: No Doubt We Will Gather in Free Palestine], *Fatah*, 29 September 1970. Photo of the group with Arafat is on page 1.
14 'An Appeal by Black Americans against United States Support of the Zionist Government of Israel', *New York Times*, 1 November 1970.
15 Nick Medvecky, personal communication with the author, 9 April 2011 and 26 April 2011.
16 Temple University, Paley Library, Special Collections, Liberation News Service Records, Pt. II – LNS Library Collection (hereafter, TULNS), Series 14: International, Mo.-Pa., Box 3, Folder 6: Palestine, Dispatches No. 1. (n.d., but 26 August 1969) and No. 2 (27 August 1969).
17 Gene Guerrero and Susie Teller, 'Palestinian Report'; Susan Teller, 'One Week in Lebanon Can Blow Your Mind'; Gene Guerrero, 'How it Came About'. All in *The Great Speckled Bird*, 4 October 1970.
18 Sharon Rose, telephone interview with the author, 3 February 2011.
19 Ibid.; Susan Teller Goodman, telephone interview with the author, 3 June 2011; Nick Medvecky, personal communication with the author, 26 April 2011; CIA Operation CHAOS document of 18 January 1971 (the document was obtained by Nick Medvecky who kindly provided the author with a copy).
20 Nick Medvecky, personal communication with the author, 5 June 2015.
21 Jean Townes, Telephone Interview with the Author, 16 January 2015; *From Refugees to Palestinians: The Birth of a Revolution* (Washington: Middle East Research and Information Project, n.d.).
22 Susan Teller Goodman, telephone interview with the author, 3 June 2011; Guerrero, 'How it Came About'. The three who remained behind eventually went to Amman and attended the conference as well.
23 TULNS, Series 14: International, Mo.-Pa. Box 4, Folder 1: Palestine, Chris Robinson and Roger Tauss, 'Palestine: They Say There is No Resistance' (4 September 1970).
24 Ibid., Nick Medvecky's dispatch (12 September 1970).
25 Guerrero and Teller, 'Palestinian Report'; Teller, 'One Week in Lebanon Can Blow Your Mind'.
26 University of Virginia, Albert and Shirley Small Special Collections Library, Social Movements Collection, Collection of Miscellaneous Printed Materials, HN1.Z993, No. 15; 'Palestine'; 'Israel Report', *MERIP*, 1, 12.
27 Guerrero and Teller, 'Palestinian Report'; Guerrero, 'How it Came About'; Gene Guerrero, telephone interview with the author, 27 May 2011.
28 FBI, 'The Fedayeen Terrorist: A Profile' (June 1970). The document contained the man's name, but it was redacted out of the version that was declassified in 2008;

document available online: https://www.governmentattic.org/docs/FBI_Monograph_Fedayeen_Terrorist_June-1970.pdf (accessed 3 March 2021).

29 He later changed his name to Abdallah Schleifer.
30 Sarah Irving, *Leila Khaled: Icon of Palestinian Liberation* (London: Pluto Press, 2012), 50.
31 New York Public Library, the Timothy Leary Papers, series IV, subseries F, 'Exile: 1967–73', box 5, folder 8, receipt from Umar al-Khayyam Hotel and Middle East Airways Customs and Currency Declaration.
32 'Letter from Timothy Leary', *San Francisco Good Times*, 18 September 1970, reprinted in Harold Jacobs, ed., *Weatherman* (New York: Ramparts Press, 1970), 517–18. The WUO emerged from the Weatherman faction of the SDS and later changed its name to the Weather Underground after SDS broke apart amid factional fighting in late 1969. Its most thorough explanation of its stance toward the Palestinian struggle came out in 1974 as part of its lengthy political statement, *Prairie Fire*. See Bernardine Dohrn, Bill Ayers, and Jeff Jones, eds, *Sing a Battle Song: The Revolutionary Poetry, Statements, and Communiqués of the Weather Underground 1970–1974* (New York: Seven Stories Press, 2006), 337–42.
33 Robert Greenfield, *Timothy Leary: A Biography* (Orlando: Harcourt, Inc., 2006), 406.
34 According to a declassified 30 December 1970 report the author obtained from the CIA.
35 Greenfield, *Timothy Leary: A Biography*, 407; Abbie Hoffman, *The Autobiography of Abbie Hoffman* (New York: Four Walls Eight Windows, 2000), 255; Elaine Mokhtefi, *Algiers, Third World Capital: Freedom Fighters, Revolutionaries, Black Panthers* (London: Verso, 2018), 114.
36 Timothy Leary, *Confessions of a Hope Fiend* (New York: Bantam Books, 1973), 170–9; Greenfield, *Timothy Leary: A Biography*, 407–11.
37 'Leary: Is Beirut Really the Hashish Capital?' [English translation], *Le Jour*, 27 October 1970, attached to a 30 December 1970 CIA report; Eric Pace, 'Leary, or a Lookalike, Appears Briefly in Beirut', *New York Times*, 27 October 1970.
38 Abdallah Schleifer, personal communication with the author, 27 April 2012; 30 December 1970 CIA report: 'Leary: Is Beirut Really the Hashish Capital?'; 'Why Did Dr. Leary Come to Beirut?' [English translation]. *al-Nahar*, 28 October 1970; and 'In Order to Maintain Friendship with the United States: The Shipping Out of Doctor Leary and his Friends' [English translation], *al-Hayat*, 28 October 1970.
39 30 December 1970 CIA report: 'Leary: Is Beirut Really the Hashish Capital?'; 'Why Did Dr. Leary Come to Beirut?' [English translation]; and 'Leary: 'Man, I Don't Know Where I'm Going', *New York Times*, 1 November 1970.

40 An image of the postcard can be found online: http://www.worthpoint.com/worthopedia/timothy-leary-signed-postcard-from-egypt-oct (accessed 15 March 2021).
41 This topic is explored in depth in Fischbach, *The Movement and the Middle East*.

Bibliography

Byrne, Jeffrey James. 'Finding the Middle East of the Insurgent Global South'. *International Journal of Middle East Studies* 52, no. 1 (2020): 146–9.

Chamberlin, Paul Thomas. *The Global Offensive: The United States, the Palestine Liberation Organization, and the Making of the Post-Cold War Order*. Oxford: Oxford University Press, 2012.

Dohrn, Bernardine, with Bill Ayers and Jeff Jones, eds. *Sing a Battle Song: The Revolutionary Poetry, Statements, and Communiqués of the Weather Underground 1970–1974*. New York: Seven Stories Press, 2006.

Dubinsky, Karen, with Katherine Krull, Susan Lord, Sean Mills, and Scott Rutherford, eds. *New World Coming: The Sixties and the Shaping of Global Consciousness*. Auburn, ME: Between the Lines, 2009.

Fischbach, Michael R. *Black Power and Palestine: Transnational Countries of Color*. Palo Alto: Stanford University Press, 2018.

Fischbach, Michael R. *The Movement and the Middle East: How the Arab-Israeli Conflict Divided the American Left*. Palo Alto: Stanford University Press, 2019.

Fischbach, Michael R. 'Palestinian Offices in the United States: Microcosms of the Palestinian Experience'. *Journal of Palestine Studies* 48, no. 1 (Autumn 2018): 104–18.

From Refugees to Palestinians: The Birth of a Revolution (Washington: Middle East Research and Information Project, n.d.).

Greenfield, Robert. *Timothy Leary: A Biography*. Orlando: Harcourt, 2006.

Hoffman, Abbie. *The Autobiography of Abbie Hoffman*. New York: Four Walls Eight Windows, 2000.

Irving, Sarah. *Leila Khaled: Icon of Palestinian Liberation*. London: Pluto Press, 2012.

'Israel Report'. *MERIP* 1, no. 4 (November 1971): 1, 7–12.

Jacobs, Harold, ed. *Weatherman*. New York: Ramparts Press, 1970.

Jian, Chen, with Martin Klimke, Masha Kirasirova, Mary Nolan, Marilyn Young, and Joanna Waley-Cohen, eds. *The Routledge Handbook of the Global Sixties: Between Protest and Nation-Building*. Milton Park, UK: Routledge, 2018.

Leary, Timothy. *Confessions of a Hope Fiend*. New York: Bantam Books, 1973.

Mahler, Anne Garland. *From the Tricontinental to the Global South: Race, Radicalism, and Transnational Solidarity*. Durham, NC: Duke University Press, 2018.

Mokhtefi, Elaine. *Algiers, Third World Capital: Freedom Fighters, Revolutionaries, Black Panthers*. Verso: London, 2018.

'Palestine'. *MERIP* 1, no. 4 (November 1971): 1.

Schayegh, Cyrus, and Yoav Di-Capua. 'Roundtable: Why Decolonization?' *International Journal of Middle East Studies* 52, no. 1 (2020): 137–45.

Weisbord, Robert G. *Bittersweet Encounter: The Afro-Americans and the American Jews.* Westport, CT: Negro Universities Press, 1970.

3

An archive of revolution retained in a filmmaker's memory: Masao Adachi and the Palestinian revolution

Dima Saqfalhait

In the past decade, there has been a growing interest in the film archive of the Palestinian revolution, sparked by the individuals who participated in its creation as well as activists, scholars and filmmakers who came across snippets of it in their research on the Palestinian revolution and were eager to see more as well as to curate, analyze and theorize their findings. For the purpose of this chapter, the film archive's importance is twofold. First, it offers an insight into the lives of Palestinians in the refugee camps in Jordan and Lebanon during the Palestinian revolution, and second, it shows the extent of international solidarity with the Palestinian cause. In the aftermath of the Oslo Accords, when the Palestinian revolution's initial aspirations of liberation and right to self-determination were removed from the table, many are now looking to the heyday of the Palestinian revolution, in an attempt to understand it, learn from it and preserve it from oblivion, especially as a significant amount of the film archive from this period was lost during the Israeli invasion of Beirut in 1982 and the subsequent departure of the Palestine Liberation Organization (PLO) to Tunisia.[1] The film archive consisted of films made by Palestinians as well as politically engaged foreign filmmakers, who visited the Palestinian camps in Lebanon and Jordan in the 1960s and 1970s, curious to witness, document and film the Palestinian revolution. One of these filmmakers was the Japanese activist, theorist and filmmaker Masao Adachi, whose interest in the Palestinian revolution led him to spend over twenty years of his life filming and participating in it.

This chapter examines Masao Adachi's life, his solidarity and film theory in light of the two films that linked him to the Palestinian revolution, namely *Red*

Army/PFLP: Declaration of World War (1971), made by Adachi during his first visit to Lebanon in 1971, and *The Anabsis of May and Fusako Shigenobu, Masao Adachi and 27 Years without Images* (2011), which was made by the French director Eric Baudelaire and narrates the twenty seven years Adachi spent in Palestinian camps. In doing so, this chapter attempts to answer an important question raised by Masao Adachi in Baudelaire's film. While reflecting on the reasons that drove him to visit the Palestinian camps in Lebanon for the first time in 1971, Adachi asks, 'What is the difference between a film "about" a struggle, and a film "in" a struggle?' This chapter takes up this question in its analysis of Adachi's films by looking to the role of film in documenting and narrating the life and work of the Palestinian revolution: the process of its production, as being part of the revolution itself; and the ability of the film to contest and reframe concepts of revolutionary participation and solidarity. It argues that unlike some of the other international filmmakers who made films 'about' the Palestinian revolution and then left, Adachi's experience living and filming in the Palestinian camps – developing close relationships and participating in the struggle for over two decades – is an example of a filmmaker working from within the struggle, as such producing films that become part of the revolution and its cultural archive as opposed to being only about it. Adachi experienced the challenges and aspirations of the Palestinian revolution and simultaneously participated in documenting it, first through his camera (in *Declaration of World War*) and second through his private memories and recollections in Baudelaire's *Masao Adachi and 27 Years without Image*.

Despite efforts to research and reassemble the Palestine film archive, the body of work written about the films made on (and in solidarity with) the Palestinian revolution is still relatively modest. In the case of Adachi, in particular, his experience filming and supporting the Palestinian revolution is often seen only within the wider context of his radical political vision and film theory, overlooking the specificity of his contribution to the Palestinian revolution. As the scholar of Palestinian cinema Nadia Yaqub writes in her book *Palestinian Cinema in the Days of Revolution*, which offers an in-depth analysis of the films made about the Palestinian revolution between 1968 and 1982, as well as the political and cultural contexts in which they were produced and screened, 'Palestinian archives are continually being erased and resisting that erasure is a key component of Palestinian activism.'[2] This chapter contributes to the body of work available on Masao Adachi and acknowledges his role in preserving the legacy of the Palestinian revolution through his cinematic work and his personal memories.

Self-representation and the establishment of the Palestine Film Unit

Since the 1948 Nakba, Palestinians only had limited control over their representation in films and photographs, which were widely disseminated by the media and humanitarian aid organizations. These images mainly portrayed Palestinians as either victims, strongly enhanced by the footage taken by humanitarian aid organizations while documenting their support for the Palestinian refugees (e.g. the American Friends Service Committee and the International Committee of the Red Cross), or as terrorists, reinforced by photos of the media coverage of the conflict. According to Zeina Maasri, after 1967, art initiatives and cultural activities in support of the Palestinian struggle started taking shape, which were then assimilated within the PLO.[3] Palestinians began to claim more agency in their self-representation through the publication of periodicals and posters, art exhibitions and films and photography that documented their struggle and activities.

The establishment of the Palestine Film Unit (PFU) in Amman in 1968 was part of an effort to express the 'emancipatory identity' of the Palestinians, which the revolution helped create, and to use it to mobilize support for the Palestinian revolution from solidarity activists and others who were fighting similar struggles.[4] The work produced by the PFU was part of a larger emerging world movement that questioned film's sole purpose as an art form and instead understood it as a medium capable of influencing the masses. PFU first started as a photography unit in 1967 when Sulafa Jadallah, who studied cinematography in Cairo, was asked to take portraits of fida'iyin before they left for military missions inside historic Palestine.[5] Then, in 1968, Hani Jawhariyyeh and Mustafa Abu 'Ali, who were both trained at the London Film School, joined Jadallah in creating the PFU. Their responsibility included filming and disseminating photographs of Fatah's military operations.[6] The PFU was eventually succeeded by the Palestinian Cinema Institute (PCI).[7]

The majority of Palestinian films created at the time, at a moment when the Palestinian national liberation movement was taking shape, were documentaries shot in black and white and made with low budgets and under difficult conditions. Most adhered to a straightforward concept that addressed the difficulties Palestinians were facing as a stateless people resisting colonial violence. They were focused more on communicating current events rather than participating in a theoretical dialogue about the nature of images.[8] Films helped construct and sustain values important for the resilience of the Palestinian revolution such as 'heroism, martyrdom, and steadfastness'.[9] They also addressed the audience as fellow supporters, engaging them and informing them about the Palestinian cause, inviting them as equals to a struggle instead of asking for their help. As described by Yaqub, an important result of these changes was the move from humanitarian to revolutionary representations of Palestinians.[10]

Attracting politically engaged filmmakers

During the late 1960s and early 1970s, the Palestinian cause was garnering unprecedented attention, due to reasons particular not only to the Palestinian revolution but also to the general political climate of the world. It was a time when many countries in Asia and Africa were gaining their independence from European colonial powers. As countries began to regain and shape their identities and practice their right to self-determination, a general climate of solidarity was taking shape among the countries of the Third World, particularly in the aftermath of the Afro-Asian Bandung Conference of 1955, the establishment of the Non-Aligned Movement in 1961, and the 1966 Tricontinental Conference in Havana. These international forums encouraged cultural and economic solidarity between Third World countries against colonialism and imperialism.[11] Moreover, as Yoav Di-Capua explains, student movements in Europe and beyond started identifying with the Palestinian struggle and highlighting the similarities between Palestine and other national liberation struggles such as those in Algeria, Cuba and Vietnam.[12] As the Palestinian revolution emerged as an emancipatory project and cause, students, solidarity activists and artists across the world began offering help and support.

In 1970, Fatah commissioned two French filmmakers, Jean-Luc Godard and Jean-Pierre Gorin, who were at the time part of the militant film collective Dziga Vertov, to make a film about the Palestinian revolution. Godard and Gorin intended to make a film titled *Until Victory*, but the production of the film was interrupted by the Jordanian civil war, also known as Black September, which was a battle between the Jordanian army and the PLO in September 1970, resulting in the death of thousands of Palestinians and the PLO's departure from Jordan to Lebanon. According to Adachi, Godard wanted to include in his film an analysis of the events of Black September, but the PLO was concerned about further provoking the Jordanian authorities and did not approve the inclusion of the analysis. The film was never finished.[13]

Godard used the footage he filmed with Gorin in 1970 to make his film *Here and Elsewhere* (*Ici et Ailleurs*, 1976) with Anne-Marie Miéville. The film was well-received internationally. Yet Godard's relationship with the Palestinian struggle ended there, at least artistically, as he returned to Paris. In 1971, the Popular Front for the Liberation of Palestine (PFLP) commissioned Japanese filmmakers Masao Adachi and Koji Wakamatsu, who were part of the Japanese New Wave,[14] to make another film about the Palestinian revolution. The result was *Red Army/PFLP: Declaration of World War* (1971).

As argued by Yaqub, the works of Jean-Luc Godard, Jean-Pierre Gorin, Masao Adachi and Koji Wakamatsu were important due to their exploration of wider topics in relation to the Palestinian struggle, including the relationship between the circulation of images and politics. They went beyond a distant documentation of the struggle as their direct relationship with the political parties enabled them to obtain a better understanding of the context and a closer engagement with the content they were filming. In addition, being from a background of politically engaged cinema enabled them to see, and in turn show, the Palestinian struggle as part of a greater struggle against imperialism. For these reasons, the works of these filmmakers have received critical attention from scholars. According to Yaqub, through their analyses of cinema, media and politics, Godard, Gorin, Adachi and Wakamatsu used the Palestinian revolution as a case study to make a theoretical contribution to the existing conversations on 'truth, representation, media circuits, and the relationships that can and cannot be formed through those circuits'.[15] This helped them make the Palestinian struggle identifiable worldwide, especially as they spoke of the importance of joining forces against the imminent danger of imperial powers.

According to Yaqub, the works of these filmmakers were influenced by military operations such as plane hijackings carried out by the Japanese Red Army (JRA) and the PFLP in 1970 and the Munich Olympics operation in 1972. Although the PFU was also interested in visibility, it worked mainly on producing and distributing films that directly served the Palestinian revolution by focusing on the local experiences of Palestinians in their daily struggle rather than on contemplating and implementing spectacular acts of violence and propaganda. Yaqub argues that '[PFU] filmmaking, and, in particular, the works of Abu 'Ali, was animated by sentiment, as well as thought, and include meditations on the meaning of commitment to a collective struggle and the difficulty and necessity of that belonging, questions that are not addressed in either *Here and Elsewhere* or *Red Army/PFLP*'.[16] This chapter questions this assumption through an examination of the work Adachi did for and within the Palestinian revolution, arguing that his work and personal experience went beyond a political and artistic interest. In what follows, this chapter argues that Adachi's life and work demonstrates a true commitment and belonging to the Palestinian revolution as a personal and collective struggle.

Adachi and student activism in Japan

Masao Adachi was born in 1939 in Fukuoka in Japan. At the age of twenty, he joined the Film Studies programme at Nihon University. He made a number of experimental films that were well-received among film critics such as *Rice Bowl* (1961), before he started making pink films. Pink films first appeared in Japan in the early 1960s and were popular in local Japanese cinemas until the mid-1980s. They are low-budget films with softcore pornographic content, made to be screened in cinema theatres. Since these films were not subject to the same strict censorship measures that targeted other forms of Japanese cinema at the time, many Japanese filmmakers used the genre of pink films to address sensitive political and social issues.

During the late 1950s, Adachi was active in the student demonstrations against Japan resigning the Treaty of Mutual Cooperation and Security with the United States, which was intended to give the United States military access to and control over Japan. The treaty had been signed in 1951, and although the new version of the treaty offered better conditions to the Japanese people in terms of limiting US influence and control, many Japanese people and organizations with different political affiliations rejected the presence of US military bases in Japan and wanted to cancel the treaty altogether.[17] Between March 1959 and July 1960, there were over twenty-seven different nationwide mass demonstrations against the signing of the treaty with the participation of students, human rights organizations, labour unions, the socialist and communist parties, farmer's cooperatives and peace groups.[18] To many people, the signing of the treaty signaled Japan's willingness to embrace a 'neocolonial status in the American imperium',[19] which was heavily rejected, particularly among Japanese student groups and artists. This political engagement and activism manifested itself through the emergence of new theories and practices in the fields of politics, art and culture in Japan, which had an important impact on film.

Student films, including the works of Adachi and his colleagues, played a vital role in depicting and shaping political activism.[20] Many Japanese filmmakers were able to poignantly and intimately document the clashes that were taking place and which they were an active part of. They also used the political struggle as a foundation for fiction films that depicted lost Japanese youth in search of meaning. Although at the time Adachi and his colleagues had little knowledge about the Palestinian cause, their activism was part of a greater student movement worldwide. During the 1960s, students started developing a new understanding of decolonization in the context of the Cold War. According to Di-Capua, who specifically writes about the student movement in Paris, student activism in the 1960s was based on 'global solidarity and intellectual critique'.[21] These students embraced theory (what was known then as philosophy) as a revolutionary weapon, much of which influenced today's postcolonial studies.[22]

When the treaty was eventually signed, it left Adachi and his generation with an overpowering sense of defeat in relation to their role in resisting the dominance of American imperialism in Japan and the rest of the world. Despite their feeling of failure, Adachi and his colleagues continued experimenting with film form and content. They were keen on exploring different genres and ways of expression, including forms of production and screening, which was part of a movement that came to be known as underground cinema.[23] This corresponded with what was happening elsewhere in the world in the late 1960s, a period that is often referred to as 'the most vibrant era of militant documentary filmmaking', directly inspired by the revolutions and decolonization struggles that were taking place around the world.[24] A Japanese avant garde movement was formed at the time by artists, filmmakers and writers who saw the potential for political practices and cultural production with a strong foundation and grounding in the everyday. They did not see a separation between politics and culture but rather saw the everyday as a site of their unification. This was a clear rejection of what Japanese liberal political intellectuals were promoting at the time, which was to depoliticize culture and the arts, making them less radical and better aligned with the values of globalization.[25]

During the beginning of the 1970s, because of his involvement with the radial student movement, Adachi began developing an interest in the Palestinian revolution's model of resistance. According to Adachi, the Palestinian refugee camps in Lebanon and Jordan were 'one of the few places of the third world where the vision of a cultural and political transformation was still an active possibility'.[26] With an interest in experimenting with political films, and due to his frustration with the situation in Japan, Adachi decided to visit Lebanon for the first time in 1971, while on his way back from the Cannes Film Festival. Adachi had already decided to stop in the Middle East to look for possible locations for his next film before his departure to Cannes. While Japanese media and other filmmakers and activists were covering the Vietnam War, Adachi felt that his peers did not pay enough attention to the political and revolutionary struggles in the Middle East. Before his trip to Lebanon, he started studying different liberation movements. In Lebanon, and particularly in the PFLP, he found what he was looking for.[27]

Adachi's first encounter with the Palestinian revolution

Adachi's visit to Lebanon was an important divergence in his life. He arrived in Beirut, along with Koji Wakamatsu, 'with a 16 mm camera, a cassette tape recorder and two walkie-talkies'.[28] With the help of fellow Japanese activist and later leader of the JRA, Fusako Shegenobu, who had already been in Beirut for months and was working with the PLFP as a translator, he met members of the PFLP, including Ghassan Kanafani and Leila Khaled. With the permission of the PFLP, Shigenobu helped Adachi and Wakamatsu meet Palestinian revolutionaries, and visit camps in Saida and Beirut, as well as PFLP military bases in the Golan Heights in Syria and in the mountains of Jerash near the borders between Jordan and Israel.[29] There Adachi found a model of resistance different to the one he had known back in Japan. Adachi's experience in Lebanon was documented in two films: *Japanese Red Army/PFLP: Declaration of World War* (1971), which he made alongside his colleague Wakamatsu upon his initial visit, and *The Anabasis of May and Fusako Shigenobu, Masao Adachi, and 27 Years without Images* (2011), which was made forty years later by the French filmmaker Eric Baudelaire.

Whereas *Declaration of World War* offers rare footage of daily life in the Palestinian camps and speeches by key figures in the Palestinian revolution, Adachi's own thoughts and private experiences are absent from the film. In one of the interviews conducted with Adachi, he stresses the importance of the filmmaker not including everything in the film's frame but rather allowing the audience to decide for themselves what they wish to focus on.[30] According to Adachi, the filmmaker can put his feelings into the film, but the audience should also be able to watch the film freely and decide on their own frames of interpretation.[31] In order to investigate the film's production and the web of relations and motivations behind it, the following section reads *Declaration of World War* alongside *27 Years without Images*, the latter of which, along with other interviews conducted with Adachi, offers an insight into Adachi's private thoughts, concerns, interests and memories of the twenty-seven years he spent as part of the Palestinian revolution.

Culture and politics in the everyday

In *27 Years without Images*, Eric Baudelaire uses segments of interviews he conducted with May Shigenobu, the daughter of Fusako Shigenobu, and Adachi to narrate the history of the JRA in Beirut and their forced deportation to Japan in 2000. In the film, Adachi speaks about the organic relationship he found between the Palestinians fighting in the battlefield and those living in the camps, giving the viewer, through his words, a unique insight into the dynamics that existed inside the camps at the time, as well as a better understanding of the logic behind the footage he chose to include in his own film, *Declaration of World War*:

> The front lines and the rear supporting groups are usually quite separate. But here, the struggle for national liberation was led by adolescents sent to the frontlines directly from the refugee camp kitchens, washing and dining rooms. The front and rear seemed as one. It was impressive. Civilian struggles can be fought like that. While in Japan, only a handful of students armed with stolen guns were fighting. I felt this was important. And that if I started with the idea that the front and the rear of the gun are connected, it could turn into something interesting. So I started filming.

What Adachi calls 'the front lines' are the Palestinian fighters in the battlefield; they are also the ones who plan the operations, promote revolutionary thought and are, at the same time, inhabitants in the camps (what Adachi calls 'the rear supporting groups'). This is evident in the footage of *Declaration of World War*, where there is no separation between a Palestinian civilian and a revolutionary – a type of revolutionary subjectivity and aesthetic that not only inspired Adachi but also one he helped promote.

In *Declaration of World War*, every act performed by Palestinians in front of the camera, regardless of whether they are in the battlefield or carrying out everyday activities in the camps, appears as a form of resistance. According to Harootunian and Kohso, Adachi used the film form as a 'basis for a rethinking of ways to reunify politics and culture'.[32] Palestinian women, children, the elders and the fighters are shown in different contexts in the refugee camps and in the battlefield eating, playing, cooking, reading, learning how to load/unload rifles and how to attack the enemy. The manifestations of Palestinian culture inside the camps are also shown as manifestations of politics, as they depict a stateless people dreaming and working towards their liberation while asserting their Palestinian identity and the fact that despite all Israeli, British and American claims, Palestinians do actually exist – and resist. The activity of the Palestinians in the film and their work towards the transformation of their individual and collective condition reflects the model of revolutionary representation in Third Cinema.

In their famous manifesto 'Towards a Third Cinema', which calls for the creation of a cinema style that breaks free from the models of First Cinema (Hollywood) and Second Cinema (European), and aims at encouraging revolutionary activism, Argentinian filmmakers Fernando Solanas and Octavio Getino refer to what they call 'the new man'. This 'new man' is to be created by the 'revolution against imperialism' in the countries of the Third World who, by shedding all previous flaws that burden him, become 'a bomb of inexhaustible power and, at the same time, the only real possibility of life'.[33] In Adachi's film, women in particular are portrayed as engaging in reinventing themselves and their role in the revolution. The same women who are shown cooking in the kitchen, are shown, in a later scene, learning how to use weapons. The film also features iconic female revolutionaries such as Leila Khaled and Fusako Shigenobu. The revolutionary subjectivity created by Adachi is one that shows the people and the revolution as one entity – two ends of the same rifle – as described by Adachi.

Furthermore, *Declaration of World War* constantly reminds the viewer that what they are watching is a propaganda film that positions itself against what is being said about the Palestinian struggle in the Western media. Adachi has expressed his influence by the playwrights Bertolt Brecht and Samuel Beckett which adds a different layer to his film.[34] As such, the film does not claim to show 'documentation' of reality as it is. On the contrary, Adachi says that he focuses on the 'relationship between the two methodologies [documentaries and fiction films]' for the purpose of demolishing the line between these two categories.[35] This sense of duality is highly present in the film. Individuals such as Leila Khaled and Ghassan Kanafani speak of the collective, but the collective also speak of the individuals. The film not only depicts people in displacement but also signals individuals out, showing a mosaic of stories of individuals fighting for their individual as well as collective liberation. The camera in certain scenes feels as invisible as a fly on the wall, whereas in others we see people directly staring at it. The film does not follow a coherent form or narrative line. It allows the audience to choose where to focus their attention. This, according to Adachi, 'is how directors can begin to close the distance between themselves and their audiences'.[36] The film mixes between a global war and the Palestinian revolution, talking about propaganda and world struggles against imperialism, and linking that to the Palestinian revolution. It shows a collective cultural manifestation of the Palestinian struggle in the camps and the battlefields, where fighters wait, chant for freedom, learn how to maneuver and occasionally stare back at the audience, as if in an attempt to secure the documentation of their own struggle and, in a way, their existence.

Fukeiron

Whereas *Declaration of World War* promotes and speaks of 'the construction of a World Red Army' against 'world imperialism', the film itself rarely shows scenes of war or combat. Instead, a lot of the footage consists of static long shots of empty fields, streets and rooms in the camps. The film opens with archival footage of a Japanese airplane hijacking and newspaper headlines. This contextualizes the film within the greater political context of the period showing that despite the different localities of the struggle, all countries are 'connected through the very system that they resisted in common'.[37] The film then moves to Lebanon, showing footage of different streets, shot in motion from the point of view of a moving car that at some point passes by the sea. The film cuts to footage of an airplane belonging to Libyan Arab Airlines, taking off, soaring in the sky (hiding the sun as it does), before the camera pans down to show a Palestinian camp for the first time. Although the voice-over talks about armed struggle, the camp itself looks surprisingly serene and no humans are visible. The footage then cuts to a TV antenna immediately after the voice-over talks about the power of Western media in shaping people's opinion worldwide.

In the late 1960s, Masao Adachi started developing an interest in the significance and meaning of space in films. At the time, he worked with the critic Masao Matsuda and his concept of 'the theory of landscape' (*fukeiron*). Adachi, along with Matsudo and five other filmmakers, made *A.K.A Serial Killer* (1969), in which they explored the way in which the Japanese government and its economic power penetrated the intimate and mundane spaces of everyday life.[38] The film depicts the landscape in which a serial killer, Nagayama, grew up, arguing that it is through the state's growing political and economic control over Japan, which materialized itself through the suffocating urbanization and homogenization of public space, that one can trace the role of the landscape in Nagayama's acts of killing.

This chapter suggests that Adachi's focus on landscape in *Declaration of World War* builds on the *fukeiron* theory. In *Declaration of World War*, traces of life begin to gradually appear in the Palestinian camps through packed clothing lines, which hint at the high number of individuals living in that space. The film shows camps whose walls are filled with bullet holes, and doors, windows and beautiful fields that at any given minute could become a battlefield. According to Adachi, landscape theory meant that 'landscape itself is a reflection of the omnipresence of power'.[39] If one is to read the film in light of this, one can see how, much like the voice-over that presents the Palestinian struggle as a unified international movement against imperialist powers worldwide, the shots of landscape become emblematic of different struggles worldwide, allowing spectators to place themselves in these empty landscapes. Noonan argues that in *Declaration of World War*, Adachi combines empty shots of space, like the ones in *A.K.A Serial Killer*, 'with propagandistic declarations to represent the power relations embedded in the global landscapes where actual struggles for power were waged'.[40] Yet the landscape shots are also particular to the Palestinian revolution, with the olive groves and guerilla fighters wearing a *kufiyya*, a symbol of the Palestinian revolution. In many instances in the film, the camera is not motivated in its movement by the fighters as much as by the landscape they are in. The camera often remains fixed on the horizon almost in a static contemplative manner, as Palestinian fighters leave the frame. This also applies to the footage taken inside the camps. Adachi's camera lingers on different angles of the camps where no action happens. This footage is also in many instances empty of people. With the traces of bullets on the walls or broken glass one can infer or predict the action that preceded the time the shot was made. This engages the audience at a deeper level with the footage. Adachi does not deliver ready stories but rather evokes different levels of engagement by the audience, encouraging them to use their imagination and to ponder their own potential revolutionary subjectivity through his landscape aesthetics.

The idea of solidarity was important to Adachi, leading him to screen the film in Europe and Japan, as well as in several Palestinian camps, thereby using the film itself to help recruit support for the Palestinian struggle. Believing that 'screening itself [to be] a form of activist movement', Adachi formed the Red Bus Screening Troupe, which became a great accomplishment for the concept of 'cinema as a movement in Japan'.[41] The screening group was established in 1971, in rejection of the capitalist film industry and the existing forms of film exhibition. It was launched in Tokyo after which the bright red microbus travelled across Japan.[42] Through screening the film, Adachi intended to invite people to join the ranks of the world revolution. According to Yaqub, Adachi performed what Getino and Solanas call a 'film act', where he travelled with his film across Japan to screen it and hold political discussions with young Japanese activists.[43] This shows Adachi's great level of engagement with the Palestinian cause. The film was no longer the goal in itself but rather a means to attract support to the Palestinian revolution.

In one interview, Adachi recalls his experience screening the film in a Palestinian camp in Lebanon. During the screening, people started looking for their dead family members in the film and crying while touching the screen. According to Adachi, whereas the film intended to enlist people in a collective movement, Palestinians did not need to see the film as they were already part of a collective movement for the liberation of their country.[44] Although made about and for Palestine, Adachi's film was not made for a Palestinian audience. Instead, the film was produced to inform, much like the films made by the PFU, the world about the Palestinian struggle. Adachi's interest in showing the film in different places and to different audiences, including Palestinians, shows Adachi as an activist 'in' the revolution. He was not solely an outsider looking in but rather a member of the revolution, who, in his film, speaks on behalf of it.

Adachi joins the Palestinian revolution

Three years later, in 1974, Adachi returned to Lebanon to make his second film. Talking about the period he spent following his return to Lebanon, Adachi remembers how Palestinians were still living in packed refugee camps in the mountain areas, far from the cities, in Sabra and Shatila, Ein el-Hilweh, Sur and Tripoli. Later in 1975, Adachi speaks of the daily struggles of surviving the bombing during the Lebanese civil war when Palestinians were fighting two wars: one against Israel and the other against the Lebanese right-wing militias. In the meantime, Palestinians worked steadily towards restoring the refugee camps from the damage of the war. This connection that Adachi could see between families and between neighbours, symbolized to Adachi 'something that united with the consciousness of the wish to restore the homeland'.[45]

Upon his return, Adachi began having a more direct role in the Palestinian revolution. He accompanied the Palestinian revolutionaries in their military maneuvers as well as in the daily activities in the camps. Adachi's close relationship with the revolutionaries quickly gave him a meaningful role in the revolution. In 1974, Adachi, while in Paris, made an announcement on behalf of the JRA. Upon his return to Lebanon, he became the official spokesperson of the JRA. In *27 Years without Images*, Adachi recalls how he mainly stayed in Lebanon because he had responsibilities, including preparing press releases and issuing statements following military operations. He adds how he believed that 'filmmaking and revolutionary struggle were one and the same'.[46] This shows Adachi's personal engagement with the revolution and the ways in which his role as a filmmaker intertwined with being a revolutionary.

Adachi constantly linked cinema and media together as important mediums for showing the truth and influence audiences. According to Adachi, a military operation scenario is not very different from a film scenario, and fighters are similar to actors in the sense that they are instructed by a detailed scenario, while the media camera plays a role similar to that of cinema in choosing what to focus on and what to ignore. Adachi never took part in military operations, nor did he participate in their planning, but he commented on how he found the reality of military operations to be far more extraordinary than his imagination. In *27 Years without Images*, Adachi recounts,

> I filmed a child growing up while I was there. He became a fine guerilla soldier, much taller than me. I filmed him as he studied, as he trained, the way he lived, I am sorry that these films were lost. ... This memory is the only thing I have left. As for everything else, I can only think that the last footage never existed.

Much like many Palestinian refugees whose memory becomes the only testimony to their forced displacement from their villages in Palestine, Adachi's own memory becomes the sole witness to the rare moments he experienced and attempted to document through his camera. His personal memories became those of the revolution.

Adachi did not make any other films about the Palestinian revolution although he continued filming extensively until his equipment and archive of over 200 hours of footage was destroyed in an Israeli raid in 1982. It was a rich archive that included intimate details of the revolutionaries' lives; footage that could only have been shot by someone actively involved in the struggle. Hana Sleiman argues that Israel's attack and seizure of the Palestinian Research Centre's archive in 1982 attest to the difficulty of preserving records when fighting for national liberation. The very act of keeping an archive poses a threat that 'exists not on the physical battlefield, but on the narrative one'.[47] With regard to Adachi, through his footage, imprinted in the memory of the filmmaker, one can begin to see how close he was to the Palestinian revolutionaries, in the camps as well as on the battlefield, surpassing the level of participation in the revolution of many other international filmmakers who documented the struggle. Without access to his archive of film, Adachi's own personal memory becomes a rich archive to countless scenarios of potential films about the revolution.

Adachi stayed in Beirut for twenty years. In an interview, he divides the time he spent in the refugee camps, following his return in 1974, into three stages. First, he returned with the intention to film a second part of *Declaration of World War*. At the time, he also worked on strengthening his relationship with the Japanese volunteers working in Lebanon. Then, he became the spokesman of the JRA, which forced him 'to adopt an underground lifestyle', especially as Lebanon was in the middle of a civil war. Survival while maintaining his activities was a challenging task. He also collaborated with the PLO on doing different cultural activities, like organizing the Palestinian Writers Conference, while living in military camps as a member of the JRA. In the third period, following the PLO's departure to Tunisia in 1982, Adachi collaborated with other people and organizations in countries that were also undergoing a revolution, while also continuing to support the Palestinians. He does not specify whether he did that from Lebanon or elsewhere. His life became more complicated with the collapse of the Soviet Union in 1991 and the labeling of the JRA as a 'terrorist organization' by the United States in 1997.[48]

In 1997, Adachi was arrested by the Lebanese police for forging his passport and was imprisoned in Roumieh prison for three years (1997–2000), along with four other members of the JRA, including Kozo Okamoto, the only survivor from the Lod Airport operation in 1972, where three members of the JRA, recruited by the PFLP, attacked Lod Airport, killing twenty-six people. A group of Palestinian and Lebanese youth held a hunger strike calling for the five Japanese prisoners to be granted asylum in Lebanon. Additionally, 150 lawyers signed a petition demanding their immediate release from prison. An exhibition showing Adachi's work was also organized to show support for the prisoners and to attract the attention of the media. Here, the concept of solidarity became reciprocal; Palestinians protested for the freedom of Adachi after he had long shown solidarity and support for their struggle.

However, Adachi was eventually deported, alongside his comrades, except for Okamoto who was granted asylum in Jordan, once they had served their sentence. Then, they were sent by a rented Russian airplane to Tokyo. Adachi was tried for entering Prague airport eight times, with a different passport each time, and for owning fake identification papers, and was sentenced and imprisoned again for the same charge he had already served time for in Lebanon. He was also denied the right to have a passport and to travel outside Japan. Adachi continued making films in Japan, some of which were influenced by his experience in Lebanon such as *Prisoner/Terrorist* (2007), which focuses on the period Okamoto spent in Israeli prisons, where he was subjected to torture but continued dreaming of freedom.

Conclusion

Unlike other international filmmakers whose contribution to the Palestinian revolution was restricted to making films to be screened at international film festivals, Adachi's commitment to the Palestinian cause went beyond his role as a filmmaker. Not only did his camera become his gun, as inspired by Getino and Solanas in their Third Cinema manifesto, but he also himself became a member of the revolution. Here perhaps lies the answer to the question that initially drove Adachi towards making his first film – the real difference between a film 'about' the struggle and a film 'in' the struggle. Adachi started filming to make a film 'about' the revolution but ended up filming material at the core of the struggle, material that was not destined to see the light yet has been immortalized through his own memory, as captured by Baudelaire in *27 Years without Images*.

Notes

1 Hend Alawadhi, 'On What Was, and What Remains: Palestinian Cinema and the Film Archive', *IAFOR Journal of Media, Communication and Film* 1, no. 1 (2013): 21; Kareem Estefan, 'Narrating Looted and Living Palestinian Archives: Reparative Fabulation in Azza El-Hassan's *Kings and Extras*', *Feminist Media Histories* 8, no. 2 (2022): 43–69; Nurith Gertz and George Khleifi, *Palestinian Cinema: Landscape, Trauma and Memory* (Edinburgh: Edinburgh University Press, 2008); Hugo Darroman, 'Towards a Decentered History of Plaestinian Revolutionary Cinema? Case Study of the Film Tall el Zaatar in the Audiovisual Archive of the Italian Communist Party', *Regards* 26 (2021): 111–27; Rona Sela 'Seized in Beirut: The Plundered Archives of the Palestinian Cinema Institution and Cultural Arts Section', *Anthropology of the Middle East* 12, no. 1, (2017): 83–114; Lubna Taha, 'On Cinema and Revolutions: Tricontinental Militancy and the Cinema of the Palestinian Revolution', Thesis, Queen's University, 2021. Available online: https://qspace.library.queensu.ca/handle/1974/28939. (accessed 9 September 2022).

2 Nadia Yaqub, *Palestinian Cinema in the Days of Revolution* (Austin: University of Texas Press, 2018), 2.

3 Zeina Maasri, *Cosmopolitan Radicalism: The Visual Politics of Beirut's Global Sixties* (Cambridge: Cambridge University Press, 2020), 173. See also Dina Matar,

'PLO Cultural Activism: Mediating Liberation Aesthetics in Revolutionary Contexts', *Comparative Studies of South Asia, Africa and the Middle East* 38, no. 2 (2018): 354–64.

4 Yaqub, *Palestinian Cinema in the Days of Revolution*, 6, 53–4; Khadija Habashneh, *Fursan al-Sinima: Sirat Wahdat Aflam Filastin* (Amman: al-Ahliyya, 2020); Nick Denes, 'Between Form and Function: Experimentation in the Early Works of the Palestine Film Unit, 1968–1974', *Middle East Journal of Culture and Communication* 7 (2014): 219–41.

5 Khadijah Habashneh, 'Shahadat: Wahdat Aflam Filastin. 'Alamah fi Tarikh al-Sinima al-Nidaliyah', *Shu'un Filastiniyah* Spring, no. 260 (2017): 17. Habashneh, *Fursan al-Sinima*; Denes, 'Between Form and Function', 219–41, no. 260, Spring 2017, p. 715.

6 Yaqub, *Palestinian Cinema in the Days of Revolution*, 54.

7 Ibid., 65–7.

8 Ibid., 49.

9 Laleh Khalili, *Heroes and Martyrs of Palestine: The Politics of National Commemoration* (Cambridge: Cambridge University Press, 2007).

10 Yaqub, *Palestinian Cinema in the Days of Revolution*, 7. See in particular Chapter one.

11 See for example, Paul Thomas Chamberlin, *The Global Offensive: The United States, the Palestine Liberation Organization, and the Making of the Post-Cold War Order* (Oxford: Oxford University Press, 2012); Zeina Maasri, Cathy Bergen, and Francesca Burke eds, *Transnational Solidarity: Anticolonialism in the Global Sixties* (Manchester: Manchester University Press, 2022); Chen Jian, Martin Klimke, Masha Kirasirova, Mary Nolan, Marilyn Young, and Joanna Waley-Cohen, eds, *The Routledge Handbook of the Global Sixties: Between Protest and Nation-Building* (London: Routledge, 2018).

12 Yoav Di-Capua, 'Palestine Comes to Paris: The Global Sixties and the Making of a Universal Cause', *Journal of Palestine Studies* 50, no. 1 (2021): 20. See also Mjriam Abu Samra, 'The Palestinian Student Movement 1948–1982: A Study of Popular Organisation and Transnational Mobilisation', PhD dissertation, University of Oxford, 2020.

13 Masao Adachi, 'Le testament que Godard n'a jamais écrit', in Le Bus de la Révolution Passera Bientôt Près de Chez Toi: Écrits sur le Cinéma, la Guérilla et l'Avant-Garde (1963–2010), ed. Nicole Brenez and Go Hirasawa, 194–204. (Pertuis, France: Rouge Profond, 2002).

14 The Japanese New Wave refers to the works of a group of Japanese filmmakers (between late 1950s and 1970s) who although were not connected by a common movement, were keen on radically innovating Japanese cinema in terms of content and form.

15 Yaqub, *Palestinian Cinema in the Days of Revolution*, 48. See also Olivia. C Harrison, 'Consuming Palestine: Anticapitalism and anticolonialism in Jean-Luc Godard's Ici et ailleurs', *Studies in French Cinema* 183 (2018): 178–91.
16 Yaqub, *Palestinian Cinema in the Days of Revolution*, 51–2.
17 Nick Kapur, *Japan at the Crossroads: Conflict and Compromise after Anpo* (Cambridge: Harvard University Press, 2018), 12–19.
18 Ibid., 19–20.
19 Harry Harootunian and Sabu Kohso, 'Messages in a Bottle: An Interview with Filmmaker Masao Adachi', trans. P. Kaffen, *boundary* 2 35, no. 3 (2008): 64.
20 Go Hirasawa, 'On Masao Adachi', trans. P. Kaffen, *boundary* 2 35, no. 3 (2008): 65–6.
21 Di-Capua, 'Palestine Comes to Paris', 20.
22 Ibid.
23 Hirasawa, 'On Masao Adachi', 66.
24 Yuriko Furuhata, *Cinema of Actuality: Japanese Avant-Garde Filmmaking in the Season of Image Politics* (Durham: Duke University Press, 2013), 120.
25 Harootunian and Kohso, 'Messages in a Bottle', 64.
26 Ibid.
27 Patrick James Noonan, 'Our Dissolution: Subjectivity, Collectivity, and the Politics of Form in 1960s Japan', PhD dissertation, University of California, Berkley, 2012, 57.
28 Furuhata, *Cinema of Actuality*, 149.
29 Ibid., 149.
30 Harootunian and Kohso, 'Messages in a Bottle', 76.
31 Ibid.
32 Ibid., 69.
33 Octavio Getino and Fernando Solanas, 'Towards a Third Cinema', *Cinéaste* 4, no. 3 (1970): 10.
34 Harootunian and Kohso, 'Messages in a Bottle', 76.
35 Ibid., 70.
36 Ibid., 76.
37 Noonan, 'Our Dissolution: Subjectivity, Collectivity, and the Politics of Form in 1960s Japan', 57.
38 Ibid., 59–60.
39 Harootunian and Kohso, 'Messages in a Bottle', 86.
40 Noonan, 'Our Dissolution: Subjectivity, Collectivity, and the Politics of Form in 1960s Japan', 61.
41 Hirasawa, 'On Masao Adachi', 67.
42 Harootunian and Kohso, 'Messages in a Bottle', 74.
43 Yaqub, *Palestinian Cinema in the Days of Revolution*, 81

44 Harootunian and Kohso, 'Messages in a Bottle', 86.
45 Ibid., 78–9.
46 Ibid., 78–9.
47 Hana Sleiman, 'The Paper Trail of a Liberation Movement', *Arab Studies Journal* 24, no. 1, (2016): 45–6.
48 Harootunian and Kohso, 'Messages in a Bottle', 80.

Bibliography

Abu Remaileh, Refqa. 'The Kanafani Effect: Resistance and Counter-Narration in the Films of Michel Khleifi and Elia Suleiman'. *Middle East Journal of Culture and Communication* 7, no. 2 (2014): 190–206.

Abu Samra, Mjriam. 'The Palestinian Student Movement 1948–1982: A Study of Popular Organisation and Transnational Mobilisation', PhD dissertation, University of Oxford, 2020.

Adachi, Masao. 'Le testament que Godard n'a jamais écrit', in *Le Bus de la Révolution Passera Bientôt Près de Chez Toi: Ecrits sur le Cinéma, la Guérilla et l'Avant-Garde* (1963–2010), edited by Nicole Brenez and Go Hirasawa, 194–204. Pertuis, France: Rouge Profond, 2002).

Alawadhi, Hend. 'On What Was, and What Remains: Palestinian Cinema and the Film Archive'. *IAFOR Journal of Media Communication and Film* 1, no. 1 (2013): 17–26.

Baudelaire, Eric. 'The Anabasis of May and Fusako Shigenobu, Masao Adachi, and 27 Years without Images', *issuu* (2014). Available online: https://issuu.com/ebaudelaire/docs/the_anabasis_libretto_eng_hd?fbclid=IwAR3YIrqQARarbKYzjCCKtrgQiXs0RAzVUOvTyfF8drvnS1JeJEJ-8GBACbs. (accessed 15 February 2022).

Chamberlin, Paul Thomas. *The Global Offensive: The United States, the Palestine Liberation Organization, and the Making of the Post-Cold War* Order. Oxford: Oxford University Press, 2012.

Darroman, Hugo. 'Towards a Decentered History of Palestinian Revolutionary Cinema? Case Study of the Film Tall el Zaatar in the Audiovisual Archive of the Italian Communist Party'. *Regards* 26 (2021): 111–27.

Denes, Nick. 'Between Form and Function: Experimentation in the Early Works of the Palestine Film Unit, 1968–1974.' *Middle East Journal of Culture and Communication* 7, no. 2 (2014): 219–41.

Di-Capua, Yoav. 'Palestine Comes to Paris: The Global Sixties and the Making of a Universal Cause'. *Journal of Palestine Studies* 50, no. 1 (2021): 19–50.

Estefan, Kareem. 'Narrating Looted and Living Palestinian Archives: Reparative Fabulation in Azza El-Hassan's *Kings and Extras*'. *Feminist Media Histories* 8, no. 2 (2022): 43–69.

Furuhata, Yuriko. *Cinema of Actuality: Japanese Avant-Garde Filmmaking in the Season of Image Politics*. Durham: Duke University Press, 2013.

Gertz, Nurith, and George Khleifi. *Palestinian Cinema: Landscape, Trauma and Memory*. Edinburgh: Edinburgh University Press, 2008.

Getino, Octavio, and Solanas Fernando. 'Towards a Third Cinema'. *Cinéaste* 4, no. 3 (1970): 1–10.

Habashneh, Khadijah. *Fursan al-Sinima: Sirat Wahdat Aflam Filastin*. Amman: al-Ahliyya, 2020.

Habashneh, Khadijah. 'Shahadat: Wahdat Aflam Filastin. 'Alamah fi Tarikh al-Sinima al-Nidaliyah'. *Shu'un Filastiniyah* 260, 2015.

Harootunian, Harry, and Sabu Kohso. 'Messages in a Bottle: An Interview with Filmmaker Masao Adachi', trans. P. Kaffen. *Boundary 2* 35, no. 3 (2008): 63–97.

Harrison, Olivia C. 'Consuming Palestine: Anticapitalism and anticolonialism in Jean-Luc Godard's Ici et ailleurs'. *Studies in French Cinema* 183, no. 3 (2018): 178–91.

Hirasawa, Go. 'On Masao Adachi', trans. P. Kaffen. *Boundary 2* 35, no. 3 (2008): 65–7.

Jian, Chen, Martin Klimke, Masha Kirasirova, Mary Nolan, Marilyn Young, and Joanna Waley-Cohen, eds *The Routledge Handbook of the Global Sixties: Between Protest and Nation-Building*. Milton Park: Routledge, 2018.

Kapur, Nick. *Japan at the Crossroads: Conflict and Compromise after Anpo*. Cambridge: Harvard University Press, 2018.

Khalidi, Rashid. *The Iron Cage: The Story of the Palestinian Struggle for Statehood*. Boston: Beacon Press, 2006.

Maasri, Zeina. *Cosmopolitan Radicalism: The Visual Politics of Beirut's Global Sixties*. Cambridge: Cambridge University Press, 2020.

Maasri, Zeina, Cathy Bergin, and Francesca Burke, eds *Transnational Solidarity: Anticolonialism in the Global Sixties*. Manchester: Manchester University Press, 2022.

Matar, Dina. 'PLO Cultural Activism: Mediating Liberation Aesthetics in Revolutionary Contexts'. *Comparative Studies of South Asia, Africa and the Middle East* 38, no. 2 (2018), 354–64.

Nassar, Maha. '"My Struggle Embraces Every Struggle": Palestinians in Israel and Solidarity with Afro-Asian Liberation Movements'. *Arab Studies Journal* 22, no. 1 (2014): 74–101.

Noonan, Patrick James. 'Our Dissolution: Subjectivity, Collectivity, and the Politics of Form in 1960s Japan', PhD dissertation, University of California, Berkeley, 2012.

Sela, Rona. 'Seized in Beirut: The Plundered Archives of the Palestinian Cinema Institution and Cultural Arts Section'. *Anthropology of the Middle East* 12, no. 1 (2017): 83–114.

Sleiman, Hana. 'The Paper Trail of a Liberation Movement'. *Arab Studies Journal* 24, no. 1 (2016): 42–67.

Taha, Lubna. 'On Cinema and Revolutions: Tricontinental Militancy and the Cinema of the Palestinian Revolution'. Thesis, Queen's University, 2021. Available online: https://qspace.library.queensu.ca/handle/1974/28939. (accessed 9 September 2022).

Yaqub, Nadia. *Palestinian Cinema in the Days of Revolution*. Texas: University of Texas Press, 2018.

Part 2
Connected Mobilizations

4

The other solidarity: Matzpen, the Mizrahi question and Palestine

Orit Bashkin

This chapter explores how Arab Jewish solidarity with the Palestinian people was conceptualized within the Israeli radical movement of Matzpen (Compass), established in 1962, during the years 1962–82. I focus in particular on the movement's few Mizrahim (Jews of Middle Eastern and North African descent). Matzpen, whose members were mostly middle-class Ashkenazi men, offered a class-based analysis of Middle Eastern politics and rejected any privilege based on Jewish ethnicity within Israel. Matzpen's history recently received scholarly attention, documenting its Israeli, Palestinian and transnational networks and relations with the New Left.[1] While Yehuda Shenhav and Tali Lev downplayed Matzpen's role in galvanizing Mizrahi Palestinian alliances,[2] I suggest that the writings of its few Mizrahi activists reveal exciting theorizing concerning the potentialities of regional solidarities situated against capitalism and settler colonialism. The short intellectual history I offer, then, focuses less on Matzpen's political undertakings and more on its Mizrahi ideologues who had much in common with contemporary Palestinian revolutionaries and the global actors who supported them. Albeit small and eventually inconsequential in changing Israeli politics, their insights might inspire our own imaginings of a different future.

Modest beginnings

After the establishment of the state in 1948, massive Jewish migration waves arrived in Israel from the Middle East. Demographic anxieties about the sustainability of a Jewish majority in Israel caused the Zionist movement to turn its attention towards the 750,000 Jews who lived in the Middle East. In tandem with intense Zionist activity, right-wing Arab ultranationalists characterized all Middle Eastern Jews as traitorous Zionists, and their persecution on this basis caused many to migrate to Israel in large numbers. In Israel, Mizrahi Jews faced horrendous poverty and discrimination based on their 'oriental origins', with many residing in terrible conditions in transit camps during the 1950s and early 1960s, and in slums and development towns for many years.[3]

Seemingly, Mizrahim shared much in common with the Palestinians who were forced to become Israeli citizens. Both communities were third-class citizens: the Palestinians' civil rights were crushed by martial law (the suspension of Israeli ordinary law in favour of military government in the years 1949–66), and the Mizrahim were brutalized by the state's careless treatment of them. In response to these conditions, radical Mizrahim joined the Israeli Communist Party (MAKI), working together with Palestinian intellectuals and organizers. These interactions between Jewish and Palestinian thinkers inspired new ideas about solidarity.[4] By 1960, however, MAKI could no longer serve as the only hub for radicals in Israel. Its Stalinist loyalties and inability to meet the challenges of Nasserism and decolonization pushed young people to search for new alternatives.

Into this vacuum entered a journal called *Matzpen*, edited by Oded Pilavsky and published by Moshe Machover in 1962. The Israeli Socialist Organization (ISO), the organization behind the journal, became synonymous with the journal's name and was known as Matzpen. The group supported Palestinians' equal citizenship and viewed its activities as part of a global effort against imperialism, Zionism and Arab reactionary regimes, favouring a united socialist Arab union in their stead. After 1967, ISO became more radicalized and grew in popularity; the original group (which numbered around 100 members) attracted more Arabs and Jews and found attentive Palestinian audiences in the West Bank. During the 1970s, ISO splintered into a few other sub-organizations, such as Ma'avak (Struggle), Avangard and The Revolutionary Communist Alliance – Red Front. Five members of the Red Front met with members of the Syrian military intelligence and were subsequently charged with espionage and jailed for treason in a trial that received massive media coverage.[5]

Matzpen's founders, Akiva Orr, an organizer and activist, and Moshe Machover, a professor of Mathematics at Hebrew University, read the American Marxist magazine *Monthly Review* and were influenced by the revolution in Cuba and the ousting of the Iraqi monarchy in 1958.[6] Their historical analysis of Zionism differed from the Palestinian interpretation, since, in their view,

British colonialism was directed against Palestinians *and* Jews; the Arab regimes during 1948, and not the Zionist movement, were Britain's most loyal servants. What gave Arab and global radicals hope, however, was Matzpen's assessment of Israel's conduct after 1948. Orr and Machover proposed that Israel was part of a broader imperialist coalition serving Western interests, whose actions conflicted with the wishes and rights of colonized people, and that Israel rejected the alliances formed at the 1955 Bandung conference in favour of a capitalist order. Moreover, the two submitted that Israeli 'retaliation' operations against the Palestinians were motivated by expansionist strategies, that the 1956 Suez War was a colonialist fantasy, and that the Palestinians were an indigenous people, denied of equal rights in and outside the state.[7]

Matzpen attracted Israeli Palestinians like Ahmed Masarwa, Da'ud Turki, and Farid Farah. It was, however, easier for Israeli Jews, albeit persecuted, to withstand the pressures exercised by the state, while Israeli Palestinians who held similar opinions or met with Palestinian revolutionaries were exposed to administrative and house arrests and media campaigns against them. The state refused to grant Matzpen a license to print an Arabic newspaper and monitored the distribution of its leaflets in Arab villages.[8] In addition, the better-organized communists were still the major political body of Israeli Palestinians running in national and municipal elections. Palestinian thinker and poet Fouzi el-Asmar described how the communists labelled Arab students who supported Matzpen as 'the orphans of Trotsky'.[9] When MAKI expelled eight members, however, including Nicola Jabra, a Trotskyist intellectual and organizer, Matzpen became more powerful.[10]

Matzpen's transnational networks expanded after 1967. Some Matzpen members resided in Europe, for educational aims and because of persecution in Israel, and they thus forged important connections with the New Left. The London-based journal, *ISCARA* (Israel Revolutionary Committee Abroad, belonging to a group of Matzpen members of the same title, established 1969), and the Paris-based journal, *Khamsin*, edited by Palestine Liberation Organization (PLO) member Leila S. Qadi and Matzpen member Eli Lobel (established 1975) publicized its views. On 3 June 1967, ISO and the Palestinian Democratic Front, a clandestine group operating inside Jordan, published a joint statement against the dispossession of the indigenous population of Palestine by Zionist colonization. It called on Israel to undergo a revolutionary transformation, abolishing 'all elements of Jewish supremacy'. 'Whether the Palestinians establish their state or, for the sake of unity, do not', the non-Zionist state will pursue a policy of merging the Israelis and Palestinians in a federal, socialist state, wherein Jews and Arabs enjoy full civil rights. The statement appeared in the *Times* a week later and in *Matzpen* after the end of the war.[11]

Matzpen reached out to French students as early as 1968 trying to play a role in their movement. The network in Europe included the British leftist public intellectual Tariq Ali and the French student activist leader Daniel Cohen Bendit, who visited Israel after being invited by Matzpen. Its activists lectured in American and European universities, often alongside Palestinian revolutionaries. Israeli embassies noted the damage caused by the organization to their propaganda efforts and prepared blacklists of its members.[12] The journals *Matzpen*, *ISCARA*, and *Khamsin* featured stories about struggles in Vietnam, South Africa, Poland, Ireland, Iraqi Kurdistan and elsewhere in the world, to show their global commitments and to draw comparisons between Zionism and other settler colonial regimes.[13]

The group connected its activities in Israel to global audiences. In January 1968 the state arrested Khalil Tu'ama, who led the Arab Students Union at Hebrew University. Tu'ama, and other Matzpen members, went to the West Bank seeking revolutionary partners. Unlike his Jewish comrades, Tu'ama was jailed for nine months for meeting with 'hostile' powers. In response, Matzpen organized demonstrations in Europe and in Israel on his behalf, and students, activists and lawyers issued letters calling for his release; signatories included intellectuals like Bertrand Russell, Jean Paul Sartre, Simone de Beauvoir, Erich Fried and Maxime Rodinson.[14] Matzpen was also engaged in campaigns to release persecuted leftists in the Middle East, like Moroccan Jewish communist Abraham Serfaty.[15]

Maztpen's intellectuals, and the thinkers affiliated with the splinter groups, resembled other Arab revolutionaries; both discussed Trotskyism and Maoism as alternatives to Soviet politics, critiqued Arab regimes and grappled with the shocks of the 1967 War and Black September. Matzpen also worked diligently to document the crimes against the Palestinians in the West Bank and Gaza, saw the PLO as the legitimate representative of the Palestinian people and reached out to Palestinian organizations in violation of the Israeli state's laws. The journal *Matzpen* printed stories about Leila Khaled, referred to King Hussein as the butcher from Jordan after Black September and condemned King 'Abdallah for his collaboration with Ben Gurion. On 21 October 1973, a letter signed by fifteen global academics and journalists, including Edward Said (the first signatory), Hisham Sharabi and Ibrahim Abu Loghud, expressed support for ISO's struggle against Zionism and Zionist illusions and called on Palestinians and Jews to support it.[16] Sa'id Hamami, the PLO representative in London from 1972 until his assassination in 1978, also published articles in *Matzpen* and was in touch with the leadership.[17]

Matzpen famously forged connections with the Democratic Front for the Liberation of Palestine (DFLP) led by Nayef Hawatmeh. On 10 March 1970 Hawatmeh penned an article that called for collaboration with Matzpen; although the movement did not understand fully the Palestinian cause, the DFLP, which upheld the ideal of a socialist and internationalist approach towards the Palestinian problem, found an ally in progressive Israelis. The DFLP translated *Matzpen*'s articles in its journal *al-Hurriya*, assuring its readers that this organization differed radically from both the Zionist Left and the Israeli communists. The relationship nonetheless came to a bitter end in May 1974 after the DFLP took 115 people hostage, mostly teenagers, in the Galilean school of Ma'alot. The raid, which cost the lives of twenty-two teenagers, exposed the fact that Matzpen and the DFLP could not agree on the meanings and means of the armed struggle. Matzpen published in its journals nuanced articles about the meanings of the armed struggles of Palestinian, Kurdish and other colonized groups and saw it as an outcome of oppression; its famous post–June War dictum stated, 'Occupation brings about foreign rule; foreign rule brings about resistance.'[18] However, its members saw the killing of the poor denizens of the Ma'alot (many of whom were Mizrahim) as serving the interests of Zionism and not the spontaneous response of the colonized masses.[19]

Mizrahi foundations: The nativist and the Arab Jew

Initially, Matzpen members did not show much interest in the Mizrahi question. As Shenhav and Lev noted, Matzpen authors discredited any attempt to discuss social injustice in Israel as detached from the Palestinian Question.[20] Jabra Nicola clarified this position in 1972, maintaining that although the global capitalist economic crisis might intensify the socioeconomic fissures between Ashkenazim and Sephardim, revolutionary consciousness among Israeli workers should only emerge as part of the anti-Zionist struggle: 'It is impossible to fight capitalism in Israel without fighting Zionism, for Zionism is the specific form of capitalist rule'.[21] Machover and Orr also used the settler-colonial paradigm against the Mizrahim. Although they acknowledged their discrimination by European Jews, they compared Mizrahim to American poor whites and the Algerian *pied noirs*. Resentful of being identified with Arabs, Blacks, or natives of any kind, deemed 'inferior' by the settlers, these Jews often sided with racist elements in Israel, like the Herut Party.[22]

From 1967, and especially from 1970 onwards, however, Matzpen members became more interested in the Mizrahi question. Matzpen had very few Mizrahi members, but those who joined the movement suggested innovative methods to facilitate Mizrahi Palestinian camaraderie and solidarity. Among the group's founders was Sephardi intellectual Haim Hanegbi, born in 1935 in Jerusalem as Haim Nissim Bejayo. Hanegbi's grandfather was the last rabbi of the Jewish community in Hebron. Growing up with both Jews and Arabs in Jerusalem, Hanegbi was influenced by the ethnic cleansing of the city in 1948, having witnessed entire villages and neighborhoods vanishing after a war.[23]

After 1967, Hanegbi underlined his profound connections with Hebron, working with its Palestinian residents against the settlers. Enraged by how the Jewish settler movement in Hebron used the history of its Sephardi community to its benefit, Hanegbi weaponized his indigenous Sephardi identity to claim affinity with the Arabs of the city. In May 1973, Hanegbi sent a letter to *Haaretz* forbidding settlers to use his family's property in Hebron, stating that he gives his share of the property to Hebron's mayor, Mr. Fahd Qawasmeh. He demanded that all descendants of the Hebronite Jewish community be consulted before any property is given to settlers. Only when the Palestinian right of return is achieved, he argued, should the Jews come back to Hebron.[24] This nativist solidarity sought to revive a shared Sephardi Arab life that historians such as Salim Tamari and Michelle Campos depicted in their studies of late-Ottoman Palestine.[25]

Hanegbi's views, however, were more than nostalgic evocations of Ottoman and mandatory Palestine, and he grounded his inquiries within his critique of Zionism. He believed that Israel could not represent all Jews. In a letter addressed to Bruno Kreisky, he wrote that 'while we reject the system of the indiscriminate armed struggle … we believe that Israeli Zionist policies are mostly responsible for the continuous mass killings of Arabs and Jews, since Zionist settlement, from its inception until the present, was, and is, at the expanse of the Palestinian masses, as it shatters their human and national rights'. He thus rejected such Israeli binaries as Mizrahim/Ashkenazim, Zionists/self-haters, and underlined the differences between socialist revolutionaries and their opponents.[26]

Hanegbi's April 1971 essay 'The Yemenites' (ha-Teymanim) argued that the labour Zionists who arrived in Palestine during the 'second Aliya' (Hanegbi used the quotation marks himself) advanced an anti-Arab line in their quest to dominate the labour force, and this line led them to cynically use Yemenite Jews.

He knew that his writing would evoke accusations of sectarian incitement and self-hate by the Zionist left, but he was proud that he based his arguments on solid research.[27] Presenting close readings of documents written by Zionist emissaries to Yemen at the beginning of the twentieth century, Hanegbi established that the Zionists perceived Yemenite Jews as cheap workers, accustomed to the region's weather, whose employment could Judify Palestinian labour. There is not much point deliberating romantically on the Yemenites Messianic longing for the holy land, Hanegbi wrote; what was needed instead was a serious inquiry into their living conditions and wages. Hanegbi ended his article by noting that the current poor living conditions and wages of Yemenite Jews were seen in Zionist circles as part of their 'pains of adjustment' into Israeli society: 'How many generations would it take to end these "pains of adjustment"? Only the gods of capitalism and the priests of Zionism should know.'[28] Hanegbi, then, proposed that the division of labour in Palestine was not based only on the exclusion of the Palestinians but also on the racialization of Jews; his critique fitted Matzpen's critique of labour Zionism, in general, and the Histadrut, in particular.[29]

Another Mizrahi leader who emerged in Matzpen was Ilan Halevi. Born as Georges Alain Albert in 1943 in Lyon, Halevi joined Matzpen with the appropriate leftist credentials. His Turkish Jewish mother delivered him in a hideaway of the French Resistance. His father, according to some accounts, was a Yemenite Jew. By the time he arrived in Israel, he had already met Malcolm X, authored articles on the condition of Blacks in the United States in Jean-Paul Sartre's *Les Temps Modernes* and published an English novel on African Americans. In the early 1960s, he moved to Africa, where he was employed at a radio station in Mali and even considered converting to Islam, in solidarity with African Muslims. He later moved to Algeria where he heard about the situation of the Palestinians from Egyptians and Syrians. In 1966, he wanted to inspect the problem closely and moved to Kibbutz Gan Shme'ul in Israel. He learned Hebrew, and joined Matzpen, and later split to lead Ma'avak. Expelled from the Kibbutz for his politics, Halevi worked for the French newspaper *Libération*. In 1975, he met sociologist Catherine Lévy, and through her connections Felix Guattari and Gilles Deleuze, who supported his pro-Palestinian views. It was in this year that he relocated to France,[30] where he increasingly began identifying as an Arab Jew:

> When my mother heard of my plans to settle here (in Israel), she worried I had become a Zionist. I quickly reassured her. … If circumstances dictate that I must be presented for what I was at birth – rather than for what I became (a

Palestinian militant, a writer and a leader of the movement) – then I would say I am first an Arab, then a Jew. People perform incredible language contortions to avoid the term Arab Jew. They speak of Oriental Jews, Yemini, Moroccan and Tunisian Jews. But we are, of course, Arab by language, culture and custom.[31]

As early as 1969, Fatah impressed Halevi. He noticed that Fatah expressed 'full solidarity ... with Jews, in Israel and elsewhere, who fight for the termination of the Zionist, racist and imperialist regime in Israel'.[32] In Matzpen, and Ma'avak, Halevi promoted the dual battle against Arab authoritarian regimes and the state of Israel. His March 1969 article analyzed the January 1969 public hanging in Iraq, whose victims included nine Jews, three Muslims and two Christians, all accused of spying for Israel. Halevi was deeply saddened by the loss of innocent lives and likewise infuriated by the Western hypocrisy that accompanied the coverage of the events. Israel and the West condemned only the murders of Jews and understood these murders only through the prism of a perpetual hatred for Jews. He was particularly bothered by the use of the term 'Arab barbarism', 'just like in the good old days of colonialism'. Halevi had nothing positive to write about the Iraqi Ba'ath party either; the Iraqi regime was an antirevolutionary dictatorship, which appropriated revolutionary causes. His condemnation of the hangings was thus understood within a search for alternatives to 'the colonial barbarism of the French and the English, the imperialist barbarism of the Americans, the genocide in Vietnam, the murderous politics of the CIA, and the (Israeli) system of collective punishment and house-demolitions'.[33]

Halevi continued developing these ideas when he returned to France in 1975. His intellectual production is quite wide but suffice here to mention his 1985 essay summing up his position about Mizrahim. Zionist racism, he observed, concerns the Arab Jews. Halevi referred to the same history explored by Hanegbi, namely the Zionist intentions to use Yemenite Jews as cheap Jewish labour, relying on the same historical sources. He then mentioned that Israeli agents planted bombs in Iraqi synagogues to panic Iraqi Jews to leave. Zionism strove toward a full exploitation of Mizrahim whose mass exodus served the Zionist movement, which now claimed that the expulsion of Palestinians was compensated by the importation of Arab Jews into Israel. Halevi reiterated that Mizrahim are the lower classes of the Israeli socioeconomic structure and, as such, are more sensitive to fascist demagogy and popular chauvinism.[34]

Halevi's view of Mizrahi history from an Arab perspective inspired unusual comparisons. After the Sabra and Shatila massacres in 1982, Halevi argued that the Israeli ruling classes blamed the Lebanese Phalangists because they were 'barbarian Arabs'. Israel used the same excuse against its Druze members of the Border Guard following the mass repression in the Gaza Strip in 1971 and 1972. When confronted with the extent of Jewish chauvinism, the state elites blamed Mizrahim for behaving like Arabs. Halevi returned here to the theme of Arab barbarism, which appeared in his writings in Israel, to compare right-wing Arab Jews to other pro-Zionist Arabs like the Phalangists and Zionist Druze, who were not only the victims of a colonial system but also its vessels.[35] There was, however, a moment when Halevi shared some untypical optimism regarding the Mizrahim. In 1975, in an interview he gave to Charles Glass, he said that many Israelis, out of selfish reasons, refuse to join the army or simply leave the state; these new social practices undo 'Zionist psychological ideological mobilization'. He also drew hope from the class struggle and social struggle that the Black Panthers embodied.[36] And he was not alone in his optimism.

The Panthers and Matzpen

A key event in the history of the Mizrahi struggle was the formation of the Israeli Black Panthers Movement in 1971. Its hub was in Musrara, a depopulated Palestinian Jerusalemite neighbourhood, turned into a Mizrahi slum, which the Israeli Panthers called Harlem-Musrara. The movement was active nationally, with a particularly strong presence in Jerusalem, organizing demonstrations between March and August 1971 that paralyzed the city and were met with police brutality. The Israeli Panthers gained local and international attention, and their protests were discussed in the government, the Knesset and the media; Israeli Prime Minister Golda Meir met with the Panthers' leadership, in an infamous encounter that was also a public relations disaster because of Meir's dismissive approach to the activists.[37]

Affiliation with the American Black Panther Party (BPP) was an unusual choice for Israelis at the time. The party, founded in 1966 in Oakland, was deeply anti-Zionist. Panthers such as the BPP leader Huey P. Newton (who visited the refugee camps in Lebanon in 1980) and George Jackson saw Israel as a Western imperialist creation, expressed support for the PLO, maintained contacts with Palestinians and compared Palestinian prisoners to Black prisoners in the United States. A staunch anti-Zionist, Malcolm X met PLO chairman Ahmad Shuqayri in 1964 and visited Palestinian refugee camps. Many in Israel, including Golda Meir, viewed the BPP as anti-Semitic.[38]

Matzpen members, in contrast, including Ashkenazim, reached out to the Mizrahi Panthers; some, like Shimshon Vigodar, even left Matzpen to be a part of the movement. Hanegbi confessed that he saw the movement as something authentic, which Matzpen hoped for, although he did not join officially.[39] Matzpen located the Israeli Black Panthers within a broader collation of oppressed groups. The radical splinter group Ma'avak argued that the campaign against the Panthers belonged to a general effort to eliminate the organizations of the radical left. Just as the joint Arab Jewish struggle for Palestine was labeled a threat to national security, the Panthers faced 'several tales about "internal terrorism" and Molotov cocktails …. The government, which for years has been engaged in displacing Arabs, and class and sectarian (*'adati*) oppression … needs new security reasoning to justify militarism and continual suppression.'[40] Not all members of the Panthers, though, shared Matzpen's pro-Palestinian positions, and not all Matzpen members upheld the Mizrahi cause. State documents from the time, however, reveal that the state feared an alliance between Matzpen and the Panthers. The chair of Knesset Domestic Affairs committee argued that while he did not wish to make light of the gravity of poverty and hardship, Matzpen's involvement led other parties to adopt the Panthers' cause.[41]

The police had a network of informants in poor Mizrahi neighborhoods, and often arrested Panthers and, at times, Matzpen members before the demonstrations themselves, based on their presumed intentions to act in a disorderly manner, typically when members were distributing leaflets or hanging posters. A Jerusalem police report on the Panthers from April 1971 noted, 'Matzpen in Jerusalem "jumped on the bandwagon" in order to exploit these boys,' hoping to use their rage for its own political causes. Matzpen members indoctrinate the Israeli Panthers, the report stated, about the Panthers in the United States, encouraging them to demonstrate and strike, emphasizing that 'if you don't take by force what you deserve, you will never get it'.[42] Matzpen, according to the report, took part in the protests, in an attempt to expand the Panthers' network to students and other leftists. The report listed Matzpen members Hanegbi and Arie Bober as involved persons. The police feared that the attention given to the Panthers by Matzpen and the communists would strengthen the group.[43] The racist report, tellingly, denied the agency of Panthers; according to the Israeli police, they could only be driven to action by Matzpen.

An earlier police account from March 1971 described how Matzpen members encouraged the Panthers to distribute posters and raise black flags. Six Matzpen members met with the Panther's leadership; Matzpen members paid for the printing of posters and bought clubs to counter police violence and attempted to connect activists in Jerusalem to those in Tel Aviv. The police, however, used Matzpen to present the Panthers as puppets of the enemies of the state. Jerusalem's mayor, Teddy Kolek, promised the police to let the public know that Matzpen was behind the protests, and police officers addressed the Panthers' activists telling them to disavow Matzpen. The police, like other public officials at the time, was concerned that the Panthers received support letters from abroad, that Arab newspapers informed their readership on the Ashkenazi domination in Israel, that Matzpen tried to convince Arab students to join the protests and that the Palestinian resistance movement wanted to enter into dialogue with them. The report concluded that these small-scale uprisings were the result of the 'stirring of educated minds conducted by marginal people'.[44] Matzpen was the 'educated minds', 'the marginal people' were the Mizrahim.

The police anxieties were not unfounded, although a considerable number of Panthers, and Robert (Reuven) Abergel, in particular, rejected Matzpen. One of the most interesting writers among the Panthers, and a supporter of Matzpen, was Kochavi Shemesh, who attended a meeting between the leaders of the American Black Panthers and their Israeli counterparts. Born in 1944 in Baghdad, Shemesh's family moved to Israel in 1950 and settled in Musrara. He studied in ultra-orthodox schools in his teens and then dropped out, initially working as a taxi driver and a waiter. In 1971, he became a Panther and published in *Matzpen*. In January 1972, he took part in a protest against the World Zionist Congress, labeling it a European organization, which does not represent world Jewry; he objected to Soviet migration to Israel, arguing that the state should privilege its discriminated population first.[45]

Shemesh founded a newspaper dedicated to Mizrahi affairs, which led to his arrest in 1972, because he had no license to print it. The state at the time demanded that editors should have a high school diploma, which he did not possess. Given the choice between paying a fine and being jailed for three weeks, he chose the latter. *Matzpen* ran a story about his unfair trail and published Shemesh's reflections from his time in jail. Shemesh admitted that he had heard much about the situation in Israeli prisons and wanted to inspect the situation closely. He recognized that Ma'asiyahu, the jail he was incarcerated at, was better than such jails as Damun, Shata or Ramleh, to which political prisoners were sent, but even the so-called reformed Ma'asiyahu shocked him to his core. He depicted the back pains the prisoners suffered due to their crumbling beds, the prisoners' poor health caused by the cold weather, their filthy toilets, indigestible food and unpaid labour. Shemesh himself was not allowed to shower for a lengthy period of time.[46]

Shemesh befriended other prisoners, among them Mizrahim and Israeli Palestinians (West Bankers and Gazans were sent to different jails), and learned about the reasons that brought them to jail. One Mizrahi prisoner was Ben 'Attar, a father of eight, who lived in a tiny apartment; when he protested his living conditions at the welfare bureau, he was jailed for three months for disorderly conduct. Shemesh discovered five more cases similar to Ben 'Attar's. He also noted,

> As a Black Panther, I won much sympathy from the prisoners, Jews and Arabs alike. The Jewish prisoners tried to uplift my spirits and entertain me. The Arab prisoners were interested in the Black Panthers and wanted to know if there were Arabs in the organisation as well. They honored me with plenty of cigarettes and shared with me the fruits and chocolate they got from their families during visits. Of interest is the composition of the population in the jail: Arabic is the spoken language in jail; the Arabs and the Arabic speaking Sephardim are the absolute majority amongst the inmates.[47]

His jailing, he concluded, shattered all notions of Jewish solidarity and camaraderie. Instead, it instilled in Shemesh a different type of solidarity, based on class, Arab culture and being socioeconomically discriminated against by the state; Ma'asiyahu cemented his solidarity with the Palestinians. Unlike Machover and Orr, Shemesh could not have benefited from global connections with the New Left. And yet he demonstrates, in the most vivid terms, how revolutionary commitments instigated instantaneous support; Palestinian prisoners, jailed for much longer periods of time than he was, shared with him their food.[48]

Shemesh's radicalism surfaced again when the entire country was in a state of frenzy over a Syrian spy ring involving Red Front activists, who were former Matzpen members. One member was a former Black Panther, a marginalized Mizrahi called Yehezkel Cohen and a friend of Shemesh. Shemesh was not surprised. He explained that all Palestinians, including the Israeli citizens, lived under occupation. The state's founders did not ask the Palestinian Israelis if they wanted to be the state's citizens, and most became Israeli by force. 'Their citizenship holds no ethical obligation', he wrote.[49] His language undid the Israeli perceptions of the Palestinian armed struggle. The occupation, according to Shemesh, brings about resistance; as long as there were no legal means for Palestinians to engage in politics, they would turn against the state in 'a violent and cruel struggle'.[50] Nevertheless, once a Palestinian state is established, those who are now called terrorists would be considered national heroes. Israel had no moral grounds in this debate: 'Can someone explain to me what is more moral: Black September in Munich, or the IDF in Kafar Qasim? The bombing of the Israeli air force in Lebanon, or the Fatah shelling of Kiryat Shmoneh?'[51] The only element that perplexed Shemesh was that radical Jews supported Syria, which, as they themselves professed in the past, sabotaged revolution in the Middle East.

The article Shemesh wrote in *Matzpen* on the October 1974 Arab League summit held in Rabat, in which twenty Arab states recognized the PLO as the sole representative of the Palestinians, could have been written by any Palestinian revolutionary. The conference, to Shemesh, was a major achievement, which brought hope to Jews and Arabs 'who aspire a shared life in a socialist regime'. The conference, he held, pushed the Hashemites from representing the Palestinians in discussing the future of the West Bank. He believed that the establishment of a Palestinian state was only a matter of time but was concerned that this independence would be restricted to the bourgeoisie, and thus he called the left to support the Palestinian working classes.[52]

Read collectively, Shemesh's three articles expose his vision of Palestinian Mizrahi solidarity. In his estimation, Arab language and culture united the disenfranchised communities of Israel, whose members were dehumanized by colonization and displacement. As a poor Mizrahi Jew, denied of free speech and political rights, Shemesh knew how meaningless Israeli citizenship was, and therefore he sympathized with Israel's Arab subjects whose rights to political representation were heavily oppressed by the state. Politics, in this regard, was not simply the business of voting. It was the ability to generate change, radicalize and revolutionize.

The Mizrahi question abroad

Initially, Matzpen's academic networks were concerned with the Palestinian cause. However, when *Khamsin* dealt with the Mizrahi question, articles written by European Jews showed much condescension. Israeli civil rights activist and chemistry professor Israel Shahak, for example, argued that the Ashkenazi community held all the real power in Israel. The Mizrahim, moreover, allowed European Jews to imagine themselves as white; the Israeli propaganda machine distributed images of fair-skinned Ashkenazi soldiers and pilots, while 72 per cent of its army recruits were in fact non-Ashkenazi. Shahak, however, contended that the longing of Mizrahim for Morocco or Iraq represented nostalgia for the semi-feudal societies they left and that they lacked any factual knowledge about contemporary Arab regimes. Moreover, Sephardi Jews now played a pernicious role in intelligence and in policing the Arabs. The solution, then, was not to engage in a struggle restricted to one community but to combat Zionism.[53] *Khamsin*, however, did publish articles on the history of Jews in Arab lands, like Yaacoub Daoud Eskandarany's class-based exploration of Egyptian Jewish history from the days of Muhammad 'Ali to 1956. Eskandarany suggested that the Jewish community was trapped; branded as strangers and as loyal to the court and to Zionism, they were objects of persecution, whether on behalf of the political police or the Muslim Brothers, and thus, mistakenly, turned to Zionism.[54]

Nevertheless, with the appearance of the Black Panthers, Matzpen activists underscored the alliance with the Mizrahim, especially in the United States, where audiences knew a thing or two about civil rights struggles and race-based discrimination. One of the most original writers on the topic was Emmanuel Dror Farjoun. Born in Safad in 1944, he already showed radical tendencies as a Kibbutz member, when he organized protests against the Vietnam War. He objected to the 1967 War and shortly after left Israel to peruse graduate and postgraduate education at MIT, where he formed friendships with the then radical Trotskyist Kanan Makiyya (who published in *Khamsin* under the name Muhammad Ja'far). Later in his life, he became a mathematics professor in Israel.[55]

Farjoun rejected the idea that Mizrahim engaged in self-hate. Israel, to him, was divided between two sectors: the bureaucratic-capitalist sector owned by the state – namely, the Histadrut and its affiliated organizations – and the private capitalist sector. Since the beginning of the Zionist colonization of Palestine, and more so under the state, the aim was to create a Jewish monopoly in certain key sectors of the economy. After 1967, a total ban on Arab labour was no longer attainable because of an acute shortage of working hands, yet Arabs were employed in mostly the private sector, officially for security reasons. The racial division of the working class influenced also Mizrahim who formed the bulk of the Jewish working class – especially in non-managerial, manual jobs. While the formula for separating Arabs from Jews was 'military service' and 'security clearance', the euphemism used for excluding Mizrahi Jews was 'education'. Settled in slums and development towns in Israel's peripheries, and deprived of decent educational institutions, their only way to secure a respectable job was to join firms owned by the state or the Histadrut, in a system where the Ashkenazim held most of the managerial jobs. Ever since the early 1950s, Farjoun explained, when large waves of Jewish immigrants arrived from Arab countries, the Zionist elite looked at them as an inferior group who must somehow be 'raised' to the true cultural level of European Jewry. Consequently, in the workplace, Mizrahim met contemptuous Ashkenazi bosses on whose goodwill their livelihoods depended. Their immediate class enemy – the boss – was most often a Labor Party bureaucrat in a Histadrut or state enterprise, which, according to Farjoun, explained their attraction to the Israeli right.[56]

Farjoun played a role in Matzpen's activities in the United States. In the spring and summer of 1970, Matzpen member Arie Bober made a speaking tour in American universities, sponsored by the Committee on New Alternatives in the Middle East (CONAME). Established in September 1969, CONAME's members were mostly radical Jews, like Noam Chomsky, Richard Falk and Irene Gendzier. CONAME promoted an end to settlements and military aid to Israel and Arab states and called for the establishment of a Palestinian state. Farjoun joined their activities.[57] CONAME helped gather Bober's lectures, and articles by his Matzpen comrades, into a book titled *The Other Israel: The Radical Case against Zionism*, which Bober edited, although Farjoun, helped by Robert Langstone, did the actual editing. The Israeli Black Panthers were a prominent topic in this book.

Bober himself took part in the Panthers' demonstrations during which he was arrested. To him, the Israeli Black Panthers spearheaded an organized struggle against socioeconomic and racial discrimination. The Israeli government and its head Golda Meir, the Knesset and the media wished to oppress this battle. The police employed brute force, mass arrests, bribes, heavy surveillance, paid provocateurs and media smear campaigns against the Panthers. Certain Mizrahim, whom Bober labelled as 'Uncle Toms', to convey to American audiences their betrayal of their racial allegiance, worked against the movement. Yet Bober noted, the Panthers gained popularity in development towns and poor neighbourhoods. Bober felt that this radicalization lost ground because the Panthers suffered from inner splits that immobilized them. But the intensified exploitation of Mizrahim became impossible to solve within the capitalist-Zionist structure of Israel and exposed the inherit problems in the ideology of massive Jewish migration, which clashed with the demands for equality, as it privileged Western Jewish immigrants. Bober predicted that more Mizrahim, in part because of Matzpen, would realize that a socialist revolution was the only solution for their predicament.[58]

Mediated by Farjoun, Matzpen tried to explain the Mizrahi struggle to North American audiences, provocatively arguing that American Jews, who migrated to Israel during the 1970s in larger numbers, and Soviet Jews, for whose rights to migrate to Israel American Jews strove, were privileged when compared to Mizrahim. Moreover, American audiences could easily identify the similarities between the Israeli and the US contexts. The oppression of communities of colour in both countries involved police violence, arrests of leaders, provocateurs sent to break demonstrations, surveillance and the arguments that demonstrations were caused by outside incitement and served the Soviet Union. Matzpen used these similarities to draw general attention to the structure of Israel and its racism towards the Palestinians and to present a more comprehensive critique of capitalism and Zionism. *The Other Israel* hence indicated that all problems in Israel, with respect to Jews and Arabs, intersected deeply with one another.

Conclusion

Matzpen never changed Israeli society. Similarly, as early as 1973, the Panthers failed in their attempts to run in national elections. Matzpen's transnational theorizing, however, opened a new space for imagining Mizrahi solidarities with the Palestinians. During the 1970s, when Palestinians discussed revolution and indigenous peoples' rights, Matzpen's Mizrahi intellectuals deliberated these issues as well. While the overwhelming majority of Matzpen members were Ashkenazi Jews, some of its members realized that the Mizrahi struggle was essential to questions of class and revolution and to the Question of Palestine itself. The writings of its Mizrahi intellectuals were intersectional, as authors considered very seriously how solidarities between Jews and Palestinians, between Mizrahim and Palestinians, and between workers of different backgrounds are formed and broken. Furthermore, the tensions characteristic of Palestinian discourses – namely, the tensions between Marxist and global revolutionary visions, on the one hand, and the belief in regional solidarities based on Arab culture, language and identity, on the other – occurred in Israel as well, as the Israeli Panthers underscored the correlations between race, ethnicity and their Middle Eastern culture. Similarly, the framing of Zionism as a settler-colonial movement, the fluctuations between revolutionary optimism and more realistic pessimism, the interests in prisoners and the disdain towards the Arab regimes could be found in the writings of both Palestinians and Mizrahi pro-Palestinian Jews. These Jewish authors were original and perceptive critics, and some of their modes of analysis, regarding intersectional struggles and settler colonialism, ring true even today.

Whereas the Israeli class-based revolution never emerged, many Matzpen members continued being active in radical organizations, particularly in the face of the occupation of Lebanon in 1982 and the massive arrests and house demolitions during the first (1987–93) and second (2000–5) Intifadas. Emanuel Farjoun worked as a mathematics professor at Hebrew University for many years and remained dedicated to leftist causes – he was a board member of The Public Committee against Torture in Israel (established 1990) and signed petitions against the occupation and in favour of conscientious objection. The most recent statement he signed, 'Declaration on the Suppression and Punishment of the Crime of Apartheid in Historic Palestine', was published in July 2021 on the online platform *Jadaliyya*.[59] Until today, he is a target of right-wing academic watch sites and their tabloid journalism.[60] Kokhavi Shemesh stayed involved in radical Mizrahi politics and even ran in national elections. Loyal to his past views, he advocated for the rights of prisoners and drug addicts and cofounded one of the first rehabilitation centres for drug addicts in Israel. Although he had only an elementary school diploma, Shemesh became a lawyer in 2003 and joined the Association for Civil Rights in Israel. Later in his life, he tried to create coalitions between Mizrahim, Soviet Jews and Ethiopians. Shemesh died on 13 May 2019.[61]

Haim Hanegbi worked as a journalist and was a member of the peace organization Gush Shalom. He initially supported the Oslo Accords, in part because of his undying admiration for Arafat and even believed for a short while that Ariel Sharon might evacuate the settlements. And yet his radicalism endured. One of his impressive projects was a 2009 photography exhibit of houses in Jerusalem, whose original owners came to visit them years after their expulsion. Nearing the end of his life, he pleaded for the Palestinian mayor of Hebron to be buried at the margins of the Muslim cemetery in the city, and the mayor, visibly moved, granted the fellow Hebronite his last wish. Hanegbi, however, was buried at the Yarkon cemetery in Israel on 2 March 2018. PA leader Abu Mazen rejected his request.[62]

Back in France, Ilan Halevi became a PLO official, representing the PLO in the Socialist International (1983) and the Madrid Conference (1991), among other venues, and Matzpen used his contacts to reach out to PLO officials, like 'Isam Sartawi. He was also a founding member of *Revue des Études Palestinians*.[63] Halevi represented the PLO in a conference in Toledo, celebrating the ecumenical cultures of al-Andalus, in which Mahmud Darwish, 'Abbas Shiblak, Sami Michael and Ella Shohat took part. PLO members jokingly blamed Israelis who refused to meet with Halevi for being anti-Semites, having rejected the *Jewish* member of the PLO delegation.[64] Although he died in France on 10 July 2013 at the age of 69, Palestinians wanted to honour, in the words of Hanan Ashrawi, their courageous comrade. In April 2019, a new street in the Palestinian town of Al-Bireh was named Ilan Halevi Street.[65]

Notes

1 For a thoughtful analysis of the appraisal of Palestinian revolutionaries of Matzpen see Maha Nassar, 'Non-Zionists, Anti-Zionists, Revolutionaries: Palestinian Appraisals of the Israeli Left, 1967–73', in *The Arab Lefts: Histories and Legacies, 1950s–1970s*, ed. Laure Guirguis, 177–81 (Edinburgh: Edinburgh University Press, 2020): Lutz Fiedler, *Matzpen: Eine Andere Israelische Geschichte* (Göttingen: Vandenhoeck & Ruprecht, 2017); Nitsah Er'el, *Matzpen: ha-matspun veha-fanṭazyah* (Tel Aviv: Resling, 2010); Joshua Blass, 'Imperialism and the Arab-Israeli Conflict: Revisions in *Matzpen*'s Historical Perspective', *Israel Studies* 20, no. 1 (2015): 134–58. See also Nira Yuval-Davis, *Matspen: ha-irgun ha-Sotsi'alisṭi be-Yiśra'el* (Jerusalem: Hebrew University, 1977); Zachary Lockman, 'The Left in Israel: Zionism vs. Socialism', *MERIP Reports*, no. 47 (1976): 3–18; David J. Schnall, 'Native Anti-Zionism: Ideologies of Radical Dissent in Israel'. *Middle East Journal* 31, no. 2 (1977): 157–74.
2 Tali Lev and Yehouda Shenhav, 'The Social Construction of the Enemy from Within: Israeli Black Panthers as a Target of Moral Panic', *Israeli Sociology* 12, no.1 (2010): 135–58; Tali Lev and Yehouda Shenhav, 'Don't Call Me a Worker, but a Panther: The Black Panthers and Identity Politics in the Early 1970s', *Theoria u-Bikort* 35 (2009): 141–64 (Hebrew); for other critiques, see Johannes Becke, 'Dismantling the Villa in the Jungle: Matzpen, Zochrot, and the Whitening of Israel', *Interventions* 21, no. 6 (2019): 874–91.
3 Orit Bashkin, *Impossible Exodus: Iraqi Jews in Israel* (Palo Alto: Stanford University Press, 2017).
4 Maha Nassar, *Brothers Apart: Palestinian Citizens of Israel and the Arab world* (Palo Alto: Stanford University Press, 2017); Hana Morgenstern, 'Beating Hearts: Arab Marxism, Anti-Colonialism, and Literatures of Coexistence in Palestine/Israel 1944–1960, 1944–60', in *The Arab Lefts: Histories and Legacies, 1950s–1970s*, ed. Laure Guirguis (Edinburg: Edinburgh University Press, 2020), 39–56; Bashkin, *Impossible Exodus*, 123–37.
5 Fiedler, *Matzpen*, 11–263; Yuval-Davis, *Matspen*, 9–71; Er'el, *Matspen*, 19–145; Eran Torbiner (Dir), *Matzpen, Anti-Zionist Israelis*, Producers: Arik Bernstein, Ami Amir–Matar Plus and Eran Torbiner, 2004 (Hebrew); Ran Greenstein, *Zionism and its Discontents: A Century of Radical Dissent in Israel/Palestine* (London: Pluto Press,

2014), 154–95; Shimshon Vigodar, 'Matzpen Movement', *Te'oria u-Bikort*, 12, no. 13 (1999), 199–203 (Hebrew); Sara Leibovitzh Dar, 'Matzpen Days', *Hadashot*, 20 November 1992 (Hebrew).
6 Fiedler, *Matzpen*, 17, 44–79; Yuval-Davis, *Matspen*, 19.
7 A Israeli (Akiva Orr and Moshe Machover), *Shalom, Shalom Ve-Ein Shalom* (Jerusalem: Bohan, 1961).
8 Er'el, *Matspen*, 206–7.
9 Fouzi el-Asmar, 'Israel Revisited, 1976', *JPS* 6, no. 3 (1977): 47–65.
10 Ran Greenstein, 'A Palestinian Revolutionary: Jabra Nicola and the Radical Left', *Jerusalem Quarterly* 46 (2011): 32–48.
11 Joint Israeli Arab Statement on the Middle East Crisis – by the Israeli Socialist Organization and the Palestinian Democratic Front (3 June 1967). Available online: https://matzpen.org/english/1967-06-03/joint-israeli-arab-statement-june-3-1967/ (accessed 3 March 2022).
12 Vigodar, 201–3, 201–3; Fiedler, *Matzpen*, 273–363; Er'el, *Matzpen*, 215–25.
13 Yuval-Davis, *Matspen*, 23.
14 Nissim Bajayo, 'The Affair of Khalil Tu'ama', *Matzpen* 41 10 May 1968 (Hebrew).
15 Comité de lutte contre la répression au Maroc, 'Pour Abraham Serfaty et ses camarades', *Khamsin* 1 30 June 1975.
16 Edward Said, Eqbal Ahmad, Ibrahim Abu Lughod and others, 'A Statement of Support in the Revolutionary Socialist List', *al-Bayanat* 71, no. 1, 10 April 1974 (Arabic).
17 'A conversation between Matzpen Member Moshe Machover and the representative of the Palestinian Liberation Organization Sa'id Hamami', *Maqalat*, 10 November 1975 (Arabic).
18 Shim'on Tsabar, Haim Hanegbi, Rafi Zichroni et al, 'Let Us Leave the Occupied Territories', *Haaretz*, 22 September 1967.
19 Naef Hawatmeh, 'For a Democratic Solution of the Palestinian Question and the Jewish Question', *Matzpen* 71, 10 March 1970 (Hebrew); 'Naef Hawatmeh Discusses: To the Sides of Peasants and Workers', *Matzpen* 57, 10 January 1971 (Hebrew); 'Naef Hawatmeh Discusses the Affairs of the Day', *al-Huriyah*, 649, 10 December 1973, (Arabic); 'An Open Letter to the DFLP', *al-Bayanat* 72, December 1974 (Arabic); Matzpen, 'On Open Letter to the Men of the Democratic Front for the Liberation of Palestine', *Matzpen* 72, 10 December 1974 (Hebrew).
20 Lev and Shenhav, 'Don't Call Me'.
21 A. Said (Jabra Nicola), 'Theses on the Revolution in the Arab East', a discussion document, 14 September 1972.
22 Moshe Machover and Akiva Orr, 'The Class Character of Israel', in *The Other Israel: The Radical Case against Zionism*, ed. Arie Bober, 55–62 (Garden City: Anchor Books, 1972).

23 Eran Torbiner (Dir), *Hebron in My Heart*, Producers: Alternative Information Center and Eran Torbiner, January 2017 (Hebrew); Ahmad Jaradat, 'Haim Hanegbi Bajayo, the Palestinian Hebronite Jew'. *IMEMC News: International Middle East Media Center*, 4 March 2018. Available online: https://imemc.org/article/haim-hanegbi-bajayo-the-palestinian-hebronite-jew/ (accessed 3 March 2022.)
24 Haim Hanegbi, 'A Letter to the Editor', *Haaretz*, 30 May 1979.
25 Michelle U. Campos, *Ottoman Brothers: Muslims, Christians, and Jews in Early Twentieth-Century Palestine* (Palo Alto: Stanford University Press, 2011); Salim Tamari, *Mountain against the Sea: Essays on Palestinian Society and Culture* (Berkeley: University of California Press, 2009).
26 Haim Hanegbi, 'Letter to Bruno Kreisky', *Matzpen* 78, 10 March 1971 (Hebrew).
27 Haim Hanegbi, 'The Yemenites', *Matzpen* 58, 10 April 1971 (Hebrew).
28 ibid.
29 ibid.
30 Farouk Mardam-Bey, 'Ilan Halevi: Palestinian Jew and Citizen of the World, 1943–2013', *JPS* 43, no. 4 (2014), 67–70; Margaret Busby, 'Ilan Halevi: Jewish Author, Journalist and Politician Who Rose to Prominence in the PLO', *The Independent*, 25 July 2013.
31 Anne Brunswic, *Welcome to Palestine: Chronicles of a Season in Ramallah*. (Scotts Valley: CreateSpace Independent Publishing Platform, 2006), 159.
32 A. Albert (Ilan Halevi), 'On Terror and Hanging', *Matzpen* 49, 10 May 1969 (Hebrew).
33 ibid.
34 Ilan Halevi, 'Zionism Today', *Arab Studies Quarterly* 7, no. 2–3, 1985, 3–10.
35 Ibid., 7–8.
36 Charles Glass, 'Jews against Zion: Israeli Jewish Anti-Zionism', *JPS* 5, no. 1–2 (1975), 69.
37 Deborah Bernstein, 'Conflict and Protest in Israeli Society: The Case of the Black Panthers of Israel', *Megamot* 25, no. 1 (1979), 65–80; Anne-Marie Angelo, *'Any Name That Has Power': The Black Panthers of Israel, the United Kingdom, and the United States, 1948–1977*, PhD dissertation, Duke University, 2013, 279–369.
38 Alex Lubin, *Geographies of Liberation: The Making of an Afro-Arab Political Imaginary* (Chapel Hill: The University of North Carolina Press, 2014), 111–42; Greg Thomas, 'Black Panther Party On Palestine: Geopolitics, Decolonization, Social Movement Studies, Race & Ethnicity, Politics & Government', *The Hampton Institute* (HI), 19 May 2021. Available online: https://www.hamptonthink.org/read/the-black-panther-party-on-palestine (accessed 3 February 2022)
39 Lev and Shenhav, 'The Social Construction'; Lev and Shenhav, 'Don't Call Me'; Vigodar, 'Matzpen'.
40 'On the Arrest of the Arab-Jewish Group', *Matzpen* 77, 10 January 1973 (Hebrew).

41 The Domestic Affairs Committee, Knesset, Discussion of the Black Panthers demonstrations, 1 June 1971, Israel State Archive (henceforth ISA). ISA-knesset-knesset-0007qmb.
42 Superintendent A. Turgemen, Deputy chief of the southern district, Jerusalem, special affairs division, 'Report on the Black Panthers'. 12 April 1971. ISA-PMO-StateDocumentsDep-0012x5t.
43 Ibid.
44 Head of Special Operation Unit, Secret Report concerning the Black Panthers, 21 March 1971. ISA-PMO-StateDocumentsDep-0011u9x.
45 Asaf Shalev, 'Mizrahi rebel: Bidding farewell to an Israeli Black Panther'. *+972 Magazine*. Available online: https://www.972mag.com/mizrahi-black-panther-kochavi-shemesh/ (accessed 10 March 2022).
46 Kokhavi Shemesh, 'A Black Panther in Ma'asiyahu', *Matzpen* 72, 10 March 1973 (Hebrew).
47 Ibid.
48 Ibid.
49 Kokhavi Shemesh, 'Your Destroyers and Those Who Made You Waste Shall Go Forth from You', *Matzpen* 67, 10 January 1973 (Hebrew).
50 Ibid.
51 Ibid.
52 Kokhavi Shemesh, 'Time Is Running Out and There's much to Do', *Matzpen* 72, 10 December 1974 (Hebrew).
53 A. Hoder (Israel Shahak), 'Oriental Jews in Israel: Collective schizophrenia', *Khamsin* 5, 10 July 1978.
54 Ya'acoub Daoud Eskandarany, 'Egyptian Jewry, Why it Declined', *Khamsin*, 5 10 July 1978.
55 Fiedler, *Matzpen*, 292, 294.
56 Emmanuel Farjoun, 'Class Divisions in Israeli Society', *Khamsin* 10 July 1983.
57 On the organizsation, see Michael R. Fischbach, *The Movement and the Middle East: How the Arab-Israeli Conflict Divided the American Left* (Palo Alto: Stanford University Press, 2019), 174–6.
58 Bober, 'Introduction' (February 1972), *The Other*, 1–17.
59 *Jadaliyya* 4 July 2021. Available online: https://www.jadaliyya.com/Details/43063 (accessed 4 April 2022).
60 Maayan Yaffe-Hoffman, 'Hebrew U. Prof. Emeritus Calls to Boycott Physics Olympiad in Israel', *Jerusalem Post*, 10 June 2019.
61 Shalev, 'Mizrahi Rebel'.
62 Aminov Eli, 'A Farewell from the Man Who Refused to Live in Hebron but Wanted to Be Buried in It', *Sihah Mekomit*, 8 March 2018. Available online: https://www.mekomit.co.il/ (accessed 2 April 2022).

63 Mardam-Bey, 'Ilan Halevi'; Busby, 'Ilan Halevi'; Fiedler, *Matzpen*, 221–9; 250–2.
64 Ella Habiba Shohat, 'A Voyage to Toledo: Twenty-Five Years After the "Jews of the Orient and Palestinians" Meeting', *Jadaliyya*, 30 September 2014. Available online: https://www.jadaliyya.com/Details/31283 (accessed 3 February 2022).
65 'An Opening of a Street in the Name of the Fighter (*munadil*) Ilan Halevi', *Dunya al-Watan*, 21 June 2019 (Arabic). Available online: https://www.alwatanvoice.com/arabic/news/2019/06/21/1252899.html (accessed 3 March 2022).

Bibliography

Aminov, Elie. 'A Farewell from the Man Who Refused to Live in Hebron but Wanted to Be Buried in It', *Sihah Mekomit*, 8 March 2018. Available online: https://www.mekomit.co.il/ (accessed 2 April 2022).

Angelo, Anne-Marie. '*Any Name That Has Power*': *The Black Panthers of Israel, the United Kingdom, and the United States, 1948–1977*, PhD dissertation, Duke University, 2013.

Bashkin, Orit. *Impossible Exodus: Iraqi Jews in Israel*. Palo Alto: Stanford University Press, 2017.

Becke, Johannes. 'Dismantling the Villa in the Jungle: Matzpen, Zochrot, and the Whitening of Israel'. *Interventions* 21, no. 6 (2019): 874–91.

Bernstein, Deborah. 'Conflict and Protest in Israeli Society: The Case of the Black Panthers of Israel'. *Megamot* 25, no. 1 (1979): 65–80.

Blass, Joshua. 'Imperialism and the Arab-Israeli Conflict: Revisions in *Matzpen*'s Historical Perspective'. *Israel Studies* 20, no. 1 (2015): 134–58.

Bober, Arie. ed. *The Other Israel: The Radical Case against Zionism*. Garden City: Anchor Books, 1972.

Bober, Arie. 'Introduction', in *The Other Israel: The Radical Case against Zionism*, edited by Arie Bober, 1–17. Garden City: Anchor Books, 1972.

Brunswic, Anne *Welcome to Palestine: Chronicles of a Season in Ramallah*. Scotts Valley: CreateSpace Independent Publishing Platform, 2006.

Campos, Michelle U. *Ottoman Brothers: Muslims, Christians, and Jews in Early Twentieth-Century Palestine*. Palo Alto: Stanford University Press, 2011.

El-Asmar, Fouzi. 'Israel Revisited, 1976'. *Journal of Palestine Studies* 6, no. 3 (1977): 47–65.

Er'el, Nitsah. *Matspen: ha-matspun ṿeha-fanṭazyah*. Tel Aviv: Resling, 2010.

Fischbach, Michael R. *The Movement and the Middle East: How the Arab-Israeli Conflict Divided the American Left*. Palo Alto: Stanford University Press, 2019.

Fiedler, Lutz. *Matzpen: Eine Andere Israelische Geschichte*. Göttingen: Vandenhoeck & Ruprecht, 2017.

Glass, Charles. 'Jews against Zion: Israeli Jewish Anti-Zionism'. *Journal of Palestine Studies* 5, no. 1–2 (1975): 56–81.

Greenstein, Ran. 'A Palestinian Revolutionary: Jabra Nicola and the Radical Left'. *Jerusalem Quarterly* 46 (2011): 32–48.

Greenstein, Ran. *Zionism and its Discontents: A Century of Radical Dissent in Israel/Palestine*. London: Pluto Press, 2014.

Lev, Tali, and Yehouda Shenhav. 'Don't Call Me a Worker, but a Panther: The Black Panthers and Identity Politics in the Early 1970s'. *Theoria u-Bikort* 35 (2009): 141–64 (Hebrew).

Lev, Tali, and Yehouda Shenhav. 'The Social Construction of the Enemy from Within: Israeli Black Panthers as a Target of Moral Panic'. *Israeli Sociology* 12, no. 1 (2010): 135–58 (Hebrew).

Lockman, Zachary. 'The Left in Israel: Zionism vs. Socialism'. *MERIP Reports* 49 (1976): 3–18.

Lubin, Alex. *Geographies of Liberation: The Making of an Afro-Arab Political Imaginary*. Chapel Hill: University of North Carolina Press, 2014.

Machover, Moshe, and Akiva Orr. 'The Class Character of Israel', in *The Other Israel: The Radical Case against Zionism*, edited by Arie Bober, 55–62. Garden City: Anchor Books, 1972.

Machover, Moshe, and Akiva Orr. *Shalom, Shalom Ve-Ein* Shalom. Jerusalem: Bohan, 1961.

Mardam-Bey, Farouk. 'Ilan Halevi: Palestinian Jew and Citizen of the World, 1943–2013'. *Journal of Palestine Studies* 43, no. 4, (2014): 67–70.

Morgenstern, Hana. 'Beating Hearts: Arab Marxism, Anti-Colonialism, and Literatures of Coexistence in Palestine/Israel 1944–1960, 1944–60', in *The Arab Lefts: Histories and Legacies, 1950s–1970s*, edited by Laura Guirguis, 39–56. Edinburgh University Press, 2020.

Nassar, Maha. *Brothers Apart: Palestinian Citizens of Israel and The Arab world*. Palo Alto: Stanford University Press, 2017.

Nassar, Maha. 'Non-Zionists, Anti-Zionists, Revolutionaries: Palestinian Appraisals of the Israeli Left, 1967–73', in *The Arab Lefts: Histories and Legacies, 1950s–1970s*, edited by Laure Guirguis, 169–86. Edinburgh: Edinburgh University Press, 2020.

Schnall, David J. 'Native Anti-Zionism: Ideologies of Radical Dissent in Israel'. *Middle East Journal* 31, no. 2 (1977): 157–74.

Tamari, Salim. *Mountain Against the Sea: Essays on Palestinian Society and Culture*. Berkeley: University of California Press, 2009.

Thomas, Greg. 'Black Panther Party on Palestine: Geopolitics, Decolonization, Social Movement Studies, Race & Ethnicity, Politics & Government'. *The Hampton Institute* (HI), 19 May 2021. Available online: https://www.hamptonthink.org/read/the-black-panther-party-on-palestine (accessed 3 February 2022)

Torbiner, Eran. Dir, *Matzpen, Anti-Zionist Israelis*, Producers: Arik Bernstein, Ami Amir–Matar Plus and Eran Torbiner, 2004 (Hebrew).

Vigodar, Shimshon. 'Matzpen Movement'. *Teòria u-Bikort* 12, no. 13 (1999), 199–203 (Hebrew).
Yuval-Davis, Nira. *Matspen: ha-irgun ha-Sotsi'alisṭi be-Yiśra'el*. Jerusalem: Hebrew University, 1977.

5

One struggle, many fronts: The National Union of Kuwaiti Students and Palestine

Kanwal Hameed

The discourse of the Palestinian revolution positioned Palestinian liberation at the forefront of an Arab struggle, linked with other Third World liberation struggles in the 1960s and 1970s. This thematic runs through the discourse found in *al-Ittihad* (The Union), the magazine produced by the National Union of Kuwaiti Students (NUKS) in editions from the early 1970s. In this chapter, I carry out a close reading of this magazine. As material produced by social actors at the time, *al-Ittihad* provides a source with which we can historicize the student movement in Kuwait and the multiple links that existed between Kuwaiti students and the Palestinian revolution. *Al-Ittihad* offers a snapshot of the discussions and developments taking place on the 'cultural front' in the region in this period. It also offers a view into NUKS' local links with parliamentarians, unionists and militants from Kuwait. This in turn gives a sense of the broader resonance of the Palestinian revolution among political movements and institutions in Kuwait.

As well as engaging with the world from which the activists were writing, and the one they were striving to create, this chapter explores the ideological and imaginary spaces to which *al-Ittihad* belongs. How, in their own words and actions, did anticolonial and anti-imperialist movements in Kuwait link themselves to their counterparts from Palestine? This chapter frames the leftist students and activists writing for and written about in the magazine as agents of history and as part of a network of revolutionaries who linked themselves materially and ideologically to other liberation struggles in the region and the world. The regional struggles included, but were not limited to, those being fought in Dhofar, Lebanon and, of course, the struggle for the liberation of Palestine. Liberation struggles across the globe addressed in the pages of *al-Ittihad* include China, Cuba and Vietnam.

The chapter addresses how Palestine was upheld as a liberation ideal by members of NUKS and how NUKS itself, as part of a broader radical tradition in Kuwait during the mid-twentieth century, positioned itself within this political landscape. Beginning with a headline from the magazine – 'Palestine is the principal issue of the Arab nation'[1] – as an entry point to historicize NUKS, the chapter explores links between NUKS and the Palestinian revolution thematically in order to think through the relationship between the 'Arab nation' and Arab leftist imaginaries at the time. It raises questions about the limits of reading Arab leftist networks and movements solely through a transnational framework. The chapter then turns to the role of students and youth as a driving force in Kuwait's political landscape, beginning with the historical support among students in Kuwait for the Palestinian cause. The circulation of university students from the Gulf in the Arab world from the 1930s onwards was foundational in developing connections among young people from disparate backgrounds, leading to their engagement with and adoption of local and regional struggles, including the liberation of Palestine.[2] Through the circulations of students and youth in the late 1960s and early 1970s and discussions in *al-Ittihad*, we see that Palestine, alongside Dhofar, was viewed as a frontline of militant struggle for leftist political actors in the region. By showing the ways in which Palestine was upheld as a liberation ideal by overlapping categories of nationalists, students, leftists and militants, the chapter sheds new light on popular politics and the radical tradition in Kuwait itself.

In this chapter, I adopt the term 'munadil' (from *nidal*, struggle), which is used widely in *al-Ittihad* to describe a person who struggles or fights for a cause. In English-language academia, it is variously translated as 'struggler', 'militant', 'activist' and 'dissident', while in popular use it refers to a person who struggles for the cause of justice and liberation. Munadil might be closer in meaning to the figure of the partisan of the French resistance, but it lacks an English equivalent that fully captures its meaning, inferences and contextual use. The use of the term is also an intervention into scholarly literature on social movements in the region. The word *jihad* (also a form of struggle, but with religious connotations) has been adopted by the International Journal of Middle East Studies (IJMES) word list, while the broadly secular term 'munadil', which encompasses a variety of forms of struggle, has not. 'Abd al-Nabi al-'Ikri, a munadil who spent time in Dhofar with the Popular Front for the Liberation of the Occupied Arabian Gulf (PFLOAG), describes Palestine and Dhofar as the 'two hot Arab arenas' linked through 'comradely solidarity between the parties of the revolutionary movement in the Arab region'.[3] I argue that for Kuwaiti students and activists at the time, both the Gulf and Palestine were crucial arenas in which liberation struggles of the broader region were being fought. This view invites us to think both about the Palestinian revolution in connection with other sites of struggle and the shifting geographies and changing scales in the anticolonial and revolutionary movements of the time. Palestine, for the leftist students of NUKS, was one among multiple registers of the anticolonial struggle, which I argue operated alongside local and regional scales and as part of a Third World and global revolution. From this perspective, the chapter considers the more intimate implications of social transformation, by looking at the formation of revolutionary subjects through the pages of *al-Ittihad*.

NUKS: Radical students and regional connections

There is an imaginative and intellectual terrain through which peoples in the Gulf struggling for liberation and social transformation between the 1950s and 1970s linked with others in the region. These links date back at least to the 1930s, and they changed course, broadened their popular bases and developed new geospatial and ideological dimensions over the forty years which followed. During this time, Palestine became the 'principal issue' of the 'Arab nation',[4] which anticolonial activists and thinkers, and the leftist activists and revolutionaries who inherited or upheld their struggles, were working to liberate, unify and build. There is a material terrain too, upon which students, workers, intellectuals and militants met, at locations including Kuwait and Palestine, Baghdad, Cairo, Beirut, Damascus, Dhofar and Aden. These spaces were 'nodal' locations, a term used by Zeina Maasri to describe sites 'connected to regional processes of decolonization' over the long 1960s.[5] Maasri's work views these nodal locations as (sometimes temporal) flashpoints across a changing landscape.

Within this network of nodal locations, connected through anticolonial liberation and anti-imperial revolutionary movements, Kuwait occupies a particular position towards the liberation of Palestine. It became host to hundreds of thousands of forcibly expelled Palestinians in the years following the 1948 Nakba. At certain times, the arrival of Palestinians to Kuwait was the result of solidarity drives – Talal Al-Rashoud's work shows how members of Kuwait's 1936 Education Council went against the wishes of British colonial authorities in Kuwait and 'drew upon their Pan-Arab networks to employ teachers to oversee Kuwait's schools',[6] after the General Strike of 1936. From the 1930s onwards, Kuwaitis and Palestinians also established connections with each other through underground political movements which intersected at other locations in the region, including Basra, Aden, Dhofar, Beirut and Cairo. At the end of the 1950s, Kuwaiti authorities also removed entry restrictions for Jordanian citizens, many of whom were originally from Palestine. Although Palestinian teachers were among the first community to establish themselves, by the time Kuwait declared formal independence from its status as a British colonial protectorate in 1961, Palestinians in Kuwait were a critical part of the work force staffing government institutions, as well as working in the oil sector and in privately owned industry. Though the life of Palestinians in Kuwait was marked by colonial-local and capitalist racial hierarchies and dynamics of separation and exclusion, there are less told shared histories among social movements of Kuwaiti citizens and non-citizens, including Palestinians, Iraqis, Lebanese and Omanis, organizing collectively through political and labour movements. Intermittently, members of these clandestine networks were punished for their political activities, particularly those thought to be communists.

In Kuwait, solidarity towards the Palestinian cause was practiced by political movements and at the popular level and, at times, as official policy. Kuwait was a key location in the emergence of Fatah and also became a hub for Palestinians in other parts of the Gulf who wanted to join the liberation struggle. In conferring diplomatic status upon the office of Fatah representatives in Kuwait, the Kuwaiti authorities arguably contributed to the PLO's own journey of state formation (initially without a physical state), through a number of political and diplomatic measures. As part of this process, the PLO worked in Kuwait to bring Palestinians in Kuwait into its own unions and coordinated with the Kuwaiti government to levy a liberation tax on Palestinian employees, initially the main source of the organization's funding.[7] Following the outbreak of the June 1967 war, the Kuwaiti ruler on 5 June 1967 issued a decree declaring that Kuwait was 'in a state of defensive war with the Zionist gangs in occupied Palestine'.[8] As well as mass demonstrations, including at the British Embassy in Kuwait, calls were made for a general strike, and labour stoppage forced the partial closure of the Kuwait Oil Company and full closure of another.[9] The worker-led embargo in Kuwait was eventually called off through negotiations by the Kuwaiti authorities, with representatives from the United States, the UK and the Netherlands. At the same time, a field hospital was established to collect donations and enlist volunteer fighters and offer medical and technical assistance. Kuwaiti foreign minister Sa'ad al-'Abd Allah agreed to supply arms to volunteer fighters on their departure from Kuwait, and health minister 'Abd al-'Aziz al-Saqr provided access to the ministry's stock of medicine and medical equipment to a medical mission of Palestinian nurses and doctors to be used in the East and West Bank. Finally, the Kuwait Red Crescent provided aid to thousands of people displaced to Jordan after the occupation of the West Bank.[10]

It is important to situate the history of NUKS within the context of the complex and at times contradictory histories of Kuwaiti Palestinian relations. While it is necessary to recognize the different and differing positions of Palestinians in Kuwait and Kuwaiti citizens, we need not always read them as separate. In fact, what might differentiate the Kuwaiti case from other solidarity movements with Palestine elsewhere in the world is that since its reception in Kuwait, the Palestinian struggle was understood by those in solidarity as a shared regional struggle. This sense of shared struggle for a liberated and united region, as I will show below, was upheld by leftist revolutionaries in NUKS and in Kuwait, even as they engaged in the register of an anti-imperial global revolution. While Palestine was not always central to struggles in Kuwait, it nevertheless persisted as a centrifugal point during this historic period for groups and movements interested in anti-imperial futures. In Kuwait, over the long first half of the twentieth century,[11] these included movements for political representation, anticolonial liberation, Ba'athists, the Movement of Arab Nationalists (MAN), communist and other leftist groups.[12] Students, teachers, secondary school and university graduates, oil industry employees, private sector workers, labour organizers and militants made up the majority of their ranks.

Secondary school students and their teachers were an important demographic in popular mobilizations, and NUKS emerged from within this radical tradition.[13] Student associations existed among Kuwaiti students at home and abroad long before the official establishment of a union in Kuwait.[14] The genesis of the union, established officially in 1964, has roots in *al-Ittihad al-Mahalli li-Talaba al-Kuwait* (The Local Union of Kuwaiti Students) at al-Shuwaikh secondary school, which declared its formation following the mass mobilizations in 1956 against the Tripartite attacks on Egypt. Establishing itself as a union for secondary school students, the group mainly agitated on material issues affecting students. It was denied permission to organize on school premises and did not last for more than two years.[15] In the 1950s, greater numbers of students from Kuwait travelled to Arab cities to pursue higher education. There, they began to form networks and join local and regional political movements and groups. By the early 1960s, Kuwaiti university students in Arab capitals were mobilizing to establish their own representative council, separate from official Kuwaiti bodies.

NUKS had links with other student organizations in the Gulf and beyond, including the General Union of Palestinian Students (GUPS), established in 1959.

The issues of *al-Ittihad* reviewed in this chapter are from the early 1970s, when the student movement was leftist and militant and connected with The Popular Revolutionary Movement (*al-Haraka al-Thawriyya al-Sha'biyya*) in Kuwait. *Al-Ittihad* described itself as 'a monthly student cultural magazine'.[16] Its price at the time was 50 fils in Kuwait, 70 fils in the Arabian Gulf and 80 fils in South Yemen. It covered issues of local concern as well as regional and international political developments and published a mixture of news, analysis and intellectual and creative works such as song lyrics and poetry. Based on the content and its distribution (in Kuwait, South Yemen and the Arabian Peninsula), the targeted readership of the magazine appears to have been students and activists in the Gulf region.

NUKS was an active political force in Kuwait in the late 1960s and early 1970s. According to 'Ali Hussain al-Awadhi, fears about student activism shaped the architectural planning for Kuwait University (opened in 1966). He argues that measures were taken to prevent the construction of a central communal space that could allow students to gather for demonstrations – as they had done at Al-Shuwaikh school in the past.[17] At the fourth NUKS executive committee meeting in 1969, a decision was taken to move the headquarters from Cairo to Kuwait University. Reflecting both the three decades during which the liberation of Palestine was part of public political discourse and action in Kuwait, as well as the language of leftist movements in the Gulf during the second half of the 1960s, the NUKS constitution was amended in 1968 to include the clause 'regarding the objectives of the federation as a trade union organization … uncovering Zionism, colonialism and reactionary schemes aimed at eliminating Arabism in the Gulf and the Arab nation's goals for freedom, socialism and unity'.[18] Despite attempts to create an official union by the university, students insisted on maintaining their independence. The union organized campaigns and strikes following the dissolution of the National Assembly in Kuwait in 1976 and the failure of the Amir to call for an election within two months.[19] Amid accusations of vote tampering, the student Islamist bloc was successful in taking the helm of NUKS in 1978, and subsequent clashes among student groups were taken as an opportunity by the government to ban student political activity at the university.[20]

Palestine: The principal issue of the Arab nation

The September 1970 issue of *al-Ittihad* featured a special focus on the NUKS fifth annual conference, held at Kuwait University from 25 to 29 July 1970 under the slogan 'a step forward in the march of the Kuwaiti student movement'.[21] The magazine cover announces some of its contents, including 'A Militant-Intellectual Conversation with the People's Front for the Liberation of the Occupied Arabian Gulf (PFLOAG)', 'A Testament to Ho Chi Min' and 'The Palestine International Symposium'.[22] The headlines give us a sense of key issues concerning members of the student union – primarily, the question of armed struggle and the anti-imperial left in the Arab world, Palestine and the Gulf as arenas of contestation and the reverberations of a world in revolt. Alongside the first article in the magazine, a photograph shows the NUKS executive committee seated before a banner with the union logo and the statement 'No to Solutions of Surrender – and Yes to the Palestinian Armed Resistance' – a reference to the US Rogers Plan initiated following the June 1967 war. Discussions on the liberation of Palestine dominate the content of the issue.

The NUKS fifth annual conference (Figure 5.1) hosted student union delegates from GUPS, Eritrea, Iraq, the UAR, Jordan and Algeria, reflecting the union's regional lines of connection.[23] The event was also attended by representatives of

Figure 5.1 NUKS fifth annual conference in Kuwait, 1970. Behind the students, a banner underneath the NUKS logo declares 'YES to Palestinian armed resistance'.
Source: From *al-Ittihad* magazine, produced by National Union of Kuwaiti Students (NUKS), September 1970.

the Kuwait Teachers Club, the Alumni Association, and the Kuwait Trade Union Workers, which demonstrates the connections between NUKS and other local political forces. The address by the executive committee, delivered by Mohammad al-Ghadiri, covers both local and regional issues and aspirations, describing NUKS as a democratic union through which students in Kuwait were able to 'serve the cause of the student in our Arabian Gulf, and the cause of our Arab peoples'.[24]

The language of *al-Ittihad* is that of anti-imperial internationalism. At the same time, however, the liberation of Palestine was still advocated for using the language of Arab nationalism. At the NUKS conference, the liberation of Palestine was articulated as the 'principal issue of the Arab nation' by GUPS delegate Rif'at Ghubeish, followed by the invocation of the MAN slogan 'from the roaring ocean to the revolutionary Gulf'.[25] The roots of Arab nationalism remained alive and entangled in the genealogy of leftist movements in the late 1960s in the region, even as they adopted a more leftist ideology and positioned themselves within the circuits of Third World internationalism. Ghubeish enmeshes the MAN slogan within a call to popular and official 'progressive forces' to support armed struggle in Palestine. In his speech, he praised the fight against imperialism by the 'oppressed peoples of the world' against the United States and its 'agent in the Arab region, Israel'.[26] He made a reference to revolutionary and militant internationalism as well as to anticolonial Arab nationalism. This dual orientation, I argue, challenges the presentation of social movements in the region, and Palestine within them, through a primarily transnational framework.

While the post-1967 landscape did see the materialization of New Leftist undercurrents in the Gulf and the wider region, the discourse of participants in these social movements did not completely depart from popular Arab nationalist ideology. The social, political and cultural work of anticolonial Arab nationalist actors over the long first half of the twentieth century was not in 'retreat'[27] after the 1967 war and not necessarily replaced with a universalist third world internationalism. The material here shows what Tareq Ismael describes as the 'rapid political, ideological and organisational transformation'[28] of the 'now defunct' MAN organization. This transformation was marked by the splintering of MAN, which, 'had given birth to most of the neo-leftist parties and groups in the Arab East'.[29] This view captures how NUKS student activists saw and spoke about themselves in the pages of *al-Ittihad* – even as new approaches and ideology were adopted, the still-suspended goal of a unified Arab region continued to be upheld.

Students and munadilun (pl. munadil) formed alliances, received support, took inspiration from and developed their strategies in relation to struggles and victories of the global anti-imperial revolution, while at the same time centring the Palestinian revolution at the heart of the Arab revolution.[30] For Ismael, the 1948 Nakba was a symbol of the inability to 'control destiny' and 'protect integrity'.[31] He holds the Nakba responsible for the radicalization of Arab nationalism from invoking Arab heritage to confronting social transformation needed for 'national survival'.[32] Through this line of thought, the liberation of Palestine endured as a central issue across the region after the 1967 war. Leftist and Third World internationalist approaches posit links between Zionism, capitalism and imperialism while maintaining a commitment to protecting the integrity, control over destiny and survival of the region as a whole. This perspective is well documented in Arabic-language sources produced by members of leftist social movements – movement materials, declarations of principles, memoirs and other texts. Revolution, for NUKS students and their peers, worked within the framework of the Arab nation (*al-umma*) alongside the national (*al-watan*). The NUKS executive committee referred to itself as a student organization 'with global ties to youth organizations across the world, and a stronger tie to the interests of the nation (*al-watan*) and the nation (*al-umma*)'.[33] This framework reflects both the historical emergence of NUKS as well as the context in which it operated – MAN had been at the helm of popular politics in Kuwait for at least a decade and played an important role in the Kuwaiti parliament since independence in 1961.

The student conference mentioned above also allows us to gain a sense of the moral and material support for the Palestinian revolution extended from other elements of Kuwaiti society. During his speech, the head of the Kuwaiti Teachers Association, Nasser al-'Usaimi, denounced attempts to eradicate the Palestinian resistance movement and expressed his association's support for liberation movements in the Arabian Gulf.[34] According to al-'Usaimi, the liberation of Palestine is 'the case that agitates the mind of every Arab, in fact every honourable *munadil*'.[35] He announced at the conference that workers in Kuwait had raised 17,000 dinars for the *fedayeen* and ended his speech with a call for revolution:

> Passionate words are no longer useful, protests and telegrams are no longer enough for the cause, nor will decisions of the Security Council or the Rogers Plan solve the case of Palestine. The revolution and support for this revolution are the actual solutions.[36]

The multilayered framing of liberation struggles in *al-Ittihad* was in keeping with revolutionary-intellectual understandings developed and practiced elsewhere in the region at the time. At the PLO Research Centre in Beirut, Haytham al-Ayyubi, head of the Military Studies division, hosted the event 'Palestine and Vietnam: A Discussion' in 1973.[37] For al-Ayyubi, drawing military lessons from the Vietnamese struggle, the centrality of 'Arabness' is strategic and responds to the need for 'an Arab base capable of playing the role of an Arab Hanoi effectively'.[38] The participants included Mohammad Kishli, writer for *Al-Hurriya* and member of the Organization of Lebanese Socialists (*Munadhamma al-Ishtirakiyyin al-Lubnaniyyin*), which emerged from MAN; Egyptian former spokesperson for Gamal Abdel Nasser and assistant to the General Secretary of the Arab League Tahsin Bashir; and Lebanese journalist and later director of the Institute for Palestine Studies (IPS) Mahmoud Soueid. Texts on the Vietnamese experience by Arab nationalist intellectual Sadiq Jalal al-'Azm and intellectual and activist Naji 'Allush (previously a leading figure in the Ba'ath movement in Kuwait[39] and a key player in securing Iraqi support for PFLOAG[40]) were among those studied in preparation for the discussion. The PLO Research Centre discussion shows the aspiration towards a united Arab region, which carried over beyond the splintering of MAN by both the nominally and the committed left-wing elements that emerged from it. Writings in *al-Ittihad* show that its writers and readers in the Gulf were engaged in this intellectual current too.

The post-Nakba orientation towards a united Arab nation was still upheld through events taking place twenty-five years later, in spite of the changed shape of the political landscape in the aftermath of the Naksa (1967) and Black September (1970). With regards to the Black September, al-Ayyubi argued that without a broader Arab revolution even 'nationalist or semi-nationalist regimes', will inevitably turn against the Palestinian revolution. He saw this as the result of Zionist violence directed against nationalist or semi-nationalist regimes in response to attacks launched by the Palestinian revolution. Unable to maintain their policy of deterrence, these regimes then use their repressive powers against Palestinian revolutionary forces. For al-Ayyubi,

> the reason for focusing on the Arabness of the revolution and the Arabness of the battle, is because this condition can make the Arab region whole ... I believe that this is the correct explanation of the principle of the Arabness of the revolution, and the importance of revolutionizing the Arab lands as a part of a struggle with the Israeli enemy'.[41]

This Arabness of the revolution, battle and region is present in the pages of *al-Ittihad*, not as a racial or ethnic identity but as a part of a liberatory project with a linguistic and historic commonality carrying the potential for unity.

I argue that this framework, which took on huge popular appeal and was a shaping factor among anticolonial, leftist and revolutionary projects should be understood as emanating largely from MAN organizations. This framework too contained limitations in its practices and approaches, including its emergence from the Arab nationalist project, which was also 'intellectually elitist, socially conservative, and highly gendered'.[42]

Al-Ittihad also features coverage of the Second World Conference on Palestine held in Amman between 2 and 6 September 1970. In a dramatic sequence of events, the opening of the conference was delayed because the Jordanian authorities refused to grant it official approval. Youth delegates arrived in Jordan while fighting between factions of the Jordanian army and the Palestinian resistance was ongoing. In light of the tense situation, GUPS appealed to the National Union of Syrian students to host the event in Damascus. According to *al-Ittihad*, the Arab and international delegations were preparing to leave Jordan when the Popular Front for the Liberation of Palestine (PFLP) intervened, insisting that the conference take place in Jordan in spite of the 'roaring of cannons and gunfire'.[43] Plans to move the conference to Damascus were cancelled, and some hours later, Yasser Arafat, the head of PLO, arrived with 300 *fedayeen* to open the symposium.[44]

Al-Ittihad's coverage of the Amman conference reflects the multiple connected registers of revolution in the region, as well as the way in which the gathering allowed both Palestinian and Kuwaiti participants to connect with other progressive forces from across the world.[45] The event brought together more than 200 representatives from student, militant and leftist organizations opposed to Zionism and imperialism. Delegates joined from PFLOAG, the Eritrean Liberation Front, the Iranian Liberation Front, the Black Revolutionary Workers from the United States, the South African Liberation Front, Cuban revolutionaries and a member of the South Vietnam Liberation Front. Speaking at the symposium, NUKS representative Mohammad al-Ghadiri drew links between the US government and reactionary Arab regimes, as well as those between the Gulf and Palestine. He also linked liberation movements in the Arab world to those in Southeast Asia, insisting that the United States, 'responsible for crimes in Vietnam, Cambodia and Laos', could not be seen as 'the dove of peace fluttering over the Middle East'.[46] He also emphasized the enduring centrality of the liberation of Palestine, foregrounding his support for armed resistance. The declared position of NUKS was to 'support, materially and morally, the revolution all over the world, with Palestine and the Arabian Gulf in the foreground, and the steadfast heroes of Eritrea' (Figure 5.2).[47]

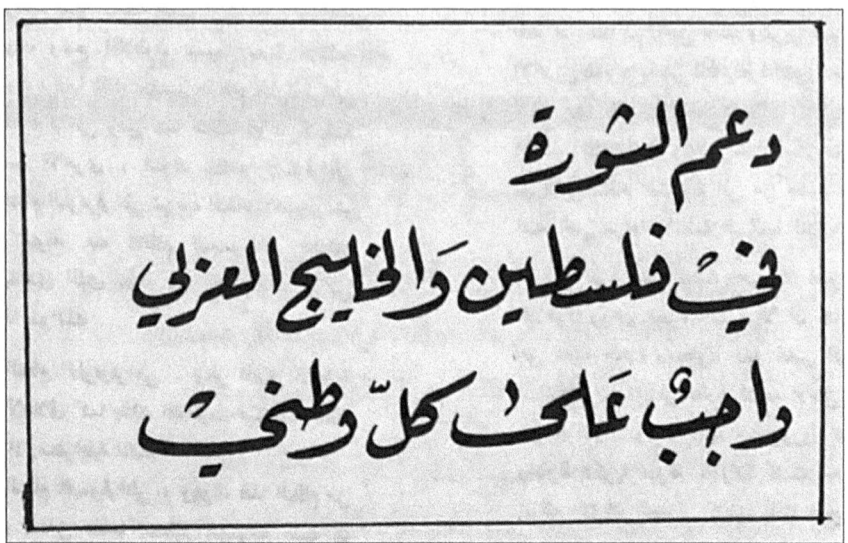

Figure 5.2 The liberatory framework proposed by the NUKS students in *al-Ittihad*, September 1970, 'support for the revolution in Palestine and the Arabian Gulf is a duty upon all patriots'.
Source: From *al-Ittihad* magazine, produced by National Union of Kuwaiti Students (NUKS), September 1970.

GUPS member Rif'at Ghubeish ended his intervention with a call for 'all Arab progressive forces (popular and official) to stand together in support of the Palestinian resistance', concluding with the PLO/Fatah slogan 'revolution until victory'.[48] The reference to 'popular and official' forces is reflective of the way in which movements were operating at the time, through popular bases and with support from allied powers. The adoption of the slogan popularized by the Fatah-led PLO also points to the consolidation of Fatah into an official body representing the Palestinian peoples, as well as its foundational role in the formation of the GUPS. The centrality of Fatah to the 1970 Amman conference indicates towards the role of the PLO in positioning the Palestinian liberation struggle within Third World liberation movements.[49]

Two fronts, one struggle: The Palestinian and the Dhofar revolutions

> The student does not live in isolation from the issues of security and his homeland, and the many issues on the table of social, economic and political

backwardness – but the issues of the Arab Gulf and Palestine are at the forefront of what preoccupies our people.[50]

In addition to Palestine, in the early 1970s, Dhofar was an epicentre for revolutionaries and anti-imperialists in the region. Two years before the 1 January 1965 Fatah military communiqué marking the beginning of the Palestinian armed struggle against colonial powers and local reactionary powers, Dhofari rebels had begun an armed rebellion. In an interview with *al-Ittihad*, Kuwaiti PFLOAG student and militant in Dhofar, Ahmad al-Ruba'i, described the struggle in the Gulf as 'fighting on two domains … the domain of [direct confrontation with] the colonisers and the domain of the reactionary classes that are interconnected with it'.[51] Al-Ruba'i was imprisoned by the Omani British forces for his participation in armed struggle and later transferred to the Kuwaiti authorities and released. In an article titled 'Notes on Kuwaiti Democracy', featured in the September 1971 issue of *al-Ittihad*, al-Ruba'i connected the Dhofari front with movements for social transformation in Kuwait: 'Parliamentary work is one domain in the programme of national, progressive work … National struggle through parliament cannot replace the liberation struggle of the masses.' The national struggle, writes Ruba'i, is centred on class struggle and the work of popular democratic organizations for liberation from the domination of foreign companies, which siphon off profits and attack the workers' movement. The second domain of struggle is through direct confrontation as exemplified in Dhofar.[52]

Coverage of the Dhofar revolution continued in the May 1971 issue of *al-Ittihad*. An analytical piece titled 'British Withdrawal and the Future of Revolution in the Arabian Gulf' presented the Gulf region as an 'epicentre' of contestation.[53] The economic interests of 'monopolistic imperialistic forces' in the Gulf were defined as oil, access to the transit route through the strait of Hormuz and markets for consumer goods. Although militants in Dhofar faced British imperial-backed troops and allies of the Omani Sultan, there was repeated reference in *al-Ittihad* to the role of the United States as an imperialist power with growing economic and military presence in the Gulf. As well as calls for solidarity with peoples struggling against US imperialism in Cuba and Vietnam, the issue also carried intimations of the Maoist ideology embraced by some segments of the Palestinian revolution and the militant Gulf Arab left. A quotation supporting armed resistance reads, 'The class that is not capable of using arms deserves nothing more than its enslavement.'[54] Dhofar linked the Gulf to Palestine in a number of ways, beginning with the lineage connecting the

Dhofar revolution to the MAN-led political sphere of Kuwait, where the Dhofari Charitable Organization was established in 1958 and worked clandestinely to recruit and mobilize members and raise money for arms.[55] Abdel Razzaq Takriti shows that Dhofar was seen by the Gulf MAN as an important site in the matrix of British control in the region. A liaison committee in Kuwait worked to supply funding and arms for Dhofari rebels, and by 1964, MAN were prepared to support the armed struggle which had initiated a series of guerrilla and sabotage operations the year before. The Kuwait branch put all its funds that year towards arming the rebels, many of whom were MAN members, and coordinated military training in Baghdad, funded partly by MAN members in Dubai.[56] As already established, as leftist groups emerged from the MAN split, elements of its framework carried over into these new formations even as they adopted a different ideology and strategy. Reading outwards from the liberation struggle, we can see that a genealogical connection existed between the liberation of Dhofar and the liberation of Palestine, established through MAN.

By reading *al-Ittihad* we can also see how events in Palestine shaped the way in which many leftists understood Dhofar. At the end of the 1960s, Kuwaiti revolutionary students and their allies used the term 'occupation' in reference to the Gulf region. Prior to this, members of social movements in the Gulf and Palestine were speaking of *al-isti'mar* (colonialism), but with the development of leftist trends we begin to see references to *al-imbirialiyya* (imperialism) and the use of *muhtal/la* (occupied) to describe the Gulf. The word 'occupation' here should not be confused by or conflated with its use by bodies such as the United Nations or the international community such as OPT – Occupied Palestinian Territories – which refers to Palestine as the fragments of its historical lands following the Zionist aggression of June 1967. Occupation as used in the context of these historical movements is used to describe all Palestinian lands under Zionist colonial control, and later used by their counterparts in the Gulf to describe British colonial military presence operating in the Arabian Gulf and peninsula.[57] Imperialism was broadly used across the movements in reference to growing US military presence in the region, as a shared enemy among Gulf and Palestinian activists. We see this in reference to Black September in the same issue of *al-Ittihad*:

> This scheme was only part of a broader plan targeting, in essence, the factions of the Arab revolution which are stubbornly fighting against imperialism and its agents. At the time the Palestinian resistance was engaged in outstanding, heroic resistance in Jordan, when the reactionary Jordanian regime aimed

at slaying the resistance by destroying the camps and militant bases. We had another September in Dhofar, where the counterforces began on September 12 to attack the revolution and arrest its political and military cadres, and spread terror against the popular forces in the Eastern region.[58]

Finally, Dhofar connected Palestine to the Gulf through material connections among leftist and revolutionary groups, namely between Gulf leftists in PFLOAG and the PFLP and DFLP. For these groups, the liberation of Palestine was an integral part of the liberation and social transformation of the entire region linked through an ideologically leftist rather than nationalist approach. The links with these and other groups and locations were lifelines to the struggle at the Dhofar front. Bahraini militant and student 'Abd-al-Nabi al-'Ikri describes this:

> The PFLOAG progressively established closer links with China, Iraq and Palestinian movements such as Nayef Hawatmeh's Popular Democratic Front for the Liberation of Palestine (PDFLP). This new support allowed the Front to take the whole of Western Dhofar in the summer of 1969. South Yemen acted as an intermediary with the Socialist bloc, but also as a sanctuary and rear base for rebels throughout the war; it also provided equipment and personnel on an extensive scale, especially at the end.[59]

There is an additional important point made here by al-'Ikri, which is that Dhofar linked Palestine with the Gulf but linked liberation struggles for both with other locations, a crucial one being Yemen. Textbooks for the revolutionary schools at the front were transported from Iraq to Aden via Kuwait Airways,[60] a media and foreign relations committee operated from Aden,[61] and a training programme was implemented by Cuban doctors in al-Ghayda in Yemen.[62] The revolutionaries at the Dhofari front also had allies among students, activists, embassy staff, media workers and leftists (including communist) groups and parties in Syria, Iraq, Libya and Algeria.[63] The Dhofar revolution also welcomed volunteers from Iraq, Saudi Arabia, Egypt, Palestine, Lebanon and Algeria.[64]

This network of liberation struggles and groups can be traced in the pages of *al-Ittihad*. The liberation of Palestine in *al-Ittihad* is a point of intersection between student unions, exemplified in an article in the December 1972 issue written by the Union of Kurdish Students in Iraq. The students write that they are learning from their brothers and sisters in the Palestinian revolution and the Arab revolutions. The writer draws on the shared imaginary of the terrain 'from the ocean to the Gulf' and links the regional struggle to Third World revolution.[65] As with Dhofar and Palestine, the links are both ideational and literal. For example, in the May 1971 issue of *al-Ittihad*, NUKS described their work to 'present the causes and public opinion of the Arab world' at the Tricontinental Conference in Cuba in 1966 and the Conference of Students Unions in Bratislava in 1971.[66] In the same issue, NUKS described itself as 'an inseparable part of the Arab students' union movement',[67] describing the collaborative work between the students' unions from Oman, Kuwait and Bahrain in Beirut.

Connections among students and the global revolution are reflected in reports from Kuwaiti students in Leningrad celebrating the fiftieth anniversary of the socialist republic with other students from the Gulf, a statement of solidarity with Arab students, workers and residents in Germany following a crackdown on them by the German government,[68] and a section on 'students in the world' in the November 1972 issue describing protests in Argentina, Beirut and Cairo.[69] As noted above, Vietnam is an exemplary struggle for the revolutionaries in this time, and the November 1972 issue of *al-Ittihad* shows a Vietnamese guerrilla fighter on its cover under the headline 'Vietnam, the Spring of Victories'.[70]

Cultivating revolutionary subjectivity

In the final section of this chapter, I argue that both *al-Ittihad* and the locations referred to in its pages should be seen as sites for the cultivation of revolutionary subjectivity through knowledge production, discussion and auto-critique. The cover image of the May 1971 copy of *al-Ittihad* (Figure 5.3) shows three male figures seated on the floor, poring over papers. There are machine guns on the floor, and the bullet magazines interlace with the papers and the students' arms and legs. The cover image of the student/intellectual, and the activist/fighter, is symbolic of the discussion running through the pages of all the issues of *al-Ittihad*, which explores the role of students' intellectual and cultural production on the path to social transformation.

There are no female participants cited in the quotes I have taken from *al-Ittihad*. This reflects the fact that among the articles which include the names of the writer (a large number of articles do not), there is only one by a female writer in the six issues of the magazine reviewed. To some extent, the women of the student movement are largely seen and not heard in *al-Ittihad*, appearing mainly in photographs, including of the NUKS executive committee, and in descriptions of activities and events.[71] At the same time, I suggest that through the inclusion of female members of the student movement – as well featuring them on the cover of the December 1972 issue – the magazine advocated a

Figure 5.3 The cover of *al-Ittihad* May 1971.
Source: From *al-Ittihad* magazine, produced by National Union of Kuwaiti Students (NUKS), May 1971.

female subjectivity that encompassed participation in public and political spheres. The visual presence of the female student activists is a reflection of the decades of women's struggles to take their place in social and political struggles, much of which has been invisible. This revolutionary subjectivity was asserted across the region through the engagement of Dhofari peasant women in armed struggle, the female militants, doctors and teachers from the wider region at the Dhofar front and Palestinian women militants from refugee camps and occupied Palestine – topics that were described in some of the magazine's issues. Student, activist and militant subjectivities, including those in NUKS, were shaped by and in turn shaped these movements. The struggle for the transformation of women's social position was situated within national liberation and revolutionary struggles, not as a separate movement. The radical female students were a part of NUKS activities, and their participation in student life and political struggles is documented in the pages of *al-Ittihad*. While the content of the magazine was largely produced by and about male students and figures, we see and read about female students taking part in demonstrations, conferences and cultural and sporting events.

In 1970, NUKS issued a list of demands for the Kuwaiti government in *al-Ittihad*, which included women's right to vote and stand as candidates in National Assembly elections.[72] In 1972, *al-Ittihad* published an article titled 'Kuwaiti Women Call for Equality' as part of its coverage of elections for the Kuwait National Assembly elections. The article calls for equal political rights for women to vote and be elected, and the right to work, including at the Foreign Ministry, in the diplomatic service and in the judiciary. It also calls for measures against the practice of polygyny.[73] Arguably, the revolutionary subject cultivated in *al-Ittihad* was not exclusively male, but a figure of the committed student militant-intellectual, both male and female. This subject is produced through the tangled web of interactions and collusions in which the liberation of Palestine and Gulf meet.

Conclusion

Al-Ittihad presents Palestine and the Palestinian revolution as a liberation ideal and shows the centrality of the Palestinian struggle to the worldview of NUKS students and activists in Kuwait in the early 1970s. Solidarity with the liberation of Palestine was both part of the students' shared imaginary and a form of revolutionary praxis. As students from the region looked outwards to the other worlds they belonged to – among progressive movements spanning the globe – they discussed the Palestinian revolution and the need to 'convince international opinion of the just nature of *our* cause [emphasis own]'.[74] Palestine was their cause. A close reading of the magazine shows that NUKS was part of a radical tradition in Kuwait and the Gulf and how in this era social actors aligned themselves against massive state and ideological powers (militarism and imperial capitalism). An important theme that emerges from the historicization of NUKS is the continued relevance of Arab unity among the leftist groups which emerged from the splintering of the MAN. In *al-Ittihad*, these social actors are envisioning the liberated Arab nation in which their alliances are articulated and exploring who *they* must become in order to gain this world.

Zeina Maasri cites Fawwaz Trabulsi to describe the contestations between visions of Lebanon as the 'Switzerland of the East' or, the 'Arab Hanoi'.[75] We see a similar contestation in the pages of *al-Ittihad*, where Gulf radicals are contesting the transformations of the Gulf into an oil-fuelled entrepot for the local bourgeoisie and their counterparts in the global ruling classes, Western capitalist governments, arms dealers and private companies. The contesting vision is of a united and liberated region which is being fought for on the revolutionary fronts in Dhofar, Palestine and Yemen as well as other locations. Through these contesting visions, local actors linked themselves and their struggles in the region to the milieu of the global revolution.

This chapter has traced the ways in which the Palestinian revolution lived ideologically and materially beyond the frontlines of Palestine and the ways in which it was upheld and linked to other movements in the region. In focussing on these linkages, this chapter de-exceptionalized both the trajectories of Palestine and the Gulf, described by many student activists as different fronts of the same battle, and showed how activists from both linked with other locations in the struggle for Third World liberation. Through a close reading of the revolutionary subjectivity posited in the magazine, this chapter ends with questions about gender and social transformation.

PFLOAG in Dhofar worked to ban polygamy, female circumcision and child marriage, and both the Palestinian and the Dhofar revolutions included female militants in their ranks. As well as class consciousness and an engagement with Third World internationalism, gender relations were evidently part of the political programme of leftist revolutionary groups operating in the region at the time. Ellen Fleischmann argues that in the emergence of a Palestinian women's movement, 'analogous to other women's movements in colonized historical contexts, Palestinian women did not define themselves solely by gender, nor did they perceive a sharp break between nationalism and feminism'.[76] These questions invite further work that engages gender as a lens to study movements for national liberation and social transformation in the region. Material produced by social movements and their members (magazines, cultural production, declarations, pamphlets and memoirs) can situate women's struggles within this context, illustrating women's historical role as agents of social change and teaching us more about the ways in which social movements operate and the social fabric is transformed.

Notes

1 Palestinian student delegate Rif'at Ghubeish quoted in *al-Ittihad*, September 1970.
2 Works by Falah al-Mudayris, Khalid al-Bassam, Rosemary Said Zahlan and the unpublished PhD thesis of Talal Al-Rashoud show education as an important site of anticolonial solidarity between the Gulf and Palestine, with the movement of teachers from Palestine to the Gulf and the movement of students from the Gulf and Palestine to other Arab capitals (Baghdad, Beirut and Cairo). For more, see Falah Abdullah Al-Mudayris, *Tatawwur al-'Alaqat al-Kuwaitiyya al-Filastiniyya wa-Athar al-Ihtilal al-'Iraqi fiha, 1921–2007 (The Evolution of Kuwaiti-Palestinian Relations, and the Effect of the Iraqi Occupation, 1921–2007)* (Kuwait: Qurtas Publishing, 2008); Khalid al-Bassam, *Kolna Fida'ak, al-Bahrain wa Qadhiya Filastiniyya 1917–1948 'We Sacrifice Ourselves for You, Bahrain and the Palestinian Cause, 1917–1948'* (Beirut: The Arab Centre for Studies and Distribution, 2005); Rosemary Said Zahlan, *The Making of the Modern Gulf States* (Reading: Ithaca Press, 2002); and Talal Al-Rashoud, *Modern Education and Arab Nationalism in Kuwait, 1911–1961*. Unpublished PhD thesis (London: SOAS, 2016).
3 'Abd al-Nabi al-'Ikri, *al-Tandhimat al-Yassariyya fi al-Jazeera wa al-Khalij al-'Araby (Leftist Organizations in The Arabian Gulf and Peninsula)* 2nd ed (Beirut: Dar Faradis, 2014), 212.
4 Rif'at Ghubeish, in NUKS/'Abd al-Muhsin al-Farhan, *al-Ittihad*, September 1970.
5 Zeina Maasri, *Cosmopolitan Radicalism: The Visual Politics of Beirut's Global Sixties* (Cambridge: Cambridge University Press, 2020), 8.
6 Talal Al-Rashoud, *Modern Education and Arab Nationalism in Kuwait*, 87.
7 Khayr al-Din Abuljubain, 'The Beginnings of the Palestine Liberation Organisation', in *Abuljebain, Jaffa, Palestine*. Available online: http://www.abuljebain.com (accessed on 7 July 2020).
8 Al-Hayat Newspaper, 6 June 1967, in *International Documents on Palestine* (Beirut: Kuwait University and the Institute of Palestine Studies, 1967).
9 'Telegram from the Mission to the Organisation for Economic Cooperation and Development to the Department of State', 12 October 1967. *US State Department, Foreign Relations of the United States, 1964–1968, Volume XXXIV*. Available online: https://1997-2001.state.gov/about_state/history/vol_xxxiv/y.html (accessed on 3 August 2020).
10 Khayr al-Din Abuljubain, 'The Setback and the Events that Accompanied It', in *Abuljebain*.

11 I take a cue from Zeina Maasri's work on Beirut's 'long sixties', and Omar al-Shehabi's work on Bahrain in the 'long twentieth century' to account for the ways in which the social movements discussed in this text can be understood through the longer context from which they emerged – discussed in the next paragraphs. For more, see Zeina Maasri, *Cosmopolitan Radicalism* and Omar Al Shehabi, 'Political Movements in Bahrain across the Long Twentieth Century (1900–2015)', in *The Oxford Handbook of Contemporary Middle-Eastern and North African History*, ed. Amal Ghazal and Jens Hanssen, 537–53 (Oxford: Oxford University Press, 2015).
12 Falah 'Abd Allah al-Mudayris, *Al-Tajamu'at wa al-Tandhimat al-Siyassiyyah fi al-Kuwait. 1938–1975 (Political Groups and Networks in Kuwait, 1938–1975)* (Kuwait: Dar Qurtas, 1994).
13 Ahmad al-Khatib, *Al-Kuwait min al-Imara ila al-Dawla (Kuwait: From Emirate to State)* 2nd ed (Casablanca: al-Markaz al-Thaqafi al-'Arabi, 2007).
14 'Ali al-Awadhi, 'al-Amal al-Tulabi … al-Qa'ida al-Asasiyya li al-Amal al-Tatawa'ee wa al-Madani (Student Activity … the Basic Pillar of Voluntary and Civic Work)', in *'Ali Hussain al-Awadhi*, 26 December 2016. Available online: https://alialawadhi.com/?p=111 (accessed on 28 July 2021).
15 Al Jazeera Documentary Channel, 'al-Talaba wa al-Siyassa (Students and Politics)', January 2014 on *Youtube*. Available online: https://www.youtube.com/watch?v=fWU8DiwAHA8 (accessed on 8 November 2020).
16 NUKS/'Abd al-Muhsin al-Farhan, *al-Ittihad*, September 1970.
17 Al Jazeera Documentary Channel, 'al-Talaba wa al-Siyassa (Students and Politics)'.
18 Ibid.
19 For more, see Clemens Chay, 'Parliamentary Politics in Kuwait', in *Routledge Handbook of Persian Gulf Politics* ed. Mehran Kamrava, 327–45 (Abingdon: Routledge, 2020), accessed 13 November 2021, Routledge Handbooks Online.
20 Ali al-Awadhi, 'Jami'a-t al-Kuwait wa Ma'raka-t al-Ikhtilat' (Kuwait University … and the Battle over Gender-Mixing)', from *'Ali Hussain al-Awadhi*, 9 April 2014 Available online: https://alialawadhi.com/?p=92 (accessed on 7 January 2022).
21 NUKS/Mohammad Salman Ghanim, *al-Ittihad*, 30 September 1970.
22 Ibid.
23 Ibid., 6–10.
24 Ibid., 5.
25 Ibid., 6.
26 Palestinian student delegate Rif'at Ghubeish quoted in NUKS/ Mohammed Salman Ghanem, *al-Ittihad*, September 1970, 6.
27 Fuad Ajami, 'The End of Pan-Arabism', *Foreign Affairs* 57, no. 2, Council on Foreign Relations, 1978, 357.

28 Tareq Y. Ismael, *The Arab Left* (New York: Syracuse University Press, 1976), 68.
29 Ibid., 70.
30 Haytham al-Ayyubi, et al. 'Palestine and Vietnam: A Discussion', *Shu'un Filastiniya*, 18 June, 1973, trans. *The Palestinian Revolution*, 2016. Available online: http://learnpalestine.politics.ox.ac.uk (accessed on 28 July 2021).
31 Ibid.
32 Ibid., 12.
33 NUKS/Mohammad Salman Ghanim, *al-Ittihad*, September 1970, 25.
34 Ibid., 12.
35 Ibid., 13.
36 Ibid., 27.
37 al-Ayyubi, et al. 'Palestine and Vietnam: A Discussion'.
38 Ibid., 19.
39 Hamad Ibrahim Abdul Rahman al-Tuwaijri, *Political Power and Rule in Kuwait*. Unpublished PhD dissertation (Glasgow: University of Glasgow, 1996), 56.
40 Abdel Razzaq Takriti, *Monsoon Revolution: Republicans, Sultans, and Empires in Oman, 1965–1976* (Oxford: Oxford Scholarship Online, September 2013), 297.
41 Ibid.
42 Ussama Makdisi, *Age of Coexistence: The Ecumenical Frame and the Making of the Modern Arab World* (Berkeley: University of California Press, 2019), 162.
43 NUKS/Mohammed al-Ghadiri and 'Abd al-Muhsin al-Farhan, *al-Ittihad*, September 1970, 15.
44 Ibid., 15–16.
45 Ibid.
46 Ibid.
47 Ibid.
48 Ibid.
49 Yezid Sayigh, *Armed Struggle and the Search for State: The Palestinian National Movement, 1949–1993*. (Oxford: Oxford University Press, [1999] 2011).
50 NUKS/Mohammed al-Ghadiri and 'Abd al-Muhsin al-Farhan, *al-Ittihad*, September 1970, 5.
51 NUKS/Mohammad Salman Ghanim, *al-Ittihad*, September 1970, 25.
52 NUKS/ Mohammad Salman Ghanim, *al-Ittihad*, September 1970, 25.
53 NUKS/'Abd al-Muhsin al-Farhan, *al-Ittihad*, 3 May 1971, 14–15.
54 Ibid., 17.
55 Abdel Razzaq Takriti, *Monsoon Revolution*, 54.
56 Ibid., 70–1.
57 Popular Front for the Liberation of Palestine (PFLP), *Muhimmat al-Marhalah al-Jadidah (Tasks of the New Stage)* (Beirut: PFLP Foreign Relations Committee, 1973).

58 NUKS/'Abd al-Muhsin al-Farhan, *al-Ittihad*, May 1971, 17.
59 'Abd al-Nabi al-'Ikri, *Al-Tandhimat al-Yassariyya*, 60–1.
60 Bassima al-Qassab, *Haq al-Holm, Bahrainiyyun fi Thawrat Dhofar (The Right to Dream, Bahrainis in the Dhofar Revolution)* (Beirut: Riad el-Rayyes Books, 2021), 70.
61 Ibid., 72.
62 Ibid., 139.
63 Ibid., 73.
64 Ibid., 199.
65 NUKS/'Abd al-Muhsin al-Farhan, *al-Ittihad*, December 1972, 10.
66 NUKS/'Abd al-Muhsin al-Farhan, *al-Ittihad*, May 1971, 17.
67 Ibid.
68 Ibid., 33.
69 Ibid., 31.
70 Ibid., front cover.
71 NUKS/'Abd al-Muhsin al-Farhan, *al-Ittihad*, September 1970, 14.
72 Ibid., 24–5.
73 NUKS/'Abd al-Muhsin al-Farhan, *al-Ittihad*, November 1972, 27.
74 Ibid., 41.
75 Ibid.
76 Ellen L. Fleischmann, 'The Emergence of the Palestinian Women's Movement, 1929–39', *Journal of Palestine Studies* 29, no. 3 (2000): 17.

Bibliography

Abuljubain, Khayr al-Din. 'The Beginnings of the Palestine Liberation Organisation', in *Abuljebain, Jaffa, Palestine*. Available online: http://www.abuljebain.com (accessed on 7 July 2020).

al-Awadhi, 'Ali. 'al-Amal al-Tulabi … al-Qa'ida al-Asasiyya li al-Amal al-Tatawa'ee wa al-Madani (Student Activity … the Basic Pillar of Voluntary and Civic Work)', in *Ali Hussain al-Awadhi*, 26 December 2016. Available online: https://alialawadhi.com/?p=111 (accessed on 28 July 2021).

al-Awadhi, 'Ali. 'Jami'at al-Kuwait wa Ma'rakat al-Ikhtilat' (Kuwait University … and the Battle over Gender-Mixing)', in '*Ali Hussain al-Awadhi*, 9 April 2014. Available online: https://alialawadhi.com/?p=92 (accessed on 7 January 2022).

al-Ayyubi, Haytham et al. 'Palestine and Vietnam: A Discussion'. *Shu'un Filastiniya*, 18 June 1973, trans. The Palestinian Revolution, 2016. Available online: http://learnpalestine.politics.ox.ac.uk (accessed on 28 July 2021).

al-Bassam, Khalid. *Kolna Fida'ak, al-Bahrain wa Qadhiya Filastiniyya 1917–1948 'We Sacrifice Ourselves for You, Bahrain and the Palestinian Cause, 1917–1948'*. Beirut: The Arab Centre for Studies and Distribution, 2005.

Al-Hayat Newspaper, 6 June 1967, in *International Documents on Palestine*. Beirut: Kuwait University and the Institute of Palestine Studies, 1967.

Al-'Ikri, 'Abd al-Nabi. *Al-Tandhimat al-Yassariyya fi al-Jazeera wa al-Khalij al-'Arabi* (Leftist Organizations in the Arabian Gulf and Peninsula) 2nd ed. Beirut: Dar Faradis, 2014.

Al Jazeera Documentary Channel. 'Al-Talaba wa al-Siyasa (Students and Politics)', January 2014 on *YouTube*. Available online: https://www.youtube.com/watch?v=fWU8DiwAHA8 (accessed on 8 November 2020).

al-Khatib, Ahmad. *Al-Kuwait min al-Imara ila al-Dawla (Kuwait: From Emirate to State)* 2nd ed. Casablanca: al-Markaz al-Thaqafi al-'Arabi, 2007.

Al-Mudayris, Falah Abdullah. *Tatawwur al-'Alaqat al-Kuwaitiyya al-Filastiniyya wa-Athar al-Ihtilal al-'Iraqi fiha, 1921–2007 (The Evolution of Kuwaiti-Palestinian Relations, and the Effect of the Iraqi Occupation, 1921–2007)*. Kuwait: Qurtas Publishing, 2008.

al-Mudayris, Falah 'Abd Allah. *Al-Tajamu'at wa al-Tandimat Al-Siyassiyyah fi al-Kuwait. 1938–1975 (Political Groups and Networks in Kuwait, 1938–1975)*. Kuwait: Dar Qurtas, 1994.

al-Qassab, Bassima. *Haq al-Holm, Bahrainiyyun fi Thawrat Dhofar (The Right to Dream, Bahrainis in the Dhofar Revolution)*. Beirut: Riad el-Rayyes Books, 2021.

Al-Rashoud, Talal. *Modern Education and Arab Nationalism in Kuwait, 1911–1961*. Unpublished PhD thesis. London: SOAS, 2016.

al-Shehabi, Omar. 'Political Movements in Bahrain across the Long Twentieth Century (1900–2015)' in *The Oxford Handbook of Contemporary Middle-Eastern and North African History*, edited by Amal Ghazal and Jens Hanssen, 537–53. Oxford: Oxford University Press, 2015.

al-Tuwaijri, Hamad Ibrahim Abdul Rahman. *Political Power and Rule in Kuwait*. Unpublished PhD dissertation. Glasgow: University of Glasgow, 1996, 56.

Chay, Clemens. 'Parliamentary Politics in Kuwait', in *Routledge Handbook of Persian Gulf Politics*, edited by Mehran Kamrava, 327–45. Abingdon: Routledge, 2020. Available online: https://www.routledgehandbooks.com/ (accessed on 13 November 2021).

Fleischmann, Ellen L. 'The Emergence of the Palestinian Women's Movement, 1929–39'. *Journal of Palestine Studies* 29, no. 3 (2000): 16–32.

Fuad Ajami, 'The End of Pan-Arabism'. *Foreign Affairs* 57, no. 2, Council on Foreign Relations, 1978.

Halliday, Fred. *Arabia without Sultans*. Baltimore: Penguin, 1979.

Ismael, Tareq Y. *The Arab Left*. New York: Syracuse University Press, 1976.

Maasri, Zeina. *Cosmopolitan Radicalism: The Visual Politics of Beirut's Global Sixties*. Cambridge: Cambridge University Press, 2020.

Makdisi, Ussama. *Age of Coexistence: The Ecumenical Frame and the Making of the Modern Arab World*. Berkeley: University of California Press, 2019.

Popular Front for the Liberation of Palestine (PFLP), *Muhimmat al-Marhalah al-Jadidah (Tasks of the New Stage)*. Beirut: PFLP Foreign Relations Committee, 1973.

Sayigh, Yezid. *Armed Struggle and the Search for State: The Palestinian National Movement, 1949–1993*. Oxford: Oxford University Press, [1999] 2011.

Takriti, Abdel Razzaq. *Monsoon Revolution: Republicans, Sultans, and Empires in Oman, 1965–1976*. Oxford: Oxford Scholarship Online, September 2013.

'Telegram from the Mission to the Organisation for Economic Cooperation and Development to the Department of State', 12 October 1967. *US State Department, Foreign Relations of the United States, 1964–1968, Volume XXXIV*. Available online: https://1997-2001.state.gov/about_state/history/vol_xxxiv/y.html (accessed on 3 August 2020).

Zahlan, Rosemary Said. *The Making of the Modern Gulf States*. Reading: Ithaca Press, 2002.

6

Palestine as rallying cry: The movement for migrant rights and the Question of Palestine in postcolonial France

Olivia C. Harrison

Transcolonial solidarity

Few international causes have generated more interest in postcolonial France than Palestine. Since the founding of the French chapter of the General Union of Palestinian Students (GUPS) in 1965, dozens of civil society organizations have been established with the explicit aim of rallying support for the Palestinian cause.[1] The Arab Israeli war of June 1967 corralled overwhelming support for Israel in France, a country that played an active, if long occulted, role in the Jewish Holocaust, with long-lasting effects on its relationship with the Jewish state. Less well-known is the role France played in the production of the Palestinian Question, from the 1916 Sykes-Picot agreement that partitioned the Levant into French and British mandates to the secret nuclear arms deals France brokered with Israel in the 1950s and 1960s.[2] But *al-naksa* (the reversal), as the 1967 war is known in Arabic, also created an opening for outspoken support for the Palestinian revolution in French leftist circles, particularly after the Palestine Liberation Organization's (PLO's) relative success at the battle of Karameh, in March 1968. Two months later, a short-lived Palestine stand in the courtyard of the occupied Sorbonne University signaled the beginnings of militancy for the Palestinian cause in France.[3] Radical organizations like the Maoist Gauche prolétarienne (Proletarian left or GP) made Palestine a central point of concern in their political platform. On invitation from Mahmoud Hamchari, the PLO's representative to France, GP militants Alain Geismar and Léo Levy travelled to the Palestinian bases and camps of Jordan in summer 1969 to demonstrate their support for the Palestinian revolution and, according to some sources, train with the *fedayeen* in anticipation of a leftist revolution in France.[4] Radical artists like Jean-Luc Godard and Jean Genet followed suit, joining the ranks of international militants like the Japanese Zengakuren and the Black Panthers, who visited, and in some cases joined, the fedayeen in the heady days of the fledgling Palestinian revolution.[5]

The early days of revolutionary solidarity with Palestine were formative, I will argue, for a particularly French strand of pro-Palestinianism, one that turned Palestine into a site of anticolonial critique in the purportedly postcolonial present. Less well-known than the expeditions of Geismar, Godard and Genet, but more significant, politically, in postcolonial France, are the grassroots mobilizations of migrant workers and students who did not enjoy the privileges of fame and mobility. Street protests, blood drives, film screenings, improvised performances and ephemeral militant publications were the tools these anonymous activists used to rally support for Palestine among migrant workers in France. In the wake of Black September, the massacre of thousands of Palestinian fedayeen and refugees by the Jordanian army in September 1970, Palestine became a rallying cry for the nascent migrant rights movement, with the founding of the first autonomous migrant workers' movement in France, the Comités pour le soutien à la révolution palestinienne (Committees in Support of the Palestinian Revolution, or CSRP). This chapter mines the extant archives of the CSRP, founded in Paris in September 1970 by North African and Middle Eastern workers and students, with the support of activists from the GP. The journals, tracts, photographs, films and video fragments that constitute the incomplete and fragmented archive of the CSRP attest to the emergence of distinctly 'transcolonial' forms of antiracist activism, rooted in anticolonial solidarity across imperial formations.[6] As we will see, the migrant rights movement in France was forged in civil campaigns to support the Palestinian revolution.

Although the focus of this chapter is pro-Palestinian activism in the early 1970s, it is worth briefly discussing the ways in which support for Palestine is characterized in French media and public discourse today, not least because this discursive framework tends anachronistically to shape scholarly work on the history of pro-Palestinianism in France. Since the second Intifada, which coincided with 9/11 and the start of the global war on terror, pro-Palestinianism in France has been framed as an 'imported conflict', one that aligns all too neatly with ethnic and religious articulations of identity. The press regularly calls on 'experts' like Alain Finkielkraut and Pierre-André Taguieff to comment on *l'intifada des banlieues*, the so-called Intifada or uprising of the *banlieues*, as the disenfranchised, majority-minority peripheries of French cities are metonymically dubbed. These scholars in turn publish best-selling essays that unambiguously equate pro-Palestinianism with anti-Semitism, now renamed 'the new Judeophobia' to divorce anti-Jewish sentiment in the *banlieue* from its illustrious European forebears.[7] Without entering into the fray of debates around the putative Judeophobia of pro-Palestinian activists – it is unfortunately the case that unapologetic anti-Semites like Alain Soral and Dieudonné Mbala Mbala have coopted the Palestinian cause to their own ends, with devastating consequences for pro-Palestinian activism in France – I want to put pressure on the notion that the Palestinian Question is an imported, that is to say *foreign*, cause in France. In fact, as closer attention to the archive of Palestine solidarity in France reveals, the Palestinian Question is a distinctly French question.

Donated to the archives of La contemporaine (Université Paris Nanterre) by the late CSRP activist Saïd Bouziri, who single handedly documented decades of migrant activism in France, the scattered documents comprising the archive of the CSRP and its successor organization, the Mouvement des travailleurs arabes (Movement of Arab Workers, or MTA), offer a rich, albeit partial, view into the workings of the first autonomous movement for migrant rights in France. As we will see, the journals, newsletters, tracts and documentary films that constitute the incomplete and fragmented archive of these movements attest to a distinctly transcolonial understanding of postcolonial migration, one grounded in the comparison between Palestinian refugees-turned-*fedayeen* and migrants-turned-militants in postcolonial France. Against the representation of migrants as unexpected or unwelcome guests, ubiquitous across the political spectrum since the 1970s, activists for migrant rights situated their struggle in continuation with the anticolonial struggles of the past and present, most notably, the Algerian and Palestinian revolutions.[8]

Before analyzing the archives of the CSRP and the MTA, I turn to a little-known documentary film that has recently been made available online, with an important omission – the eight-minute opening sequence on the Palestinian revolution that framed the struggle of migrant workers in France as an anticolonial movement. Symptomatic of the elision of the central role Palestine has played within grassroots antiracist movements in France, the distribution of this documentary film nevertheless attests to a renewed interest in migrant movements in twenty-first century France – including, paradoxically, the Palestinian Question.

'We are the *fedayeen* of Palestine'

One of a few dozen militant documentaries about the plight of migrant workers in 1970s France, *Compter sur ses propres forces* (self-reliance) attests to the centrality of the Palestinian Question in the antiracist movement forged in the struggle for migrant rights in postcolonial France.[9] It is, to my knowledge, the only film that frames this struggle in terms of solidarity with Palestine, although several pro-Palestinian documentary films – most notably, *Palestine vaincra* (Palestine shall overcome, 1969) and *Biladi* (My country, 1972) – were regularly screened at CSRP meetings and rallies to draw parallels with the condition of migrant workers in France.[10] As such, it offers a rare glimpse of the role of the Palestinian revolution in the early days of antiracist militancy in France, offering an audiovisual supplement to the incomplete and scattered archive of the CSRP.

In 2019, the film's director, Yannis Tritsibidas, digitized an abridged version of the film and posted *Compter sur ses propres forces* on YouTube.[11] Produced by the militant film collective Atelier pour un cinéma de lutte (Workshop for a cinema of struggle) in collaboration with the CSRP, the sixty-minute, 16mm black and white film begins with an eight-minute sequence, in Arabic and French, on the Palestinian revolution, and ends with a two-minute long audiovisual montage that weaves together the struggles of the Arab masses, from Palestine and Morocco to France. Although the introductory sequence has been lost, the final montage clarifies the iconic role played by the Palestinian revolution in the struggle for migrant rights in postcolonial France. First delivered in Arabic, and then in a slightly accented French voice-over, the rallying cry that overlays the closing shots of *Compter sur ses propres forces* articulates the unity of these struggles, even as the moving and still images scramble the coordinates of the map of anticolonialism and antiracism. A close-up shot of a photograph of the fifteen-year-old Djellali Ben Ali, gunned down by the companion of his concierge on his own doorstep, appears as the voice-over intones 'we are the fedayeen of Palestine', while an aerial view of a rally to protest racist crimes reveals marchers bearing Palestinian flags next to giant portraits of the victims of racist violence (Figure 6.1). Nor is the Palestinian revolution the banner of Arab workers alone. At the massive funeral for Pierre Overney, a Maoist activist killed by a security guard at the automobile factory Renault-Billancourt, it is the Palestinian flag that accompanies his portrait in the cortège. 'Our strength is our unity,' proclaims the narrator, mobilizing Maoist discourse against colonization and occupation in Palestine, state repression in Morocco and capitalist exploitation and racist crimes in France.

Figure 6.1 Antiracist protest with Palestinian flags. Screen shot of *Compter sur ses propres forces*. Courtesy of Yannis Tritsibidas.

It is important to note that Palestine does not figure in the film as a symbol of Arab unity, at least not in the official idiom of pan-Arabism prevalent in state rhetoric at the time. The shot that follows the opening sequence on Palestine – the first shot in the abridged version available on YouTube – shows two CSRP activists, their faces shrouded in darkness against the bright light pouring in through the window behind them, speaking of the importance of September 1970 in rallying migrant workers in France. Known as Black September, the killing of thousands of fedayeen and civilians in the Palestinian bases and refugee camps of Amman by King Hussein's troupes in September 1970 symbolized the betrayal of the Palestinian revolution by Arab regimes – *la réaction arabe* (the Arab reactionaries) as they are dubbed in the film – and triggered massive protests across the Arab world, including within migrant communities in postcolonial France. Ironically, the brutal excesses of a corrupt and authoritarian Arab regime can be credited with rallying postcolonial migrants against racism in France. Nor are nominally pro-Palestinian Arab regimes off the hook, as the CSRP's mobilizations against the abuses of the postcolonial Moroccan and Tunisian governments make clear. 'September 1970 united the Arab masses in France,' explains the CSRP activist. 'The Arab worker knows that here in France he is continuing the struggle of his brothers in Morocco.' In the film's audiovisual montage, these words are illustrated by still and moving images, including a photograph of protestors – their faces whited out to protect their identity from French and Moroccan police forces – bearing the banner 'Let us save the condemned of Marrakesh' alongside giant Palestinian flags. The postcolonial Arab regimes are allied with the colonizers of old in oppressing Palestinians and migrant workers in exchange for lucrative arms or oil deals with France. The French Interior Ministry, for its part, notoriously shared intelligence with its counterparts in North Africa, such that migrants deported to their home countries might face arrest and torture upon arrival. Palestine is the cause that unites the Arab masses against their oppressors, in the Arab world and in postcolonial exile.

The CSRP was the first antiracist organization to invoke Palestine in a multidirectional critique of colonialism and racism in the purportedly postcolonial era. In the following section, I analyze the extant archives of the CSRP and the MTA, animated by Arab workers and students alongside militants from the GP. In this reading, the CSRP is not a 'footnote' in the history of French Maoism or, for that matter, the Palestinian liberation movement.[12] It is, on the contrary, an autonomous movement for migrant rights, forged in the Palestine solidarity movement. Unlike the other pro-Palestinian groups in France, like the GP's Comités Palestine, whose primary goal was to inform the public about the colonization of Palestine and rally its support, for the CSRP solidarity with Palestine was a given. Its mission was to use 'Palestine as rallying cry', connecting the predicament of migrant workers in postcolonial France to the Question of Palestine.[13] Against the image of the migrant as an unexpected or unwelcome guest, the CSRP turned the North African migrant worker into a figure of resistance in the postcolonial metropole. As the CSRP put it in their December 1970 'Communiqué and appeal to all workers in France', 'Brother workers, the Arab workers in France today all recognise themselves in the struggle of the Palestinian people.'[14] The archives of the CSRP make it possible to sketch a portrait of the pro-Palestinian, antiracist movement that emerged in the wake of Black September, connecting the movement for migrant rights in postcolonial France to the most iconic anticolonial struggle of the time – the Palestinian revolution.

Palestine and the 'immigrant cause'

On 11 February 1971, the sixth issue of the CSRP's bilingual publication *Fedaï: Journal de soutien à la révolution palestinienne* (Fedayee: News bulletin in support of the Palestinian revolution) published an unsigned story, titled 'Dis-moi mon frère' (Tell me my brother) in French, 'hadith yadur fi maqha 'adi' (Conversation overheard in a neighborhood café) in Arabic. The story takes the form of a Socratic dialogue about the status of the Palestinian revolution, five months after Black September. 'Tell me my brother, the Zionists and other reactionaries ... say that the Palestinian Resistance is over, that the Palestinian people are finished,' queries one worker. Not so, responds his comrade, 'Our fedayeen continue to fight, every day they attack the invaders, bearing their weapons ....Our people have become a people of combatants.'

The story offers few surprises at the level of content and tone: Black September was the first major reversal of the fledgling Palestinian revolution, which had 'transformed a multitude of refugees into a people of combatants' with the Karameh victory of March 1968.[15] As in other parts of the world, pro-Palestinian activists in 1970s France – a small but vocal minority composed of migrant workers and far-left militants – were fascinated by the figure of the fedayee, whose stylized profile, complete with *kufiyya* and Kalashnikov, adorned the posters, magazines and ephemeral publications of these fringe movements, including *Fedaï*, the newsletter of the CSRP. 'Dis-moi mon frère' is in this sense representative of the militant and militarized image of revolutionary Palestine that prevailed in radical left publications in post-68 France, from the newsletters and communiqués of the many Palestine committees formed in the wake of the June 1967 Arab Israeli war to the short-lived publication of the clandestine Maoist party Gauche prolétarienne, *Lutte palestinienne: Journal de soutien à la la lutte du peuple palestinien* (Palestinian struggle: Journal in support of the struggle of the Palestinian people), which ran two issues in March and June 1969.[16]

What is remarkable about 'Dis-moi mon frère', and what distinguishes the CSRP from other Palestine solidarity movements in France, is the dynamic of recognition it stages between migrant workers and Palestinians. Whether the dialogue between the two workers was overheard in a café and fictionalized or, more likely, invented, it betrays a slippage from solidarity ('our Palestinian brothers') to identification ('our people') that is more than simply rhetorical. That the two workers are not identified by nationality or even ethnicity – they are not named as Arab workers – only underscores the political, as opposed to identitarian, nature of this identification. If it is true that there is a Maghrebi genealogy to pro-Palestinianism in France – 'Maghreb-Palestine, même combat' as the title of a September 1970 *Fedaï* story has it – 'Tell me my brother' speaks to a singularly French form of antiracism in 1970s France – a critique, by the former colonial subjects of France's empire, of the legacies of colonialism and the persistence of racism in the postcolonial metropole.[17]

Abdellali Hajjat has convincingly argued that the militants of the CSRP were 'the first "political immigrants" … who considered France as a terrain of struggle for the "immigrant cause"'. Where previously migrants in France mobilized around 'the national cause' (Algerian independence during the war, miners' strikes in Hassan II's Morocco, and state repression of dissident groups like Perspectives in Bourguiba's Tunisia), the CSRP forged a new type of political activism, one that has only gained in visibility since then – a grassroots antiracist movement pegging the struggle for equality in postcolonial France to anticolonial struggles worldwide and, most saliently, Palestine.[18] Founded in the wake of Black September by students and workers from Morocco, Algeria, Tunisia, Syria, Lebanon and Palestine, the CSRP brought the vocabulary of decolonization to bear on the realities of racialization in postcolonial France.[19] The new decolonial idiom they disseminated in the form of tracts, communiqués, magazines and popular theatre has, I argue, deeply structured the grassroots antiracist movements that followed in their wake, from the MTA, founded by CSRP members in June 1972, to the so-called Beur movement that coalesced around the 1983 Marche pour l'égalité et contre le racisme (March for equality and against racism) and more recent antiracist collectives like the Indigènes de la république (Natives of the republic).[20]

Little known in comparison with the more media-savvy movements that would follow, the CSRP nevertheless achieved a remarkable following among migrant workers in 1970s France. If some CSRP activists did not shy away from militant actions – sometimes at great personal cost – the organization's primary focus was grassroots organizing.[21] Demonstrations, strikes, walkouts, film screenings, magazines, flyers, cartoons, spray-paint, fundraising and blood donations were the main weapons of the CSRP. An undated tract published after a massive rally for Palestine in October 1970 places the quotidian tasks of antiracist activism within the 'combat for liberty' of migrant workers: 'In cafés we have conversations around photographs, we read the newspaper of the fedayeen. In the factories, on the streets, in buses, we post flyers under the nose of racist bosses.'[22] The café conversation staged in 'Dis-moi mon frère' offers a reconstituted archival trace of the micropolitics of activism – two workers in a café are already a militant cell. This local, ultra-democratic form of politics was of great importance to the CSRP, which drew relatively modest crowds to their rallies, ranging from several hundreds to several thousands. And yet their presence was ubiquitous. The increasingly repressive measures taken by the police, who arrested or deported several CSRP activists, offer a paradoxical testament to the movement's visibility in postcolonial France.[23]

The June 1967 and October 1973 Arab Israeli wars elicited mass demonstrations in support of Israel and an 'unleashing of hatred' against Arabs.[24] In the context of the 1971–3 oil crisis and the 1972 attacks in Munich, there was scant room for solidarity with Palestine. And yet attempts to contain or suppress CSRP activism cannot be explained by the predominance of pro-Israeli sympathies in France alone. The police repression that was exercised upon pro-Palestinian migrant workers had a distinctly French colonial genealogy, as a February 1971 CSRP tract makes clear:

> Fifteen days ago, *Minute* (a fascist journal that supported the assassins of the OAS [the Secret Armed Organization, a French militia active during the Algerian war of independence]) published a cover story titled: out with the Algerians! [*dehors les Algériens!*] The enemies of Palestine are the same as those who in France expel Arab workers from a *foyer* [a state-run boarding house for migrant workers] in Suresnes without housing them somewhere else. They want to stop us from supporting the struggle of our Palestinian brothers by all means: they arrest and condemn our comrade Hamza Bouziri to a six-month prison sentence, they want to scare people by parading their cops everywhere; they want to sabotage the demonstration in support of Palestine that was held at Barbès; they deport a comrade from the CSRP.[25]

The police repression of migrant activism – expulsions, arbitrary arrests, deportations – is implicitly connected here to an emerging racial discourse that is itself tributary to one of the most extreme forms of colonial racism, that of the *ultras* who fought to keep Algeria French. But what is remarkable is the politics of recognition that undergirds this critique. In a nearly paratactic juxtaposition – from the OAS and the far-right journal *Minute* to what, a few years later, militants from the Gauche révolutionnaire (Revolutionary left) would characterize as 'racist campaigns designed to facilitate the "control of immigration"' – France becomes an 'enemy of Palestine'.[26] Drawing a straight line from colonial-era racial terror to anti-immigrant discourses, and from the Question of Palestine to the migrant question, the tract portrays the antiracist struggle in clearly anticolonial terms.

There is no small degree of irony to the fact that pro-Palestinian activists of the first grassroots antiracist movement in France were perceived as foreign – why deport a pro-Palestinian migrant otherwise? – effectively buttressing the far-right's argument that immigrants should go home ('dehors les Algériens!').

And yet the invocation of Algeria in the tract has, I argue, the reverse effect: the Palestinian Question concerns migrants because France colonized Algeria and is now oppressing its former colonial subjects. In the words of Bouziri, the Palestinian Question is an 'integral part' of the struggle of migrants in France.

On 29 December 1970, CSRP activist Hamza Bouziri – brother of Saïd Bouziri, the archivist of the CSRP – was arrested while handing out pro-Palestinian tracts at the Citroën factory in Nanterre, in the outskirts of Paris. In a statement issued from prison, Bouziri explains his decision to go on hunger strike:

> I am in solidarity with the struggle of all other political prisoners in France who are struggling against the penitentiary system to obtain their political rights. But also, inspired by the glorious example given to us by our comrades from the FLN [National Liberation Front] who were detained during the Algerian war, going on hunger strike is for me a way to actively support the Palestinian Revolution.... The Palestinian Revolution is an integral part of the Revolution of all the peoples of the world who struggle for justice and liberty.[27]

It is striking that Bouziri does not call upon the notion of sovereignty in his statement – the declared goal of both the Algerian and the Palestinian revolutions – but rather the very Republican notions of justice and liberty. Using a tactic, the hunger strike, associated with anticolonial struggles rather than the age of revolutions, Bouziri translates Enlightenment ideals into the idiom of anticolonialism. Invoking the example of Algerian revolutionaries imprisoned during the long war of independence – a war that ended only eight years prior to his action – Bouziri inscribes the struggle of migrant workers in France in a broader anticolonial struggle that includes the Question of Palestine in its purview.

The stakes were already high when Bouziri initiated the first hunger strike in the history of the movement for migrant rights in France.[28] By 1972, the antiracist movement was on high alert. In the context of rising unemployment and a full-blown housing crisis, particularly for migrant workers confined to *foyers* and *bidonvilles* (shantytowns), the Marcellin-Fontanet circulars of January and February 1972 linking legal residency to employment and housing produced the first generation of *sans-papiers* (undocumented migrants) in France. At the same time, a series of racist crimes, often unpunished or inadequately sanctioned, were terrorizing migrant communities in France.[29] The urgency of the moment called for a radicalization of the antiracist movement. The CSRP stepped up its activities: rallies, strikes, meetings and mobilizations in support of the occupation of vacant buildings by *les mal-logés* (the poorly housed).[30]

Without changing the militant logo or main title of its journal – *Fedaï*, framed by two drawings of a Kalashnikov – the CSRP shifted its centre of gravity from pro-Palestinian activism to the migrant struggle. But Palestine did not disappear from the pages of the journal. On the contrary, the ways in which Palestine was mobilized within the antiracist struggle in France became even more explicit in the final issues of *Fedaï*.

On 23 February 1972 – two days before it was banned – *Fedaï* published what was to be the last issue of its iteration as the 'Journal in support of the Palestinian revolution'. Titled 'Pour arrêter les crimes racistes descends dans la rue!' / 'linanzal ila al-sharī'a hata nawqif al-jara'im al-'ansuriya' (Go down into the streets to stop racist crimes), the cover story offers an allegory of Palestine as a rallying cry in the struggle against racism in France. Visually, what jumps out is not the text but an overexposed black and white photograph of Palestinians marching toward the camera in military fatigues, waving Palestinian flags above their heads. A boy, perhaps ten years old, leads the march, his flag jutting out into 'the street' of the French title, just below, and parallel to, the Kalashnikov that strikes a diagonal line through the capital 'I' of *Fedaï*. The fact that the journal is printed in greyscale makes it somewhat difficult to read the block letter text superimposed on the black and white image (Figure 6.2):

> Today there is a new wave of assassinations and a new campaign of racist intoxification. The circular of the Minister of Labor Fontanet says that one must not give work to immigrants. So the bosses are firing, like at Renault: Sadock Ben Mabrouk and José [Duarte].
>
> The government maintains unemployment to keep salaries low and turn us into the bosses' slaves and the Minister of Work wants to spread the idea that migrant workers are responsible for unemployment.
>
> And so in Paris, the parallel police and the racist networks commit a series of attacks against migrant workers. It's a new offensive by the fascists to pit the French against migrants, to bring Arab workers down on their knees.
>
> But we will not go down on our knees.
>
> Jellali Ben Ali in Barbès
>
> Aït Abdelmalek in Belleville
>
> Abdallah Zahmoul 16 years old found dead in the 19th [*arrondissement*]
>
> It has to stop

Below the image, overlaid with this call to take to the streets, an appeal calling for the solidarity of French workers clearly links colonial and postcolonial

Figure 6.2 Front page of *Fedaï*, no. 15 (23 February 1972). Fonds Saïd Bouziri, La contemporaine.

subjection and calls for the right to political subjecthood in the postcolony: 'Here we are far from our homeland, we came here to work because in our country we live in great hardship, and don't forget the remainders of colonialism that persist in our countries. We want to live like the other, like all the other, workers. We will fight for our rights until the end.'[31] The image of the marching Palestinians, apparently unrelated to the content of the cover story, is a palimpsestic reminder of the conditions that brought Moroccans, Algerians and Tunisians to France. The rights they claim in France are the same rights that they were denied as colonial subjects – equal treatment under the law.

Published on 15 July 1972, the first issue of *Fedaï, nouvelle série: Journal des travailleurs arabes* (Fedayee, new series: News bulletin of Arab workers) documents the transcolonial understanding of racism that was so central to the nascent antiracist movement. Here the counterpoint is lexical as well as visual, embedded in the postcolonial language used, unselfconsciously in this case, to speak of racism in France. According to the cover story on the killing of Rezki Arezki, gunned down in Lyon by a neighbor on 6 June 1972, among the 2,500 demonstrators assembled at the rally on 17 June many raised 'FLN [Algerian] and Palestinian flags' alongside portraits of the victim. When a French person takes the mic to denounce racist crimes, 'an old immigrant interrupts him to say, "I want to say that we are not against all *pieds-noirs*…. The majority of French people, the majority of *pieds-noirs*, are not racist. They are with us."' An Algerian worker leaving the demonstration agrees: 'We demonstrated calmly to show that we are not racist against the *pieds-noirs*, nor against the French. We are against the racists, against the bosses who take us for slaves.'[32]

It is telling that both migrants use a term designating European settlers in Algeria – *pieds-noirs*, literally 'black-feet' – to speak of white people in France. Although they use it in positive rather than negative terms – not all 'settlers' are racists, many are our allies – their appropriation of a term forged in the colony speaks volumes of the distinctly colonial genealogy within which racist acts such as the murder of Arezki are placed. It also serves as a reminder of the reasons for the presence of North Africans in France: yesterday's colonized subjects are today's migrant workers. The fact that protestors waved Algerian and Palestinian flags at the rally further serves to visually anchor antiracism within a broader anticolonial struggle that connects the revolutionary past (Algeria) to the revolutionary present (Palestine and France).

The CSRP journal's subtitular shift from *Journal in support of the Palestinian revolution* to *Journal of Arab workers* foregrounds the organization's main arena of activism – migrant rights. But as the palimpsestic cover of the last issue of

Fedaï: Journal de soutien à la révolution palestinienne makes clear, it also signals the naturalization of the equation between anticolonialism and antiracism. The dissolution of the CSRP and founding of the MTA in spring 1972 represents a shift in tone rather than substance.[33] The MTA's publications continued to foreground the struggle for migrant rights in France alongside the Palestinian revolution and pro-democracy movements in the Maghreb, taking for granted the homology between these disparate but interconnected sites of anticolonial struggle. The result was a particularly trenchant diagnosis of the historical links between past and present forms of oppression, one that merits to be revisited in the context of the ongoing migrant crisis and renewed forms of antiracist activism in France today.

Conclusion: *Intifada des banlieues*?

Against the 'strategies of erasure' that divorce current forms of migrant solidarity from the history of pro-Palestinian activism in postcolonial France, the study of the first autonomous movement for migrant rights reveals that the Palestinian Question is intimately connected to the emergence of anticolonial antiracist movements in France.[34] In mobilizing this archive, I am working against accepted understandings of 'antiracism' in France, where the term conveys a depoliticized notion of human rights, and non-governmental organizations such as the Mouvement contre le racisme et pour l'amitié entre les peuples (Movement against racism and for friendship between peoples, or MRAP) or the Socialist Party–backed SOS racisme, rather than autonomous movements for migrant rights.

To specialists of postcolonial France, the term 'antiracism' might also convey the Beur (*Arabe* in back-slang) generation of the 1980s, as the children of France's postcolonial migrants were dubbed by the liberal media, in a thinly veiled attempt to 'ethnicize' what was first and foremost a political movement.[35] As activists have amply documented, the grassroots antiracist movement of the 1980s entered the mainstream at the cost of the political demands foregrounded in the very title of its foundational event – the March for Equality and Against Racism that departed Marseille in October 1983 and culminated in December of that year with the arrival of more than 100,000 demonstrators in the streets of Paris, a great many of them proudly donning Palestinian *kufiyyas*, as evidenced in the photographic archive of the movement.

If the central role of Palestine in the emergence of grassroots antiracism in postcolonial France has been one of the casualties of the institutionalization of antiracism, the archive of the first autonomous movement for migrant rights shows ample evidence of distinctly transcolonial forms of antiracist militancy, grounded in solidarity with Palestinians. Ironically, the expression *Intifada des banlieues*, usually deployed to highlight the foreignness of pro-Palestinianism in France, constitutes proof that the Palestinian Question is, also, a question for postcolonial France.

Notes

1 I thank Dr. Michael Turcios for the vital research he completed on my behalf in the Saïd Bouziri archives held at La contemporaine (formerly Bibliothèque de documentation internationale contemporaine or BDIC) at the Université Paris Nanterre. For a thorough account of pro-Palestinian organizations in France from the 1960s to the present, see Marc Hecker, *Intifada française: De l'importation du conflit israélo-palestinien* (Paris: Ellipses, 2012) and Alexandre Mamarbachi, 'Émergence, construction et transformations d'une "cause". Sociologie historique des dévouements en faveur de la "cause" des Palestiniens: 1960–2010. Recherche historique et enquête ethnographique', Phd dissertation, Université Paris Nanterre, 2020. Yoav Di-Capua gives a fascinating overview of Arab student activism in support of the Palestinian cause in 1960s Paris from the point of view of Israeli spies. Yoav Di-Capua, 'Palestine Comes to Paris: The Global Sixties and the Making of a Universal Cause', *Journal of Palestine Studies* 50, no. 1 (2021): 19–50.

2 For a detailed history of France's role in the partition of the Levant, the establishment of the Jewish state and Israel's nuclear program, see Samir Kassir and Farouk Mardam-Bey, *Itinéraires de Paris à Jérusalem: La France et le conflit israélo-arabe*, vol. 1 (Washington, DC: Institut des Etudes Palestiniennes).

3 The Palestinian stand at the Sorbonne was quickly taken down to avoid confrontations with Zionist students. Kassir and Mardam-Bey, *Itinéraires de Paris à Jérusalem*, vol. 2, 167.

4 Geismar has denied allegations that Fatah offered military training to GP militants. Marc Hecker, 'Un demi-siècle de militantisme pro-palestinien en France: Evolution, bilan et perspectives', *Confluences Méditerrannée* 86 (2013), 200.

5 In spring 1970, Jean Luc Godard, Jean-Pierre Gorin and Armand Marco travelled to Jordan and Lebanon to make a film about the Palestinian revolution. The film was never made, but Godard and Anne-Marie Miéville used the footage to make *Ici et ailleurs* (*Here and elsewhere*), a sympathetic satire of Third Worldism. On the heels of his clandestine visit to the United States to support the embattled Black Panther Party, iconoclastic writer Jean Genet spent several months in the bases of Jordan,

from October 1970 to April 1971, and then from September to November 1971. The moving texts he wrote about the fedayeen, drafted with compelling urgency after the September 1982 Phalangist massacres of the Sabra and Shatila refugee camps in Israel-occupied Beirut, gave the Palestinian revolution its *lettres de noblesse* in French literature. Jean Genet, 'Quatre heures à Chatila', *Revue d'Etudes Palestiniennes* 6 (1983): 3–19. Jean Genet, *Un captif amoureux* (Paris: Gallimard, 1986).

6   Françoise Lionnet and Shu-mei Shih were the first to use the expression *transcolonialism* to describe the network of relations between formerly and still colonized sites across heterogeneous imperial formations. Françoise Lionnet and Shu-mei Shih, 'Thinking Through the Minor, Transnationally', in *Minor Transnationalism*, ed. Françoise Lionnet and Shu-mei Shih, 1–23 (Durham, NC: Duke University Press, 2005), 11.

7   Pierre-André Taguieff, *La nouvelle judéophobie* (Paris: Mille et une nuits, 2002). Alain Finkielkraut, *Au nom de l'autre: Réflexions sur l'antisémitisme qui vient* (Paris: Gallimard, 2003). All translations are my own unless otherwise noted.

8   For a nuanced critique of the representation of the migrant as guest, see Mireille Rosello, *Postcolonial Hospitality: The Immigrant as Guest* (Palo Alto: Stanford University Press, 2001).

9   The title *Compter sur ses propres forces* is drawn from a chapter of Mao Zedong's 'Little Red Book', translated into English as 'Self-Reliance and the Arduous Struggle'. Mao Zedong, *Quotations from Chairman Mao Tsetung* (Peking: Foreign Language Press, 1972).

10 Several of the militant pro-Palestinian documentary films produced in the early 1970s have recently been made available online. Francis Reusser, 'Biladi', Vimeo video, 22 April 2020. Available online: https://vimeo.com/410696668 (accessed 2 February 2021). Idioms Film, 'L'Olivier, by Groupe Cinéma de Vincennes 1976'. Vimeo video, 24 June 2020. Available online: https://vimeo.com/432062 498 (accessed 2 February 2021). For a non-exhaustive list of militant films about Palestine, see Guy Hennebelle, *Guide des films anti-impérialistes* (Paris: Editions du Centenaire, 1975). On the collaborations between pro-Palestinian filmmakers in the 1970s and the fledgling Palestinian cinema industry, see Nadia Yaqub, *Palestinian Cinema in the Days of the Revolution* (Austin: University of Texas Press, 2018).

11 Yannis Tritsibidas, 'Compter sur ses propres forces', YouTube video, 3 May 2019. Available online: https://www.youtube.com/watch?v=1DKkKUdnFSw (accessed 2 February 2021).

12 I borrow this formulation from Abdellali Hajjat: 'Writing the history of the Comités Palestine and the MTA as a footnote of the GP's history would completely impair the object of research'. Hajjat, 'Les comités Palestine (1970–1972): Aux acism du soutien de la cause palestinienne en France', *Revue d'Études Palestinennes* 98 (2006): 57. In her study of Jewish-Muslim relations in France, Maud Mandel draws

extensively from state and police archives to demonstrate that 'Hajjat downplays Fatah's role in the establishment of the Comités Palestine [CSRP]', even though she notes factual errors in, for example, a state department report she consults to make this claim, and acknowledges that police reports 'often portrayed foreign laborers as passive'. Maud Mandel, *Muslims and Jews in France: A History of Conflict* (Princeton: Princeton University Press, 2014), 113, 215–17, 37–56. I have made the deliberate choice to tell the story of the CSRP on the basis of the movement's own archives, rather than the state and police archives evidencing attempts to control it.

13 To my knowledge, Edward Said was the first to use the expression 'Palestine as rallying cry' in describing the catalyzing effect of the Palestinian revolution in popular revolts across the Middle East. Edward W. Said, *The Question of Palestine* (New York: Vintage, 1979), 125.

14 Comité de soutien à la révolution palestinienne, 'Un communiqué et un appel à tous les travailleurs en France!', December 1970 tract, ARCH/0057/01, Fonds Saïd Bouziri, La contemporaine (hereafter FSB-LC).

15 'Dis-moi mon frère', *Fedaï* 6 (11 February 1971): 1, ARCH/0057/04, FSB-LC.

16 For a non-exhaustive list of the Palestine committees extant in France and elsewhere in Europe at the time of the founding of the CSRP, see Hajjat, 'Les comités Palestine', 19.

17 'Palestine-Maghreb: même combat', *Fedaï: Bulletin des comités de soutien à la révolution palestinienne* (25 September 1970): 2, ARCH/0057/04, FSB-LC. On the central importance of Palestine in postcolonial Maghrebi literature and thought, see Olivia C. Harrison, *Transcolonial Maghreb: Imagining Palestine in the Era of Decolonization* (Palo Alto: Stanford University Press, 2016).

18 Hajjat, 'Les comités Palestine', 56.

19 The CSRP were founded at the Maison du Maroc (the 'Moroccan House' at the Cité universitaire) shortly after Black September, by Arab students and 'Arab Maoists', including the Tunisian students Saïd and Hamza Bouziri, and the Palestinian Ezzedine Kalak, president at the time of the General Union of Palestinian Students (GUPS), active in France since 1965 and future representative of the PLO in France. Other founding members, many of them known only by their pseudonyms, included the Franco-Syrian student Gilles 'Fathi', the Franco-Lebanese student Thérèse, the Algerian migrant worker Mohammed 'Fedaï' and the Moroccan migrant worker Mohamed 'Mokhtar' Bachiri. Abdellali Hajjat, 'Éléments pour une sociologie historique du Mouvement des Travailleurs Arabes (1970–1976)' (MA Thesis, École des Hautes Études en Sciences Sociales / École Normale Supérieure, 2005), 12.

20 Broadcast via print journalism, photography and television, the Marche pour l'égalité et contre le racisme is to this day the standard bearer for grassroots antiracism in France. In January 2005, a collective of grassroots antiracist

activists published an online petition calling for the constitution of a 'postcolonial anticolonial' movement in France, 'Nous sommes les indigènes de la république!' (We are the natives of the republic). Breaking with the mainstream antiracist discourses that have dominated representations of racism in France since the founding of the Socialist Party–backed organization SOS racisme in 1984 – discourses centred round universal, republican ideals of equality, tolerance and secularism – the appeal insists on situating systemic racism in the *longue durée* history of the French empire and its aftermath, including the history of colonial and postcolonial migration. 'Nous sommes les indigènes de la république!', Parti des indigènes de la république, January 2005. Available online: http://indigenes-republique.fr/le-p-i-r/appel-des-indigenes-de-la-republique/?fbclid=IwAR1bIn_th5Ccr1F4VchwUqp8VGcyYHmvKL-Wo6xUHoZloxXNEAu7caO7c2o (accessed 3 February 2021).

21 Christian Riss, one of the militants involved in throwing Molotov cocktails into the Jordanian embassy on the day of King Hussein's visit to the Elysée Palace, 23 July 1971, was gravely wounded during a police interpellation. Hajjat, 'Les comités Palestine', 66.

22 'Avec les fedayins tu résiteras', undated tract, ARCH/0057/01, FSB-LC. The 'newspaper of the fedayeen' is undoubtedly *Fedayin*, a magazine launched by PLO representative Mahmoud Hamchari in 1969, staffed by Arab Maoists and distributed by the GP. According to Hajjat, Hamchari's *Fedayin* and the CSRP's *Fedaï* shared several contributing editors. Hajjat, 'Les Comités Palestine', 63. Although the CSRP refrained from promoting any particular Palestinian party's agenda, its positions are recognizably those of Fatah.

23 On the 'wave of expulsions' targeting pro-Palestinian migrant activists, see the Secours rouge tract, 'Commission centrale immigrés. Note aux comités de base', March 1971, ARCH/0057/01, FSB-LC. The Secours rouge was a Maoist migrant rights organization allied with the CSRP. *Fedaï* was banned on 25 February 1972, and 3000 copies of the journal were seized. Hajjat, 'Éléments pour une sociologie historique', 43.

24 Kassir and Mardam-Bey, *Itinéraires de Paris à Jérusalem*, vol. 2, 157.

25 'Tous unis nous vaincrons'. February 1971 tract, ARCH/0057/01, FSB-LC.

26 'Plan de travail de la rentrée', *Peuples en lutte: Bulletin du mouvement anti-impérialiste des Comités Indochine-Palestine* 7 (6 September 1973): 2, F/DELTA/RES/0579/26, FSB-LC. C.I.P. The Organisation armée secrète (Secret Armed Organization or OAS), a paramilitary organization intent on blocking Algerian independence, carried out a number of terrorist attacks in France in the final years of the Algerian war and remained active after independence.

27 Hamza Bouziri, 'Grève de la faim', *Fedaï* 6 (11 February 1971): 2, ARCH/0057/04, FSB-LC.

28 To the best of my knowledge, Hamza Bouziri was the first immigrant to go on hunger strike in France, inaugurating the *sans-papier* (undocumented) movement that would culminate with the occupation of the Saint Bernard Church in 1996. For an overview of hunger strikes in the early 1970s, including Hamza's brother Saïd Bouziri's much more publicized 1972 hunger strike, see Daniel A. Gordon, *Immigrants and Intellectuals: May '68 and the Rise of Anti-Racism in France* (Pontypool: Merlin Press, 2012), 126–32.

29 The murder of Djellali Ben Ali, a fifteen-year-old Algerian killed by a white Frenchman in the working-class neighborhood of La Goutte d'Or (Paris 18e) on 27 October 1971, was the first racist crime to mobilize migrant workers *en masse*. A rally convened by the CSRP drew 4,000 protestors to Barbès on 7 November 1971, including French writers and intellectuals such as Jean Genet, Jean-Paul Sartre, Michel Foucault and Claude Mauriac. Abdellali Hajjat, 'Alliances inattendues à la Goutte d'Or', in *68: Une histoire collective, 1962–1981*, ed. Philippe Artières and Michelle Zancarini-Fournel, 525–6 (Paris: La Découverte, 2018). For a painstaking reconstitution of racist murders from 1970 to 1991, see Fausto Giudice, *Arabicides: Une chronique française, 1970–1991* (Paris: La Découverte, 1992). Tahar Ben Jelloun offers a more summary, if equally harrowing, list of the victims' names in his classic analysis of French racism. Tahar Ben Jelloun, *French Hospitality: Racism and North African Immigrants*, trans. Barbara Bray (New York: Columbia University Press, 1999), 47–51.

30 See the undated manuscript issue of *Fedaï* subtitled, 'Pour des logements déscents! [*sic*]', which includes a call to occupy vacant buildings. 'Vive la résistance des mal-logés contre la misère', *Fedaï* (n.d., c. April 1972): 5, ARCH/0057/04, FSB-LC.

31 'Pour arrêter les crimes racistes descends dans la rue!', *Fedaï* 15 (23 February 1972): 1, ARCH/0057/04, FSB-LC.

32 'Pour la première fois depuis la guerre d'Algérie, nous étions 2,500 dans la rue le 17 juin contre les racistes', *Fedaï* n.s. 1 (15 July 1972): 2, ARCH/0057/04, FSB-LC.

33 There is no consensus on the exact date of the creation of the MTA. I follow Rabah Aissaoui, Hajjat and Gordon, who give June 1972 as the likely launch date of the MTA. Rabah Aissaoui, *Immigration and National Identity: North African Political Movements in Colonial and Postcolonial France* (London: Tauris, 2009), 212. Hajjat, 'Les comités Palestine', 72. Gordon, *Immigrants and Intellectuals*, 128; note 34 p. 270.

34 I borrow the expression 'strategies of erasure' from poet and migrant rights activist Philippe Tancelin. 'On Bearing Witness: Conversation between Bouchra Khalili, Phillipe Tancelin and Alexandre Kauffmann', in *The Tempest Society*, ed. Bouchra Khalili, 81 (London: Book Works, 2018).

35 On the 'racialization of urban rebellions', see Abdellali Hajjat, *The Wretched of France: The 1983 March for Equality and Against Racism*, trans. Andrew Brown (Bloomington: Indiana University Press, 2022), 65–6. Historian Gérard Noiriel is

also critical of what he calls 'the ethnicization of the discourse on immigration', including the appropriation of the *verlan* term *Beur* (*Arabe*) to speak of the activists of the March for Equality and Against Racism, redubbed Marche des Beurs in both left- and right-leaning media. Gérard Noiriel, *Immigration, antisémitisme et racisme en France* (Paris: Fayard, 2007), 588–667.

Bibliography

Aissaoui, Rabah. *Immigration and National Identity: North African Political Movements in Colonial and Postcolonial France*. London: Tauris, 2009.

Ben Jelloun, Tahar. *Hospitalité française: Racisme et immigration maghrébine*. Paris: Seuil, 1984. Translated by Barbara Bray as *French Hospitality: Racism and North African Immigrants*. New York: Columbia University Press, 1999.

Biladi. Dir. Francis Reusser. Geneva: Le CinéAtelier Sàrl, 1971.

Compter sur ses propres forces. Dir. Yannis Tritsibidas. Vincennes: Groupe Cinéma de Vincennes, 1973.

Di-Capua, Yoav. 'Palestine Comes to Paris: The Global Sixties and the Making of a Universal Cause'. *Journal of Palestine Studies* 50, no. 1 (2021): 19–50.

Finkielkraut, Alain. *Au nom de l'autre: Réflexions sur l'antisémitisme qui vient*. Paris: Gallimard, 2003.

Fonds Saïd Bouziri. La contemporaine: bibliothèque, archives, musée des mondes contemporains. Paris: Université Paris Nanterre.

Genet, Jean. *Un captif amoureux*. Paris: Gallimard, 1986. Translated by Barbara Bray as *Prisoner of Love*. New York: New York Review of Books, 2003.

Genet, Jean. 'Quatre heures à Chatila'. *Revue d'Études Palestiniennes* 6 (1983): 3–19. Translated by Daniel R. Dupêcher and Martha Perrigaud as 'Four Hours in Shatila', *Journal of Palestine Studies* 12, no. 3 (1983): 3–22.

Giudice, Fausto. *Arabicides: Une chronique française, 1970–1991*. Paris: La Découverte, 1992.

Gordon, Daniel A. *Immigrants and Intellectuals: May '68 and the Rise of Anti-Racism in France*. Pontypool: Merlin Press, 2012.

Hajjat, Abdellali. 'Alliances inattendues à la Goutte d'Or', in *68: Une histoire collective, 1962–1981*, edited by Philippe Artières and Michelle Zancarini-Fournel, 525–31. Paris: La Découverte, 2018.

Hajjat, Abdellali. 'Éléments pour une sociologie historique du Mouvement des Travailleurs Arabes (1972–1976)'. MA thesis, École des Hautes Etudes en Sciences Sociales/École Normale Supérieure, 2005.

Hajjat, Abdellali. 'Les comités Palestine (1970–1972): Aux origines du soutien de la cause palestinienne en France'. *Revue d'Études Palestinennes* 98 (2006): 74–92. Translated by Rayya Badran as 'Comités Palestine (1970–72): On the Origins of Solidarity with the Palestinian Cause in France', in *Transnational Solidarity: Anticolonialism in the Global Sixties*, edited by Zeina Maasri, Cathy Bergin, and Francesca Burke, 54–76. Manchester: Manchester University Press, 2022.

Hajjat, Abdellali. *The Wretched of France*, Translated by Andrew Brown. Bloomington: Indiana University Press, 2022.

Harrison, Olivia C. *Transcolonial Maghreb: Imagining Palestine in the Era of Decolonization*. Palo Alto: Stanford University Press, 2016.

Hecker, Marc. 'Un demi-siècle de militantisme pro-palestinien en France: Évolution, bilan et perspectives'. *Confluences Méditerrannée* 86, no. 3 (2013): 197–208.

Hecker, Marc. *Intifada française: De l'importation du conflit israélo-palestinien*. Paris: Ellipses, 2012.

Hennebelle, Guy. *Guide des films anti-impérialistes*. Paris: Éditions du Centenaire, 1975.

Ici et ailleurs. Dirs. Jean-Luc Godard and Anne-Marie Miéville. Sonimage/INA/Gaumont, 1974.

Kassir, Samir, and Farouk Mardam-Bey. *Itinéraires de Paris à Jérusalem: La France et le conflit israélo-arabe*. 2 vols. Washington, DC: Institut des Études Palestiniennes, 1993.

Kauffmann, Alexandre, Bouchra Khalili, and Philippe Tancelin. 'On Bearing Witness: Conversation between Bouchra Khalili, Phillipe Tancelin and Alexandre Kauffmann', in *The Tempest Society*, edited by Bouchra Khalili, 78–88. London: Book Works, 2018.

Lionnet, Françoise, and Shu-mei Shih. 'Thinking Through the Minor, Transnationally', in *Minor Transnationalism*, edited by Françoise Lionnet and Shu-mei Shih, 1–23. Durham, NC: Duke University Press, 2005.

L'olivier. Dirs. Ali Akika, Guy Chapoullie, Danièle Dubroux, Serge Le Péron, Jean Narboni, and Dominique Villain. Vincennes: Groupe Cinéma de Vincennes, 1976.

Mamarbachi, Alexandre. 'Émergence, construction et transformations d'une "cause". Sociologie historique des dévouements en faveur de la "cause" des Palestiniens: 1960–2010. Recherche historique et enquête ethnographique'. Phd dissertation, Université Paris Nanterre, 2020.

Mandel, Maud. *Muslims and Jews in France: A History of Conflict*. Princeton: Princeton University Press, 2014.

Noiriel, Gérard. *Immigration, antisémitisme et racisme en France, XIXe-XXe siècle: Discours publics, humiliations privées*. Paris: Pluriel, 2007.

Palestine vaincra. Dir. Jean-Pierre Olivier. Cinéastes Révolutionnaires Prolétariens, 1969.

Rosello, Mireille. *Postcolonial Hospitality: The Immigrant as Guest*. Palo Alto: Stanford University Press, 2001.

Said, Edward W. *The Question of Palestine*. New York: Vintage, 1992.

Taguieff, Pierre-André. *La nouvelle judéophobie.* Paris: Mille et une nuits, 2002. Translated by Patrick Camiller as *Rising from the Muck: The New Anti-Semitism in Europe* (Chicago: Ivan R. Dee, 2004).

Yaqub, Nadia. *Palestinian Cinema in the Days of Revolution.* Austin: University of Texas Press, 2018.

Zedong, Mao. *Quotations from Chairman Mao Tsetung.* Peking: Foreign Language Press, 1972.

Part 3
Transnational Cultural Production

7

Presence and visibility in Cuban anticolonial solidarity: Palestine in OSPAAAL's photography and poster art

Fernando Camacho Padilla and Jessica Stites Mor

Few causes connected distant movements during the late 1960s and beyond like that of the fate of Palestine.[1] The extension of authority over a former mandate territory (UNGA Resolution 181, 29 November 1947) confirmed the sanctioning of settler colonialism by the United Nations (UN).[2] Wars between the new Israeli state and its neighbours also revealed the strategic role that powerful imperial forces might exercise against pan-Arabism and the national independence of Arab-majority states. The show of imperialist force in events like the 1967 Six Day War galvanizsed political organizations, trade unionists, anticolonial nationalists and revolutionary leftists across the global South. For many leaders, solidarity with Palestine became a key front in a revolutionary alliance against imperialism. The 1969 Pan African Cultural Congress held in Algiers went so far as to include the contested boundaries of Palestine in their map of Africa.[3]

For Cuba, forging Third World alliances during this period was a chief priority of the revolutionary government. Supporting non-state actors, mostly left-wing organizations, in their struggle for revolution was a central objective of Cuban foreign policy.[4] Cultural institutions including the Casa de las Américas, the Cuban Institute of Cinematography Arts and Industries, the National Council of Culture and the National Union of Cuban Writers and Artists, among others, were tasked with internationalist initiatives, in the hope that Cuba could spread its influence on behalf of these revolutionary movements.[5] Strategically, offering solidarity to Palestine provided an expedient way to court relationships with important figures in the Middle East and North Africa.[6] Solidarity between Cuba and Palestine also presented the opportunity for Cuban internationalists to shape a particular view of solidarity, crafting a worldview that elaborated

Cuban revolutionary goals and placed cooperation at its centre. This chapter outlines the central features of Cuban Palestinian relations during the era of decolonization and the Cold War and expands on the cultural methods employed by Cuba to shape a narrative of the Palestinian struggle. Specifically, it examines the Cuban revolutionary state's use of visual media to construct a visible presence in solidarity with armed struggle in Palestine. We argue that photography, poster art and illustration produced by the Cuban state were successful in advertising Cuba's alliance with key figures in the Palestinian nationalist struggle and in shaping a narrative of anti-imperialist struggle that most benefited Cuba's objectives.

The Organization of Solidarity with the Peoples of Asia, Africa, and Latin America (OSPAAAL) was the primary organization established to carry out the internationalist project of the Cuban Revolution. Founded during the Tricontinental conference, held in Havana in January 1966, OSPAAAL was charged with coordinating solidarity activities between movements across the three regions. From the beginning, OSPAAAL adopted Palestinian nationalism as one of its main solidarity causes, using it to focus attention on ongoing projects of colonialism. The visibility of displaced Palestinians, political leaders and militants in OSPAAAL's publications, such as the *Tricontinental* magazine and bulletin, shaped a narrative and drew attention to a Cuban vision of South-South solidarity. The use of visual communication as a form of transnational cultural politics formed an important part of Cuba's strategy to mobilize support not only for Palestine but also for a particular vision of internationalist anticolonialism.[7] This effort was central to a larger project of worldmaking that emerged across anticolonialist internationalist spaces through exchange and negotiation of new forms of international cooperation. Cuba's shaping and rendering of narratives of Palestinian struggle were used as an instrument of persuasion in framing connected struggles and in positioning possible transnational responses. We focus our analysis on the images published by the *Tricontinental* magazine between the years 1967 and 1976.

This study contributes to the emerging field of Latin American–Middle Eastern relations, which has recently begun to flourish. Over the past few decades, several scholars have examined Cuba's internationalist policy in different arenas.[8] Several recent publications have begun to uncover details about Cuban–Palestinian relations.[9] While access to available records in Cuba is difficult, those from outside, such as those in the United States as well as US allies, tended to exaggerate or misrepresent Cuba's actions in the name of fighting communism. This problem also persists in the Middle East, where Palestinian archival materials were often destroyed. Those held in Lebanon, for instance, were removed and relocated to Israel by the Israeli Army during the occupation.[10] In this study, we consult previously unused primary sources, including the only comprehensive collection of materials produced by OSPAAAL, and interviews with key individuals who participated in the production of Cuba's foreign policy. We also interviewed archivists and producers of visual materials used in OSPAAAL publications, press agencies that maintained image archives and diplomats that oversaw the impact of Cuban solidarity on struggles in the Middle East. These sources offer new perspectives on how strategies of visual communication were produced and circulated to support Cuban–Palestinian relations and also how the Palestinian cause bacame a major solidarity cause in Cuba.

Historical context of Cuban–Palestinian relations

Before Fidel Castro's revolution of January 1959, Cuba had little political contact with the Arabic-speaking world. Despite connections made between anticolonial and antiracist intellectual figures and organizations in Mexico and the Caribbean, Cuba remained somewhat removed from major movements elsewhere. Most diplomatic discussions were held through international organizations. These took place primarily at regional *convenios*, or treaty-making conventions; the League of Nations, before its dissolution; and, subsequently, through the Organization of American States and the UN. Notably, along with India, Cuba had voted against the partition of Palestine at the General Assembly of the UN on the grounds that it was a non-democratic and coercive measure.[11] The same year, the British plan for the partition of India was announced, and most Latin American delegations, while abstaining from the vote, viewed these related events as an extension of British colonialism. Cuba defended the rights of the Palestinians against the objectives of Zionists and their British allies.

While long-standing diasporic ties existed between the Middle East and Cuba throughout the colonial and post-independence period, these did not translate into strong positions on politics in the region. Contingents of Siro-Lebanese and Palestinians migrated to the Americas from the late Ottoman period to the wars surrounding the foundation of the state of Israel.[12] During the most intense period of debate around the British mandate system, Jews also migrated to Cuba.[13] Many of these new arrivals played an important role in the early years of the Cuban Communist Party,[14] which formed a part of the 26 of July Movement that brought Castro to power. The Cuban revolution of 1959 captured the attention of national liberation movements around the world, including that of Palestinian nationalists. The circulation of Third World intellectuals interested in decolonization and national liberation shifted over the course of the decade from European capitals like Paris and Prague to revolutionary capitals of Algiers, Dar es-Salaam and Havana. Soon, Fidel Castro was given awards and recognition by Arab revolutionary governments for his solidarity with their cause. Algeria presented Castro with an award in early March of 1959, the first accepted by the Cuban leader, and the United Arab Republic presented him with an award the following November.[15] These awards evidence the early political connections and sympathies that Cuba had with charismatic nationalist leaders in the Middle East and North Africa.

According to Algerian National Liberation Front (FLN) leader Alfred Bérenguer, who visited Cuba in 1959, around five or six Algerians travelled to Cuba to participate in the revolution alongside Fidel Castro in the Sierra Maestra.[16] The connection between Cuba and the Algerian FLN intensified quickly, and one of the earliest foreign policy decisions of the new Cuban revolutionary government was to actively support the liberation of Algeria in 1961. Cuba sent weapons to assist in the revolution, and once the French withdrew, Cuba sent doctors, medical supplies and equipment, and soldiers to confront an attack from Morocco on the Sahara in 1963.[17] This early relationship with Algeria would inspire in Castro an interest in the fate of North African and Middle Eastern independence and decolonization movements, and Cuba's foreign relations would be extended in the region throughout the 1960s and 1970s.

Revolutionary Cuba's first official contact with Palestinians in the Middle East came when Ernesto 'Che' Guevara[18] led a delegation to visit Gaza in July 1959, on route from a trip to Egypt to meet with Gamal Abdel Nasser.[19] Nasser hosted many national liberation movement delegations in Cairo, and soon after the visit, Cuba and Egypt strengthened their political ties. Cuba sent various delegations to Cairo, one of which included Fidel's brother, Raúl Castro, who also visited Gaza in 1960. In 1962, Che Guevara opened an operations office for Fatah in Algiers, where Cubans would have constant contact with Palestinians. During their trips to Egypt, Cubans met with Palestinian political figures, including Ahmad Shuqayri, who served as Chairman of the Palestine Liberation Organization (PLO) from 1964 to 1967.[20] Just a few months after the creation of the PLO in 1964, its first official political delegation travelled to a handful of Latin American countries to promote solidarity. The emissaries were Yasser Amro, Salim Barhoum and Jeries Rumman whose mission was to try to convince

Latin American governments to take a stand against Israel at the UN.²¹ The same year, Che Guevara met Abu Jihad, one of the founders of the PLO, and al-Afif al-Akhdar, a Tunisian Marxist intellectual, in Algiers.²² Abu Maizar, who was also in attendance, became responsible for the Palestine Office and for Fatah in Algiers after 1965.²³

Political contact between Cuban and Palestinian political actors increased steadily after the Tricontinental conference, held in Havana in January 1966. At the conference, 82 national delegations met in Havana and for the first time brought Latin American leaders into more direct dialogue with their counterparts among the Afro-Asian solidarity bloc. Castro championed a Latin American vision of solidarity between formerly colonized regions and emphasized the connectedness between Latin American revolutions and ongoing struggles for national liberation elsewhere. Moroccan leftist intellectual Mehdi Ben Barka²⁴ was appointed secretary general of the Tricontinental after meeting Che Guevara in Algiers and helped plan the conference.²⁵

The first Palestinian delegation was formally welcomed to Cuba to attend this 'Tricontinental Conference', as it would come to be known. After almost two weeks of discussions, the political commission of the conference issued a resolution in favor of the Palestinian people and condemned the aggression of the Israeli Defense Forces. It read as follows:

1. The Conference warns against what is called Israeli technical and financial aid and considers it a new disguised method of US imperialism and neocolonialism.
2. The Conference request all progressive parties and committees to multiply their efforts to combat Zionist infiltration and penetration in their countries and to abrogate the various agreements concluded with Israel.²⁶

All five of the delegates to the Palestine commission were members of the PLO with close connections with the Syrian government.²⁷ These leaders belonged to an earlier generation than those who would take control of the PLO following internal transformations after 1967 and the rise of the resistance organizations, but they cemented a strong foundation for Cuban–Palestinian ties.

In early 1967, Cuba's political relations with Egypt began to slowly deteriorate. After the Six Day War, Egypt had begun to call for peace with Israel, creating a distance between Cairo and the revolutionary leadership in Algiers. Both Moscow and Washington expected Nasser to distance himself from Cuba's foreign policy and Che Guevara's *foquista* insurgent strategy. Castro, along with other PLO leaders, was also increasingly sceptical of Nasser's initiatives within both Egypt and the Non-Aligned Movement (NAM), which seemed to be increasingly 'Bonapartist'.[28] More radical Palestinian Arab organizations emerging from the Arab Nationalist Movement (ANM) were concentrated in Beirut, making it easier for the Cuban government to strengthen collaborations.[29]

Osvaldo Cárdenas, chief of the Africa and Middle East department of the Cuban Secret Services, and Ulises Estrada, close confidante of Che Guevara and Manuel Piñero, head of Cuban security, travelled from Cairo to Lebanon, and then to Syria over the border to Jordan, where they met with Arafat. They were the first Cuban representatives to formally meet with Arafat and to discuss what role Cuba might play in supporting Palestinian nationalism.[30] During the visit, they also toured the al-'Asifa guerrilla camp along the Jordan River, home to the armed wing of Fatah. After Black September (1970–1), Lebanon became the main 'bridge for the liberation of Palestine',[31] and until the Israeli invasion of Lebanon in 1982, Beirut was the city where most of the meetings between Palestinian and Cuban delegations took place. Throughout the early 1970s, Cuban journalists from *Prensa Latina*, which was founded in 1959 to confront media campaigns against the Cuban revolutionary process,[32] interviewed Palestinian leaders in Lebanon such as Arafat, Ghassan Kanafani and George Habash, and their declarations were published in different Cuban newspapers and magazines. The main journalist from *Prensa Latina* who reported from the Arab states during these years was Osvaldo Ortega Nejme, a Cuban with Syrian background,[33] who was later joined by other Cuban journalists from *Prensa Latina*, such as Irma Cáceres and Moisés Saab, also posted in Beirut. PLO representatives in the Lebanese capital began to travel to Cuba more often beginning in late July 1970.[34] During these years, the first Palestinians arrived in Cuba to receive education, and some of them married Cubans and became active in solidarity activities.[35]

During the Fourth NAM summit held in Algiers during 5 to 9 September 1973, Castro and Arafat met in person for the first time. The PLO was also invited at this meeting to formally participate in the NAM. The summit hosted fourteen other national liberation movements from Asia, Africa and Latin America, and the Palestinian cause was represented alongside these other movements. At this meeting, Libyan leader, Muamar Mu'ammar Muhammad Abu Minyar al-Gaddafi, sent a critical message to Cuba: solidarity with Palestine and the Arab cause was not compatible with formal relations with the Zionist state. A few days later, Castro broke off diplomatic relations with Israel. Bilateral relations have remained unrepaired, despite the fact that political contacts and channels of communication were never fully closed. As the Cuban embassy in

Tel Aviv had played a key role in gathering information related to the occupation of Palestine until then, Beirut became even more important as a site of contact.

In the middle of November 1974, Arafat visited Cuba for the first time after participating in the UN General Assembly, receiving a lot of attention from the Cuban media.[36] After his visit, in early 1975, the PLO officially set up diplomatic representation in Havana, which in 1982 became an official embassy. In the coming years, more Palestinian delegations arrived on the island, not only from the PLO but also from other organizations, such as the Popular Front for the Liberation of Palestine (PFLP). Farouq Qaddoumi, who headed the PLO headquarters in Beirut beginning in 1973, travelled on several occasions to Havana, and George Habash became good friends with several Cuban diplomats, such as Ernesto Gómez Abascal.[37] Nayef Hawatmeh from the Democratic Front for the Liberation of Palestine (DFLP) visited Cuba, as well, on four occasions from 1977 to 1987. Arafat continued to visit Cuba on several occasions, mostly to participate in political events taking place in the island such as *El festival de la juventud* (Festival of Youth) in 1978. The Sixth NAM summit took place in Havana in 1979, a major diplomatic coup for Castro whose status and influence within the movement had begun to rise. In the opening speech of the summit and later at the thirty-fourth session of the UN General Assembly, Castro stated:

> As I stated in my speech at the Sixth Summit: …we are not fanatics. The revolutionary movement has been brought up in the hatred of racial discrimination and pogroms of any kind, and from the depths of our souls, we repudiate with all our strength the ruthless persecution and genocide which, in its time, Nazism unleashed against the Jewish people. But I can find nothing more similar to that in our contemporary history than the eviction, persecution and genocide that is being carried out today against the Palestinian people by imperialism and Zionism. Stripped of their lands, driven out of their own homeland, dispersed throughout the world, they are an impressive example of abnegation and heroism, and they are the living symbol of the greatest crime of our times.[38]

Castro and Arafat also met a number of times during these years, in Moscow and in Managua, Nicaragua, after the Sandinista revolution. By 1975, the *Tricontinental* began to republish photographs of Arafat and his speeches. This trend would continue as the PLO began to attract more of Cuba's attention.

During the Lebanese Civil War (1975–90) and the Israeli invasion (1982–5), Cuba's connections with Fatah and the PLO increasingly included military support. In 1978, Cuba and the PLO signed a secret agreement of military cooperation, and Cuba began training Palestinians in guerrilla warfare strategies, mostly at the guerrilla training camp *Punto Cero* in Guanabo.[39] Cuba also received many Palestinian students, and by 1985 there were around 500 in total, mostly located in *La Isla de la Juventud*, the place where most foreign students in the country stayed. Cuba consistently condemned the crimes committed against Palestinian refugees in Lebanon, such as the massacres of Sabra and Shatila in 1982. After 1983, Cuba tried to reconcile the different Palestinian factions' leaders from various organizations in the Middle East and also in Havana.[40] During this period, Cuba had a clear preference for the PFLP and the DFLP and other radical organizations as relations with the PLO deteriorated due to their rapprochement with Egypt. This could be noticed in important dimensions, for example, the militancy of the Palestinians who received scholarships to study in Cuba (mostly from the PFLP), the composition of delegations of Palestinian organizations arriving in the island and the ranks of Cuban authorities who received them in Havana. At that time, PLO representatives in Cuba did not have a prominent presence nor an active role in social events. Nevertheless, Castro and Arafat kept good personal relations.

Anticoloniality and the visibility of Palestine in OSPAAAL's cultural production

As part of its internationalist campaign to raise awareness of the Palestinian cause, OSPAAAL published various materials on the Palestinian situation. As the formal office designated to carry out transnational solidarity activities beyond Havana,[41] OSPAAAL's principal aim was to coordinate associated organizations to fight against imperialism and to promote revolutionary socialism. Its publication strategy mirrored this objective. From the beginning, the organization was active in printing magazines, bulletins and posters in solidarity with distant struggles. Of particular interest were those that could echo and clarify Cuba's alliance with revolutionary struggles and illustrate central themes of its foreign policy objectives, such as its position on Israel and its support for specific organizations of Palestinian national liberation. During the early years of publishing, from 1966 to 1970, OSPAAAL endeavoured to communicate Cuba's solidarity efforts to a wide audience and thereby to inspire the support of other parties for distant causes.

The conflict between Israel, Palestine and the Arab nations of the Middle East became a major subject of writing and analysis within the pages of the

Tricontinental magazine and bulletin, and a delegation from OSPAAAL visited Gaza as early as 1967.[42] For this reason, Arabic also became one of the official languages of dissemination, and most posters that were circulated after 1967 included Arabic text, alongside Spanish, English and French. Some publications were also translated into Arabic, mostly those that were printed in Beirut in the lead up to the Israeli invasion of 1982. Melba Hernández, general secretary of OSPAAAL and wife of Jesús Montané, a member of the Central Committee of the Cuban Communist Party, asked a Cuban resident in Beirut, Mayra Díaz Arango, to be responsible for this goal of the magazine. Translations were made by the Lebanese writer Arlette Khoury.[43] As the involvement of Cuba within Third World struggles increased, the magazine and its artwork became more committed to a narrative of interconnectedness, and artistic influences from other parts of the world were increasingly incorporated in OSPAAAL's design work. The artistic style of OSPAAAL was simple and direct. Its illustrators, poster artists and cover designers made use of straightforward iconography to deliver powerful messages. Jocular critiques of imperialist powers, including the United States and Israel, were illustrated by colourful, playful imagery.[44] Due to the success and popularity of Cuban revolutionary designs, this iconography was able to cross ideological borders and found its way into the publicity strategy for all types of political projects.[45] As Zeina Maasri describes, visuality inconspicuously commands power, and it connects and relates ideas, provoking reactions that exist on both the rational mind and through the subjective experience of viewing.[46]

The narrative approach of OSPAAAL publications was to connect a particular vision of the Palestinian conflict that aligned with the priorities of the revolutionary state in its support for displaced Palestinians and the guerrilla activities of Palestinian organizations and their allies. In 1970, a book titled *Palestine: Crisis and Liberation* was published in English by OSPAAAL in order to disseminate information throughout non-Spanish speaking countries. The book includes a general overview of the situation alongside testimonies of Cuban journalists and visitors to Palestine, A. Zapata and Teófilo Acosta.[47] These testimonies privilege the importance of armed militancy within the Palestinian political organization, centre the soldier's experience and the process of becoming a revolutionary, moving away from particulars of the struggle to focus on ideological principles. A poster made by OSPAAAL artistic director Alfredo Rostgaard of a Palestinian soldier was used as the cover illustration. In 1970, Palestinian fighters appear on the cover of one issue of the bulletin and on the inside cover of another issue of the magazine. In the *Tricontinental*

Bulletin no. 57, a colourful painting appears, inspired by a photograph taken that same year of a Palestinian fighter by Hani Jawhariyyeh, one of the founders of the Palestine Film Unit.[48] The illustration connects the reporting work of Palestinian photographers and cinematographers working on the front lines with the colourful, bold imagery of the Cuban revolution. It suggests a presence, on the ground, of Cubans, soldiers, reporters and dignitaries, aligned with the cause. Another image (Figure 7.1) is of a Palestinian soldier standing in front of a large face of Che Guevara.

The iconography of the Palestinian fighter, weilding a Kalashnikov and wearing a *kufiyya*, became popular among solidarity movements with Palestine. OSPAAAL reproduced this imagery across its printed material,[49] representing guerrilla warfare as central to revolutionary struggle, suggesting through the choice of weapon an anti-Americanist vision that at this moment reflected Cuba's position on the Soviet Union as an ally.[50] It also centred the *kufiyya* as a symbol of nationalism. The iconic *kufiyya* as a part of a combatant's uniform became more regular in graphic depictions of Palestinian militants, and despite transformed revolutionary rhetoric in the wake of Soviet support for Cuba, this image remained consistent until the 1990s. This iconography would be repeated by artistic exhibitions in solidarity with Palestine across the globe.[51]

OSPAAAL's artists depicted solidarity with Palestine as equivalent to support for national liberation elsewhere. While the text of the magazine and bulletin publications detailed the activities in camps, the experiences of soldiers and the thoughts of important political leadership in Palestine, visual representations of the struggle underlined the message that a particular hierarchy of struggle should take precedence over others.[52] The notion that such struggles were at the centre of breaking down a world order set in place by imperial, capitalist interests meant that national liberation had to be a priority over other goals. It also created a direct connection between the struggles for freedom and equality within powerful countries like the United States to the goals of anti-imperialism (Figure 7.2). Artists for the magazine and bulletin depicted other African and Middle Eastern struggles for liberation with similarly strong visual references to Cuban and Latin American revolutionary iconography.

Building on the argument made by African American militants that Black art could be used as a weapon to transform culture and thought, the publications echoed visual idioms of the Black Power movement in the United States. Using bold colours, particularly yellows, oranges and reds, against thick black lines, artists abstracted images of struggle and portraits of armed revolutionary heroes. Envisioning the struggle of Palestine as akin to the struggle against race-based

Figure 7.1 *Tricontinental* magazine, no. 19–20 (1970), inside front cover

oppression and ongoing colonialism set the struggle directly at odds in forums like the UN with the competing narrative of Israeli independence. OSPAAAL posters, of which fifteen were dedicated exclusively to solidarity with Palestine,[53] created a symbolic visual language that was immediately accessible to audiences receiving *Tricontinental* publications. Pro-Palestinian designs inspired by the artwork of OSPAAAL were also published by Arab revolutionaries in countries

Figure 7.2 *Tricontinental* magazine, no. 31 (1971) pp. 117, 119

such as Algeria, Egypt, Syria and Iraq. The influence and exchange among these countries, regions and even continents were far reaching, particularly in Lebanon.[54]

Images were explicitly designed to enhance texts written by leading intellectual figures of liberation movements. Speeches and interviews with figures like Arafat, pronouncements by Luís Cabral, Hô Chi Minh, Guevara and others were accompanied by graphics and posters that called for specific acts and days of solidarity. Art historians have suggested that the use of minimalism and an aesthetic that mirrored highly reproduceable, cinematic poster art visually suggested that the struggle for liberation had found its way into the idiom of the times.[55] OSPAAAL's poster art iconographically connected the ideological struggles of Latin American revolutions to those of Vietnam, Palestine, the Congo and oppressed groups in the United States. They also visually suggested that individual causes could be considered from within a comparative frame. Images of armed militants engaged in similar activities, drawn in similar styles, and fighting similar-looking, if not the very same, enemies, connected struggles across continents.

These posters also visually framed Castro's desire that solidarity action in the Middle East move away from Nasserist compromises. Nasser's influence in the NAM, acting as something of a gatekeeper to the region, had limited Latin American internationalist approaches to solidarity action with Arab nations in international institutions and had left the NAM more open to the influence of competing new figures like Anwar Sadat, who quickly abandoned Egpyt's efforts to foster a Palestinian state. Appealing to the deep anticolonialism and antiracism that had brought together many nations within the Afro-Asian bloc at the UN, the *Tricontinental* magazine and its poster art emphasized traditional Arab dress in its depictions of struggles in the Middle East, not the more modern style adopted by Nasser. They empasized pan-Arabism as inerhently anticolonial and militant, without reference to regional leadership, liberatory but not nationalist. They also emphasized clothing style and skin tones that were clearly meant to suggest non-white, non-European Middle Easterners. Notably, one of the most prominent images includes such a figure with the barrel of a gun doubling as sunglasses (Figure 7.3).

OSPAAAL's Palestine posters utilized basic shapes, bold colours, contrast and minimalist presentation to suggest simplicity. The Question of Palestine, and of the displaced Palestinian diaspora, was one which required a similar approach. To be stateless was not a different problem than that of national liberation or decolonization. The artistic renderings and textual narrative of

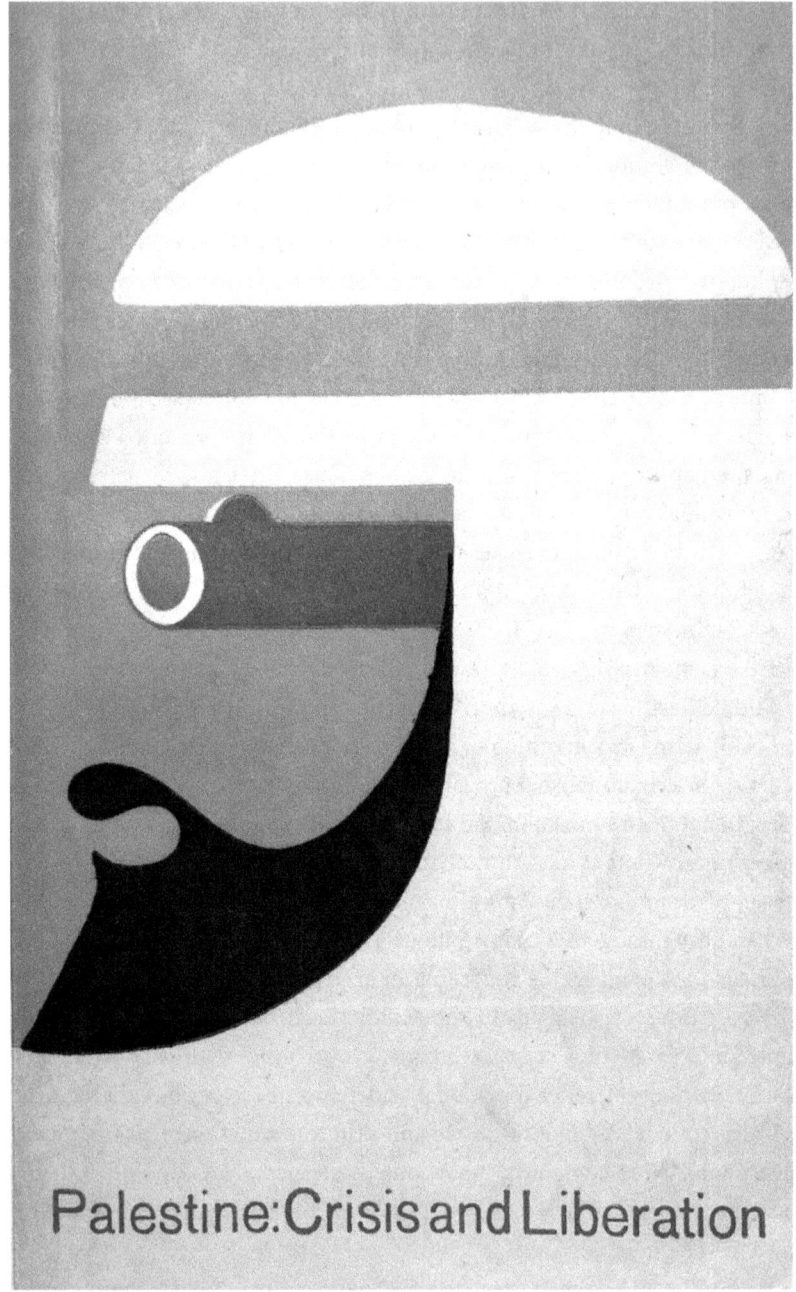

Figure 7.3 Book cover also used in poster art, *Palestine: Crisis and Liberation* (1970). Cover by Alfredo Rostgaard.

OSPAAAL's publications mirrored Cuba's strategy at the UN. It pressed upon Latin American and Middle Eastern delegations, especially the Afro-Asian bloc, the prioritization of national liberation struggles. Framing this form of solidarity as a necessity in combating colonialism, racism, apartheid and US intervention, Cuba urged other delegations to embrace armed conflict. These posters made in similar style featured not only Palestine and Palestinian figures but also Syria, Lebanon, Mehdi Ben Barka, the Polisario Front in Western Sahara and even Egypt and South Yemen.[56] They confronted dominant positions on Middle Eastern conflict at the UN, which often followed Egypt's lead, countering with more radical interpretations. Photographic images included in the reporting and analysis of the Palestinian cause in *Tricontinental* publications depicted Palestinian refugees as agents in their own struggle, as possessing their own revolutionary chic. This became increasingly the case as Cuba drifted away from the PLO.

It is curious that the authorship of the photographs published in the *Tricontinental* magazine is generally unknown. Not only are names of photographers not printed, but they are also not recorded in the photographic archive of OSPAAAL. In this way, while the photos of the Cuban revolution are linked to world-renowned photographers such as Raúl Corrales, Gilberto Ante or Alberto Díaz, alias *Korda*, most of the imagemakers responsible for Middle Eastern coverage remain practically anonymous. Most likely due to the sensitivity of the subject and the politicized nature of the positions being taken by the organization, it was convenient not to disclose the source of images, particularly those from camps and active sites of military activity. In contrast, while most of the OSPAAAL posters are not signed, their authorship is generally known due to style and artistic detail. Photographs published in the *Tricontinental* magazine and bulletin came from many different sources. Many came directly from the national liberation movements themselves and from various national press agencies. Many photos also came from *Prensa Latina*, Cuban newspapers such as *Granma* and foreign embassies and political representatives in Havana. OSPAAAL photographs were sometimes even just reproduced, 'borrowed' or 'taken', from foreign journals and magazines.[57] Due to the US blockade, the Cuban government did not respect many international copyright policies.

Most of the photographs of Palestinians used by the *Tricontinental* after 1973 were given to Cubans by other Palestinian organizations. When Cuban journalists visited camps, mostly in Lebanon and Syria, they took pictures themselves. The photographs and reports from camps in the publications underlined the primacy of ongoing imperial threats. They centred on the violent nature of conflict between Palestine and Israel. Many articles about Syria and Lebanon even included mention of the Palestinian cause and displaced peoples, connecting the struggles against French colonialism to that of the ongoing territorial expansion of the Zionist state. Several articles featured children, youth and images of military training. Unlike images used to frame other struggles in Africa and even the Middle East (e.g. Dhofar or Western Sahara), no pictures in the magazine or poster art featured Palestinian women with weapons, reflecting the fact that very few images of women were included in general, despite their occasional presence, a fact we attribute to respect for regional gender politics. Some of the articles also include discourses of Arab leaders, situating the journalistic narration of the event within the scaffold of emerging authority in the region. Cuba supported the right of Palestinian decolonization, framing the conflict in such a way as to make clear Cuba's pursuit of enforcement if not broadening of interpretations of what the UN provisionally promised newly independent nations.

OSPAAAL's publications emphasized clear ideological leadership. The presence of a central figure, often almost overfilling the frame, was repeated across the published images of the magazine. Photographs of youth, soldiers, politicians, intellectuals, workers and others were unmissable reflections of Cuba's ideological vision of the centrality of the social to revolutionary political experiments. Representations of conflict would deliberately connect the narratives presented by leading figures of the left to images of armed combatants. In the case of Palestine, Arafat's centrality in dictating the revolutionary posture is as unmistakable as is deference to the leadership of the Palestinian intellectuals and leadership in Beirut after 1973.

Presence, evolving relationships and images of solidarity in struggle

In the third issue of the *Tricontinental* magazine in 1967, a photo essay on Palestine appears with the title, 'Palestino: "Comandos Tormenta" (Palestine: "Storm Commandos")' (Figure 7.4). Largely without captions, several black and white photographs appear, depicting men preparing for battle in Fatah training camps. Most of the men appear shirtless, though a few are wearing simple fatigues and caps or helmets. These images are followed by a series of six photographs that mirror those taken of the Nakba by Palestinian photographers. Images of refugees fleeing for their lives appear over the

Palestine in Cuban Anticolonial Solidarity 183

La efectividad de las acciones ha sido reconocida por el gobierno de Tel Aviv.

Figure 7.4 *Tricontinental* magazine, no. 3 (1967), p. 67

caption 'the reason for existence of the commandos'. A note cites the number of Palestinians that became refugees in the process of the attacks of the Israeli military on 5 June 1967. Joining the ranks of Palestinains already taking refuge in Jordan, Egypt, Syria, Gaza, Lebanon and Iraq, those fleeing appear to be photographed from a distance, from precarious angles and amid debris from a fallen aircraft, suggesting disorder and imminent danger. The faces of the refugees are not visible, just as those in the training camps are also obscured, making it difficult to identify any individual, portending, as does the subsequent text, that these refugees are combatants in the making.

The accompanying article, by Teófilo Acosta, who is also the photographer, makes note of the conditions of those fleeing for their safety and makes it clear that the Israeli troops that oversee and direct their movement shout at them in English. With slogans that assert that the land has been claimed by the Israeli state, they reflect the British soldiers that previously enforced the League of Nations mandate. Acosta addresses the readership of the three continents, asking them to make up their own minds about the status of Fatah's militancy. Interviewing an anonymized Syrian-based Palestinian leader, Acosta reports that the militant activities of one clandestine group began in 1959, with the support of Syria and Algeria, under the banner of national liberation. To the interviewee is also attributed an admonishment against adopting a racialized framework for the struggle against the state of Israel. The combatant argues that, unlike other organizations, they don't intend to 'push the Jewish settlers into the sea' but rather to confront the project of the state of Israel as inextricably tied to North American, as a replacement of British, imperialism in the region.[58] Uncoupling the state of Israel from the UN and its British imperial history to connect it to US ambitions in the region makes a crucial move in terms of framing the conflict. Unlike photos of the Nakba, which captured Palestinians 'at the exact point in which they ceased to be citizens and were turned into refugees indefinitely', as Issam Nassar explains, these photos offer a mode of passage between two interconnected experiences.[59]

Another issue of the *Tricontinental* presents a series of fourteen black-and-white photographs from a Fatah training camp, all without caption, following the reporting of 'A. Zapata' (Ulises Estrada) on the progress of the Palestinian cause.[60] An emphasis on the heroic guerillas, Fidel Castro and Che Guevara, as inspiration, dominate the narrative. The first photograph is of a lone boy soldier, standing at full attention, centred in the frame. He stares across the deserted landscape with his back to debris that could be the wreckage of a plane or a makeshift tent. The next photos are all camp scenes, training exercises, and small

Figure 7.5 *Tricontinental* magazine, no. 9 (1968), p. 75

groups of soldiers, mostly unidentifiable outlines, until the last three, which depict combatants climbing across ropes through the trees.

Included are also four nearly identical photographs, as if repeated motion shots, of young militants in the camp jumping over the blaze of a fire. Their toes just clear the sparks that reach upwards from a shallow firey pit, dug roughly in the shape of a burial plot (Figure 7.5).

Athletic, strong and capable, the youths in the images are assembled in a comradeship of readiness. The two most prominent themes in the photography of the issues in the late 1960s and early 1970s are of ruins of bombed out locations (see issue no. 13) and young soldiers performing acrobatic and technical skills in Fatah training camps (issues no. 12, 14 and 24). Some are edited to a modern style, capturing a quality of reiteration and reverberation that echoes the cinematic. Others resemble shapes suggestive of the crude quality of destruction. The images tell the story of colonial displacement. But rather than concentrate on tragedy and victimhood, however, they emphasize agency. They depict refugees as strong and capable militants in the making, symbols of a new revolutionary consciousness.

By 1972, the *Tricontinental* magazine published an increasing number of stories on Palestine. In an issue otherwise dedicated to Vietnam, an article on Palestine appears following a story on US 'General Issue', or GI, Veterans. The article on veterans explains how many solidiers returning from Vietnam had themselves formed a movement against the war. The issue suggests a connection between these stories indirectly in its cover art. The cover features the large smiling face of Richard Nixon, under the words 'For President', with bullet holes as if the campaign sign had been used for target practice, and on the inside cover, formatted similarly, with a swastika across Nixon's forehead. The connecting of Nazism with Nixon and Vietnam with Palestine foregrounds an article written by Nayif Hawatmeh, Secretary General of the DFLP, on questions related to combat in the struggle for Palestinian rights. The piece advocates for an Arab Socialist Federation and for the greater recognition of the founding of the state of Israel as a continuation of British imperialism in the region with US support.[61]

Despite the increasing recognition and influence of the PLO at the UN after 1974, Cuba's commitment to solidarity with Palestinian organizations only grew. As the *Tricontinental* publications evidence, 1974 seemed to mark an increase in urgency rather than deferral to Palestinain leadership at the UN or in negotiations with Israel. Numbers 36 and 37 of the magazine, published in 1974, both included striking illustrations of Stars of David, one with a photograph of a tank protruding from the centre, another with a daggerlike point dripping what might be blood onto the ground. Antother features a skull and crossbones similar to the design of poison labels in the centre of the star. This repetition of the symbol of Israeli nationalism equated with violence and death accompanies a chronology of Zionist attacks from 1938 to October of 1973. Described as an ongoing genocide, the issues include reporting on chemical warfare used against Palestinian farms, alongside the damning testimony of an Israeli soldier on genocidal tendencies of the state and a poem by Mahmud Darwish, editor of the journal *Shu'un Filastiniyya* (*Palestinian Affairs*). These permutations of narrative and visual communication about the Palestinan struggle reflected ongoing reorientations and repositionings of Cuban foreign policy. The visual elements created contiuity between issues and policy shifts, while suggesting through symbolic language subtleties of the argument, such as a move from national liberation rhetoric to a position against Israel as a genocidal state, akin to the Nazi regime. The subtleties of this shift would not be missed on OSPAAAL's intended audiences. In fact, the image of Palestinian militants became the most prominent of those that figured in OSPAAAL's publications long after 1975, reflecting the way that visual revolutionary aesthetics continued to command inflence even after revolutionary rhetoric strategies had changed.

Conclusion

Cuba and its practices of solidarity with Palestine became a global reference point during the Cold War, not only for their actions and political support but also because of the highly successful campaigns organized by OSPAAAL. Reporting on Palestine in the *Tricontiental* magazine and bulletin shows shifts in Cuba's foreign policy and its connections in the Middle East. It demonstrates Cuba's priorities between the earlier period of inflence at the NAM and its longer entanglements at the UN. Cuba's highly visible demonstration of solidarity with Palestine created a vehicle to shape and transmit ideological positionings. It also allowed Cuba to craft important alliances beyond those available at the level of the nation state. Reporting on Palestine increased in the 1980s, as outrage during the Israeli invasion and occupation of Lebanon sparked a wide international debate. By this period, the number of ongoing national liberation struggles in the global South was quite limited, and many newly formed states found that any ties to revolutionary militarism might invite unwanted divisions at home and sanctions from abroad. Thus, Cuba's ongoing support for militancy was increasingly exceptional.

Notably, OSPAAAL's publications avoided representing factionalism within the Palestinian ranks. It offered no critical views of Palestinian organizations, keeping its appraisal of the conflict focused on Israeli aggression and complicity of other powers, such as the UN, the United States and Great Britain, while providing a voice for leadership outside and within the PLO. The Question of Palestine allowed OSPAAAL to keep attention focused on anti-imperialism, offering a means by which to also describe the ongoing and increasing intervention in Latin American nations by the United States as a similar problem. OSPAAAL continued until July 2019, when the Cuban government decided to finally close its doors.[62]

Notes

1 This publication results from the following research projects: 'Nuevos actores en las relaciones internacionales contemporáneas durante los procesos de descolonización de África, Asia y América Latina (1810–1990). Redes políticas, alianzas y cooperación Sur-Sur', funded by *Comunidad de Madrid* through a multi-year agreement with *Universidad Autónoma de Madrid*, V PRICIT (Reference: SI1/PJI/2019-00493); 'Photographing Revolution: Images of Cuban Solidarity in Transnational Contexts' funded by the Social Sciences and Humanities Research Council of Canada (Reference: 435-2020-0492, Research Ethics Certificate H20-02570). See Yoav Di-Capua, 'Palestine Comes to Paris: The Global Sixties and the Making of a Universal Cause', *Journal of Palestine Studies* 50, no. 1 (2021): 19–50.
2 Hillel Schenker, 'The International Community's Role in Israeli History', *Palestine - Israel Journal of Politics, Economics, and Culture* 20, no. 2–3 (2015): 101–6.
3 For more on this event, see George W. Shepherd, 'Reflections on the Pan-African Cultural Conference in Algiers', *Africa Today* 16, no. 4 (1969): 1–3.
4 See Aldo Marchesi, *Latin America's Radical Left Rebellion and Cold War in the Global 1960s* (Cambridge: Cambridge University Press, 2019) and Alberto Martín Álvarez and Eduardo Rey Tristán. 'La dimensión transnacional de la izquierda armada', *América Latina Hoy* no. 80 (2018): 9–28.
5 See Rebecca Gordon-Nesbitt, *To Defend the Revolution Is to Defend Culture: The Cultural Policy of the Cuban Revolution* (Oakland: PM Press, 2015).
6 Cuba also supported the struggle of other stateless Arab peoples, such as the Dhofaris and the Sahrawis.
7 Interference Document 11. *El diseño a las armas. Los carteles y publicaciones cubanos de la Organización en Solidaridad con los Pueblos de África, Asia y América Latina (OSPAAAL)* (New York: Interference Archive, 2015) and J. C. Robert, 'Disseminating

the Tricontinental', in *The Routledge Handbook of the Global Sixties: Between Protest and Nation-Building*, ed. C. Jian, M. Klimke, M. Kirasirova, M. Nolan, M. Young, and J. Waley-Cohen, 517–47 (New York: Routledge, 2018).

8 See Anne Garland Mahler, *From the Tricontinental to the Global South: Race, Radicalism, and Transnational Solidarity* (Duhram: Duke University Press, 2018); Piero Gleijeses, *Visions of Freedom: Havana, Washington, Pretoria, and the Struggle for Southern Africa 1976–1991* (Chapel Hill: University of North Carolina Press, 2013); Piero Gleijeses, *Conflicting Missions: Havana, Washington, and Africa 1959–1976* (Chapel Hill: University of North Carolina Press, 2002); Kail Argyriadis, Giulia Bonacci, and Adrien Delmas, eds, *Cuba and Africa, 1959–1994: Writing an Alternative Atlantic History* (Johannesburg: Wits University Press, 2020); Christine Hatzky, *Cubans in Angola: South-South Cooperation and Transfer of Knowledge, 1976–1991* (Madison: University of Wisconsin Press, 2015); Damian Fernández, *Cuba's Foreign Policy in the Middle East* (Boulder: West View Press, 1988).

9 Robert Henry, 'Global Palestine: International Solidarity and the Cuban Connection', *Journal of Holy Land and Palestine Studies*, 18, no. 2 (2019): 239–62; Carlos Fernando López de la Torre, 'Encuentros solidarios en épocas revolucionarias. La Revolución Cubana y el Frente Sandinista de Liberación Nacional ante la causa palestina', *Crítica y emancipación. Revista latinoamericana de ciencias sociales* 7, no. 15 (2015): 45–106; David Kopilow, *Castro, Israel and the PLO* (Washington DC: The Cuban-American National Foundation, 1984); and Federico Vélez, *Latin American Revolutionaries and the Arab World: From Suez Canal to the Arab Spring* (Burlington/Surrey: Ashgate, 2016).

10 Hana Sleiman, 'The Paper Trail of a Liberation Movement', *Arab Studies Journal* 24, no. 1 (2016): 42–67, 48–50.

11 Ignacio Klich, 'Cuba's Opposition to Jewish Statehood in Palestine, 1944–49: A Critical Review of Varying Interpretations', *Middle East Journal* 51, no. 3 (1997): 405–6.

12 Rigoberto Menéndez Paredes, 'Del Medio Oriente a la mayor isla del Caribe: los árabes en Cuba', in *Contribuciones árabes a las identidades iberoamericanas*, ed. Lorenzo Agar Corbinos, 17–46. (Madrid: Casa Árabe, 2009).

13 Reinaldo Sánchez Porro, 'Tradición y modernidad: Los judíos en La Habana', *Cuadernos de Historia Contemporánea* 18 (1996): 176–89.

14 Adriana Hernández Gómez de Molina, '¿Judío, o comunista? Una polémica de los 30´ en Cuba', *Temas Americanistas* 43 (2019): 217–30.

15 Full list of the different awards given to Fidel Castro: *Fidel Castro. Soldado de las ideas.* Available online: http://www.fidelcastro.cu/es/reconocimientos/todos (accessed 20 February 2022).

16 Alfred Bérenguer, *Un curé d'Algérie en Amérique latine, 1959-1960* (Algiers: Editions nationales algériennes, 1966), 138.
17 Piero Gleijeses, 'Cuba's First Venture in Africa: Algeria, 1961-1965', *Journal of Latin American Studies* 28, .no. 1 (1996): 159-95.
18 Dario de Urra Torriente, *Che. El embajador viajero. África 1959-1965* (La Habana: Editorial José Martí, 2019).
19 Omar Fernández Cañizares, *Un viaje histórico con el Che* (La Habana: Ciencias Sociales, 2005).
20 Shuqayri gave a negative impression to the Cubans, despite their sympathies for the Palestinian cause. Interview by email with Domingo Amuchastegui (2018).
21 Carrie Cunningham, *Meaning Train: Essays on Religion and Politics* (Bloomington: Archway Publishing, 2019).
22 Ammon Kapeliouk, *Arafat* (Pozuelo del Alarcón: Editorial Espasa Calpe, 2005) and Fadi Bardawil, *Revolution and Disenchantment: Arab Marxism and the Binds of Emancipation* (Durham: Duke University Press, 2020), 173.
23 *The Palestinian Revolution*, Interview with Abu Mayzar, 2011. Available online: http://learnpalestine.politics.ox.ac.uk/uploads/sources/58ec897ef13bf.pdf (accessed 2 May 2021).
24 For a complete biographical information, see Nate George, 'Travelling Theorist: Mehdi Ben Barka and Morocco from Anti-colonial Nationalism to the Tricontinental', in *The Arab Lefts: Histories and Legacies, 1950s-1970s*, ed. Laure Guirguis, 127-47. (Edinburgh: Edinburgh University Press, 2020).
25 Jorge Serguera Riveri, *Che Guevara: La clave africana* (Jaén: Liberman Grupo Editorial, 2008), 341-3.
26 *Tricontinental*, no. 19-20 (1970). 223.
27 They included Ibrahim Abu Sitta, a Jordanian, who was at the time president of the executive committee of the PLO; Husni Khuffash Saleh, Jordanian secretary general of the General Confederation of Palestine Workers; Zuhayr Rayyis, a Jordanian and editor of *Palestina*, a newspaper from Gaza; Abd Al Karim Al Karmi, a Syrian official of the Syrian Ministry of Information and member of the Syrian Communist Party; and Dr. Salah Heddin Dabbagh, Lebanese Palestinian and Director of Foreign Affairs for the PLO. Roger Faligot, *Tricontinentale. Quand Che Guevara, Ben Barka, Cabral, Castro et Hô Chi Minh préparaient la révolution mondiale (1964-1968)*. (Paris: La découverte, 2013), 338-9.
28 Jessica Stites Mor, *South-South Solidarity and the Latin American Left* (Madison: University of Wisconsin Press, 2022).
29 After the defeat of the Six-Days War in 1967, revolutionary positions and subversive armed struggle increased because, among other reasons, of the difficulty of directly facing the Israeli army. See Yezid Sayigh, *Armed Struggle and the Search for*

State. *The Palestinian National Movement 1949–1993*. (Oxford: Oxford University Press, 1997).
30 Interview by email with Osvaldo Cárdenas (2019).
31 Fawwaz Traboulsi, 'De la Suisse orientale au Hanoi arabe: une ville en quête de rôles', in *Beyrouth*, ed. Jad Tabit, 39 (Paris: Institut français d'architecture, 1999).
32 The first director was Jorge José Ricardo Masetti, a journalist and close friend of Fidel Castro and Ernesto Guevara, who disappeared in 1964 in Salta, Argentina, during a guerrilla operation.
33 Menéndez Paredes, 'Del Medio Oriente a la mayor isla del Caribe', 27.
34 *Granma*, 31 July 1970, 8.
35 Regla Fernández González, *Cruzadas de amor: cubanas en el Medio Oriente* (La Habana: Editorial José Martí, 2016). This publication gives interesting information about the ordinary lives of Palestinian and Cuban couples in connection with major cooperation activities.
36 *Granma* followed-up the visit in detail with long articles and many pictures. See *Granma*, 15–19 November 1974.
37 Interview with Regla Fernández Gonzalez, wife of Ernesto Gómez Abascal (Havana, 14 July 2019).
38 Address by Commander in Chief Fidel Castro, President of the Councils of State and Ministers and President of the Non-Aligned Movement, at the thirty-fourth Session of the United Nations General Assembly, New York City, 12 October 1979. Available online: http://www.fidelcastro.cu/en/discursos/speech-delivered-34th-session-united-nations-general-assembly-new-york-city (accessed 25 February 2022).
39 Juan Reinaldo Sánchez, *La vida oculta de Fidel Castro* (Barcelona: Ediciones Península, 2014), 110–29.
40 Fernández, *Cuba's Foreign Policy*, 72–3.
41 The only partial history of OSPAAAL has been written by Blasson Borges and Lenay Alexandra, in *Des «faits» qui parlent. Étude comparative du project de communication de quatre ONG à Cuba et au Costa Rica*, 173–228 (Louvain: Presses universitaires de Louvain, 2009).
42 Interview by email with Domingo Amuchastegui (2018).
43 Interview by email with Leonel Nodal, Cuban Journalist and husband of Mayra Díaz Arango (2020).
44 See Alfons González Quesada, *Mi tío no se llama Sam. Estados Unidos en la gráfica cubana*. (Barcelona: RM Verlag, 2016).
45 Trisha Ziff ed., *Che Guevara: Revolutionary and Icon* (New York: Abrams Image, 2006).
46 Zeina Maasri, *Cosmopolitan Radicalism: The Visual Politics of Beirut's Global Sixties* (Cambridge: University of Cambridge, 2020), 1.

47 Ulises Estrada Leiscalle was a well-known member of the Cuban intelligence service and later a diplomat of the Ministry of Foreign Affairs. He sometimes used the pen name A. Zapata. He had a close relation with Che Guevara and a sentimental relationship with Tamara Bunke, alias Tania. Later in his life he became director of the *Tricontinental* magazine. Estrada also played a significant role in several episodes of Cuban foreign relations. Like him, many Cuban political actors abroad participated in a variety of roles and on several continents.
48 Hani Jawhariyyeh (1939–76) was a Palestinian photographer, cinematographer and co-founder of the Palestine Film Unit. He is known for his images of Palestinian freedom fighters of the 1960s and 1970s. He was killed in 1976 while in Lebanon documenting a battle. In 1982, during the Israeli invasion of Lebanon, Jawhariyyeh's work was seized by the Israeli army and transferred to the Israeli military archive, where it still is located. See for images https://p21.gallery/exhibitions/the-void-project-the-found-archive-of-hani-jawherieh.
49 This machine gun also became a symbol of resistance and liberation in the global South. For more see Mikhail Kalashnikov and Elena Joly, *Kalashnikov: The Gun That Changed the World* (Malden: Polity Press, 2006). See also Anna Clayfield, 'Militarized by Moscow? Re-examining Soviet Influence on Cuba in the 1970s', in *Cuba's Forgotten Decade. How the 1970s Shaped the Revolution*, ed. Emily J. Kirk, Anna Clayfield, and Isabel Story, 71–85 (Lanham: Lexington Books, 2018).
50 Paula Barreiro López, 'Un Vietnam en el campo de la cultura: objetos promiscuos en el arsenal de la guerrilla', in *Atlántico Frío. Historias transnacionales del arte y la política en los tiempos del Telón de Acero*, ed. Paula Barreiro López (Madrid: Brumaria, 2019), 131–9.
51 Catherine Dossin, 'The Brush and the Kalashnikov: The Political Vision of the Jeune Peinture from Paris to Beirut', in *Past Disquiet. Artists, International Solidarity and Museums in Exile*, ed. Kristine Khouri and Rashe Salti, 279–96 (Warsaw: Museum of Modern Art in Warsaw, 2018).
52 By the time of the creation of OSPAAAL, Algeria had already gained its independence, but visuality of its struggle still influenced the following solidarity campaigns. The first photobook in solidarity with an Arab cause was published by Dirk Alvermann, *Algeria* (Berlin: Rütten & Loening, 1960). Also available online: https://youtu.be/rM0vgOWU8q0 (20 February 2022).
53 OSPAAAL printed a total of 333 posters (Richard Frick *The Tricontinental Solidarity Poster*, 2002) of which 37 depicted conflicts in the Middle East (11, 1 % of the total).
54 See Maasri, *Cosmopolitan Radicalism*, 8–9.
55 Lincoln Cushing, ¡*Revolución!: Cuban Poster Art* (San Francisco: Chronicle, 2003).
56 Cuban artists who designed the poster in solidarity with Palestine by year were Alfredo Rostgaard (1968), Rafael Morante Boyerizo (1971, 1982), Tony Évora (1967), Berta Abelénda Fernández (1968), Rafael Enríquez Vega (1980, 1983),

Alberto Blanco González (1983), Gladys Acosta (1977), Ramón González Alonso (1975), Rolando Córdova Cabeza (1979), Andrés Hernández (1974), Olivio Martínez Viera (1973), Lázaro Abreu Padrón (1968), Victor Manuel Navarrete (1978), and Jesús Forjans Boade (1968). Most OSPAAAL posters are available online: http://www.ospaaal.com/ (22 February 2022). Damian Viñuela and José Menéndez. *El cartel de la Revolución. Carteles cubanos entre 1959 y 1989*. (La Habana: Ediciones Polymita, 2017).

57 Interview with Maria Antonia Bornot, *Prensa Latina*, Image Archive, Havana, (2021); interview with Eva Dumenigo, OSPAAAL archivist, Biblioteca Casa Editorial Abril, Havana (2021); and interview with Rafael Enriquez, OSPAAAL poster artist, Havana (2021).
58 *Tricontinental*. no. 3 (1967): 73.
59 Nasser Issam, 'Photography of the Oppressed: On Photographing the Palestinian Refugees', *International Journal for History, Culture and Modernity* 8 (2020): 39.
60 *Tricontinental*. no. 9 (1969): 58–72.
61 *Tricontinental*. no. 31 (1972).
62 Fernando Camacho Padilla and Eugenia Palieraki, 'Hasta Siempre, OSPAAAL!', *NACLA Report on the Americas* 51, no. 4 (2019): 410–21.

Bibliography

Alvermann, Dirk. *Algeria*. Berlin: Rütten & Loening, 1960.
Argyriadis, Kail, Giulia Bonacci, and Adrien Delmas, eds. *Cuba and Africa, 1959–1994: Writing an alternative Atlantic history*. Johannesburg: Wits University Press, 2020.
Bardawil, Fadi. *Revolution and Disenchantment: Arab Marxism and the Binds of Emancipation*. Durham: Duke University Press, 2020.
Barreiro López, Paula. 'Un Vietnam en el campo de la cultura: objetos promiscuos en el arsenal de la guerrilla', in *Atlántico Frío. Historias transnacionales del arte y la política en los tiempos del Telón de Acero*, edited by Paula Barreiro López, 117–54. Madrid: Brumaria, 2019.
Bérenguer, Alfred. *Un curé d'Algérie en Amérique latine, 1959–1960*. Algiers: Editions nationales algériennes, 1966.
Borges, Blasson, and Lenay Alexandra. *Des «faits» qui parlent. Étude comparative du project de communication de quatre ONG à Cuba et au Costa Rica*. Louvain: Presses universitaires de Louvain, 2009.
Camacho Padilla, Fernando, and Eugenia Palieraki, 'Hasta Siempre, OSPAAAL!'. *NACLA Report on the Americas* 51, no. 4 (2019): 410–21.
Clayfield, Anna. 'Militarized by Moscow? Re-examining Soviet Influence on Cuba in the 1970s', in *Cuba's Forgotten Decade. How the 1970s Shaped the Revolution*, edited

by Emily J. Kirk, Anna Clayfield, and Isabel Story, 71–85. Lanham: Lexington Books, 2018.

Cunningham, Carrie. *Meaning Train: Essays on Religion and Politics.* Bloomington: Archway Publishing, 2019.

Cushing, Lincoln. *¡Revolución!: Cuban Poster Art.* San Francisco: Chronicle, 2003.

Di-Capua, Yoav. 'Palestine Comes to Paris: The Global Sixties and the Making of a Universal Cause'. *Journal of Palestine Studies* 50, no. 1 (2021): 19–50.

Dossin, Catherine. 'The Brush and the Kalashnikov: The Political Vision of the Jeune Peinture from Paris to Beirut', in *Past Disquiet: Artists, International Solidarity and Museums in Exile,* edited by Kristine Khouri and Rashe Salti, 279–96. Warsaw: Museum of Modern Art in Warsaw, 2018.

Faligot, Roger. *Tricontinentale. Quand Che Guevara, Ben Barka, Cabral, Castro et Hô Chi Minh préparaient la révolution mondiale (1964–1968).* Paris: La découverte, 2013.

Fernández, David. *Cuba's Foreign Policy in the Middle East.* Boulder: West View Press, 1988.

Fernández Cañizares, Omar. *Un viaje histórico con el Che.* La Habana, Ciencias Sociales, 2005.

Fernández González, Regla. *Cruzadas de amor: cubanas en el Medio Oriente.* La Habana: Editorial José Martí, 2016.

Frick, Richard. *The Tricontinental Solidarity Poster.* Bern: Commedia-Verlag, 2002.

George, Nate. 'Travelling Theorist: Mehdi Ben Barka and Morocco from Anti-colonial Nationalism to the Tricontinental', in *Arab Lefts: Histories and Legacies, 1950s-1970s,* edited by Laure Guirguis, 127–47. Edinburgh: Edinburgh University Press, 2020.

Gleijeses, Piero. *Conflicting Missions: Havana, Washington, and Africa 1959–1976.* Chapel Hill: The University of North Carolina Press, 2002.

Gleijeses, Piero. 'Cuba's First Venture in Africa: Algeria, 1961–1965'. *Journal of Latin American Studies* 28, no. 1 (1996): 159–95.

Gleijeses, Piero. *Visions of Freedom: Havana, Washington, Pretoria, and the Struggle for Southern Africa 1976–1991.* Chapel Hill: The University of North Carolina Press, 2013.

González Quesada, Alfons. *Mi tío no se llama Sam. Estados Unidos en la gráfica cubana.* Barcelona: RM Verlag, 2016.

Gordon-Nesbitt, Rebecca. *To Defend the Revolution is to Defend Culture: The Cultural Policy of the Cuban Revolution.* Oakland: PM Press, 2015.

Hatzky, Christine. *Cubans in Angola: South-South Cooperation and Transfer of Knowledge, 1976–1991.* Madison: University of Wisconsin Press, 2015.

Henry, Robert. 'Global Palestine: International Solidarity and the Cuban Connection'. *Journal of Holy Land and Palestine Studies* 18, no. 2 (2019): 239–62.

Hernández Gómez de Molina, Adriana. '¿Judío, o comunista? Una polémica de los 30´ en Cuba'. *Temas Americanistas* no. 43 (2019): 217–30.

Interfence Document 11. *El diseño a las armas. Los carteles y publicaciones cubanos de la Organización en Solidaridad con los Pueblos de África, Asia y América Latina (OSPAAAL)*. New York: Interfence Archive, 2015.

Kalashnikov, Mikhail, and Elena Joly. *Kalashnikov: The Gun That Changed the World*. Malden: Polity Press, 2006.

Kapeliouk, Ammon. *Arafat*. Pozuelo del Alarcón: Editorial Espasa Calpe, 2005.

Klich, Ignacio. 'Cuba's Opposition to Jewish Statehood in Palestine, 1944–49: A Critical Review of Varying Interpretations', *Middle East Journal* 51, no. 3 (1997): 405–17.

Kopilow David. *Castro, Israel and the PLO*. Washington DC: The Cuban-American National Foundation, 1984.

López de la Torre, Carlos Fernando. 'Encuentros solidarios en épocas revolucionarias. La Revolución Cubana y el Frente Sandinista de Liberación Nacional ante la causa palestina'. *Crítica y emancipación. Revista latinoamericana de ciencias sociales* 7, no. 15 (2015): 45–106.

Maasri, Zeina. *Cosmopolitan Radicalism: The Visual Politics of Beirut's Global Sixties*. Cambridge: University of Cambridge, 2020.

Mahler, Anne Garland. *From the Tricontinental to the Global South: Race, Radicalism, and Transnational Solidarity*. Duhram: Duke University Press, 2018.

Marchesi, Aldo. *Latin America's Radical Left Rebellion and Cold War in the Global 1960s*. Cambridge: Cambridge University Press, 2019.

Martín Álvarez, Alberto, and Eduardo Rey Tristán. 'La dimensión transnacional de la izquierda armada'. *América Latina Hoy* 80 (2018): 9–28.

Menéndez Paredes, Rigoberto. 'Del Medio Oriente a la mayor isla del Caribe: los árabes en Cuba', in *Contribuciones árabes a las identidades iberoamericanas*, edited by Lorenzo Agar Corbinos, 17–46. Madrid: Casa Árabe, 2009.

Nasser, Issam, 'Photography of the Oppressed: On Photographing the Palestinian Refugees'. *International Journal for History, Culture and Modernity* no. 8 (2020): 38–57.

Sánchez, Juan Reinaldo. *La vida oculta de Fidel Castro*. Barcelona: Ediciones Península, 2014.

Sánchez Porro, Reinaldo. 'Tradición y modernidad: Los judíos en La Habana'. *Cuadernos de Historia Contemporánea* no. 18 (1996): 176–89.

Sayigh, Yezid. *Armed Struggle and the Search for State. The Palestinian National Movement 1949–1993*. Oxford: Oxford University Press, 1997.

Hillel Schenker. 'The International Community's Role in Israeli History'. *Palestine: Israel Journal of Politics, Economics, and Culture* 20, no. 2–3 (2015): 101–6.

Serguera Riveri, Jorge. *Che Guevara: La clave africana*. Jaén: Liberman Grupo Editorial, 2008.

Shepherd, George. W. 'Reflections on the Pan-African Cultural Conference in Algiers'. *Africa Today* 16, no. 4 (1969): 1–3.

Sleiman, Hana. 'The Paper Trail of a Liberation Movement'. *Arab Studies Journal* 24, no. 1 (2016): 42–67.

Stites Mor, Jessica. *South-South Solidarity and the Latin American Left*. Madison: University of Wisconsin, 2022.

Traboulsi, Fawwaz. 'De la Suisse orientale au Hanoi arabe: une ville en quête de rôles', in *Beyrouth*, edited by Jad Tabit, 28–41. Paris: Institut français d'architecture, 2001.

Tricontinental. *Palestine: Crisis and Liberation*. Havana: Instituto del Libro, 1970.

Urra Torriente, Dario de. *Che. El embajador viajero. África 1959–1965*. La Habana: Editorial José Martí, 2019.

Vélez, Federico. *Latin American Revolutionaries and the Arab World: From Suez Canal to the Arab Spring*. Burlington/Surrey: Ashgate, 2016.

Viñuela, Damian, and José Menéndez. *El cartel de la Revolución. Carteles cubanos entre 1959 y 1989*. La Habana: Ediciones Polymita, 2017.

Young, Robert. J. C. 'Disseminating the Tricontinental', in *The Routledge Handbook of the Global Sixties: Between Protest and Nation-Building*, edited by C. Jian, M. Klimke, M. Kirasirova, M. Nolan, M. Young, and J. Waley-Cohen, 517–47. New York: Routledge, 2018.

Ziff, Trisha, ed. *Che Guevara: Revolutionary and Icon*. New York: Abrams Image, 2006.

8

Palestinian voices in the *Tricontinental*: Revolutionary journalism and the literary history of Palestine solidarity

Anna Bernard

In 1979, the Cuban state-sponsored periodical *Tricontinental Bulletin* published a special issue 'dedicated to the Arab people's struggle against aggressive Zionism'.[1] The lead article by Nazim Abu Nidal – identified as the President of the Union of Writers and Journalists of Palestine in Lebanon – is emphatically titled 'The Reason for Internationalist Solidarity with the Palestinian Revolution'. Abu Nidal argues that the Palestinian struggle deserves the reader's support not simply because of the justness of its cause but also because of its strategic importance to the global fight against capitalism and imperialism:

> [T]he Palestinian and Arab liberation movements play the part of the Irish 'lever' … for the world capitalist system, through whose main arteries Arab oil runs … Internationalist solidarity with the Palestinian and Arab liberation movements and the participation alongside them in obtaining victories will deal mortal wounds to imperialism, even now reeling from sharp economic, social and political crises.[2]

Abu Nidal's statement is notable for not only its rousing tone and Marxist vocabulary but also its explicit assurance that the Palestinian struggle is crucial to the future 'victory of mankind', by which he means the advent of revolutionary socialism.[3] His declaration has a ritual quality to it: rather than developing his claims in detail, Abu Nidal affirms the righteousness of positions that he assumes the *Tricontinental*'s readers already hold. His authority is derived both from his mobilization of an internationally recognized set of references that were well established by the late 1970s and from his identity as a Palestinian; the latter gives his appeal a sincerity and urgency that an identical call for solidarity from a non-Palestinian would lack.

This chapter addresses the *Tricontinental* publications as a key site for Palestinians' international promotion of their revolution in the long 1970s. The Palestinian revolution took on particular prominence during this period as a site of continuing national liberation struggle at a time when many of the Asian and African anticolonial independence movements of the 1950s and 1960s had run their course. Like Fernando Camacho Padilla and Jessica Stites Mor (this volume), I take my examples from the *Tricontinental Bulletin* (1966–80) and *Tricontinental* magazine (1967–98), which were published and distributed in Spanish, English, French and sometimes Arabic and Italian by the Havana-based Organization of Solidarity with the Peoples of Asia, Africa and Latin America (OSPAAAL).[4] These periodicals articulated an explicitly Third Worldist, internationalist and revolutionary solidarity with struggles in Palestine, southern Africa, Central America, Puerto Rico, Vietnam, Cambodia, Korea, Western Sahara, Angola and more. They documented the movements' challenges and successes, analyzed their strategies and tactics, and – most importantly – celebrated their continued resistance, which they presented as part of a popular struggle against capitalist imperialism that would eventually triumph. A statement that closes a 1975 English-language issue of the *Bulletin* (no. 97) sums up the publications' stance: 'We are optimists because we are fighters and we are fighters because we are optimists.'[5]

The *Tricontinental* constitutes an increasingly well-known if still understudied archive. An emerging body of scholarship focusing on the inaugural (and only) Tricontinental Conference in Havana in January 1966 and its legacy often draws on the *Tricontinental* as evidence for its accounts.[6] The Tricontinental Conference joined Latin America to the Afro-Asian 'worldmaking' project declared at the Bandung Conference in 1955, but it articulated a more radical internationalist and anticapitalist vision than its predecessor.[7] OSPAAAL, which arose from the conference, was funded by the Cuban government until its dissolution in 2019, with the stated mission of 'coordinat[ing] revolutionary organizations worldwide'.[8] The *Tricontinental* publications, along with the iconic posters that came folded inside the magazine, were the main vehicle through which OSPAAAL disseminated its ideas internationally.[9] Robert Young suggests that the Cuban government conceived of this material as 'anti-propaganda, since it was directed against the misinformation and anti-leftist propaganda circulated by the world's capitalist press'.[10]

While there has been some important work on the representation of Palestine in the *Tricontinental*,[11] this remarkable archive of revolutionary journalism, theory, poetry and prose deserves more recognition and investigation by scholars of the history of international solidarity with Palestine. In this chapter, I consider a selection of pieces published in the *Tricontinental* between 1971 and 1979 from the perspective of the literary history of Palestine solidarity.[12] The *Tricontinental* archive reminds us that there are models for the kind of internationalist solidarity that we need today, and that literature in all its forms is an indispensable site for imagining and building such a solidarity. I examine not only what Palestinian voices in the *Tricontinental* say but also how they say it, focusing on the form, style and address of different kinds of profiles of Palestinian leaders and fighters, specifically interviews and testimony. These texts demonstrate Palestinians' role in globalizing their revolution by foregrounding their subjects' own (often translated) words, which like Abu Nidal's typically emphasize the Palestinian revolution's contribution to a worldwide struggle against capitalist imperialism. Thus, as Nate George observes, the *Tricontinental* 'provided a unique platform for Palestinians to narrate their own personal and collective histories, as well as the space to advance their own political aims'.[13] But this was a reciprocal endeavour, since the *Tricontinental* also presents the Palestinian revolution as a source of inspiration for readers, employing a transnational vocabulary and iconography of revolutionary heroism and asserting the movement's exemplarity for other struggles.

This line of enquiry builds on my interest in the role that cultural production plays in movements of international solidarity, especially solidarity with Palestine, from the long 1970s to the present.[14] While the *Tricontinental* texts mostly do not fall within the creative genres of fiction, drama or poetry, they play an equally important role in constructing *an other aesthetics*, through which 'worldviews that support the collective struggle to make and defend [another] possible world' beyond the present conjuncture are not only reflected but also constituted.[15] These texts promote a lexicon of heroism and struggle, experiment with journalistic conventions and find ways of dramatizing Palestinian fighters' political and military analysis alongside – and often in place of – accounts of their lives. Recognizing the forms and techniques of such works as examples of aesthetic practice in themselves is crucial to our understanding of how the literature of international solidarity makes its case. This remains a rare approach in dominant formations of both history and literary studies: the former tends to privilege the content of revolutionary texts over their forms, and the latter (with some notable exceptions[16]) tends to disregard revolutionary texts as a proper subject for analysis.

In what follows, I address this gap by highlighting ways in which Palestinian speech is represented in the *Tricontinental* in the long 1970s and examining the kind of solidarity between Palestinian protagonists and readers that these representations seek to develop. I also discuss some of the pitfalls of the *Tricontinental*'s formulations of solidarity, not least its problematic representations of women. I focus on the interview and testimony forms not only because they are among the most common genres used to represent Palestinians in the *Tricontinental* but also because they underline the challenge of engaging critically with forms that are not typically recognized as literary. This challenge becomes particularly apparent when considering the Latin American *testimonio*, which has attracted significant literary-critical attention,[17] alongside the interview, which has not. Looking at these forms together makes it possible to appreciate the features and techniques that they share as well as those that are distinct and to see both forms as examples of literary craft.

The point I want to emphasize above all is that in these texts Palestinians rarely speak as victims or solely on the basis of their experience, but instead they are presented as analysts, strategists and leaders. This framing derives from the *Tricontinental*'s political stance – namely, its rejection of a humanitarian understanding of the Palestinian struggle and its celebration of Palestinian armed resistance – but it also stems from specific editorial and narrative decisions by contributing journalists like Osvaldo Ortega and Moises Saab, as I discuss below. This approach is relevant beyond the specific site of Cuba and beyond the period of armed struggle that the *Tricontinental* championed. Instead of an asymmetrical solidarity relation based on the recognition of suffering, the *Tricontinental* promotes a camaraderie that is based not only on shared political commitments but also admiration for and deferral to Palestinians' fortitude and insights.

The *Tricontinental* as an international platform

Before I turn to specific examples, the *Tricontinental*'s significance as a venue for Palestinian self-representation requires further elaboration. After all, the *Tricontinental* was hardly the only international platform where Palestinians spoke for themselves in the long 1970s – as the chapters in this volume demonstrate – and unlike some other sites of cultural production of the period it was not run by Palestinians. International outlets that were Palestinian led include the *PFLP Bulletin*,[18] an English-language monthly published from Beirut by the Popular Front for the Liberation of Palestine (PFLP) in the 1970s and 1980s; the *PLO Information Bulletin*, published in English from Beirut by the Palestine Liberation Organization (PLO) from 1975–91; *Arab Palestinian Resistance*, published in English from Damascus by the Palestine Liberation Army (PLA) from the 1960s to the 1980s; *Fateh*, published in English, French and Italian from Beirut by Fatah in the 1960s and 1970s; *International Documents on Palestine*, an English-language annual produced by the Institute for Palestine Studies in Beirut from 1967 to 1981, alongside their flagship academic journals *Journal of Palestine Studies* (1971–present) and *Revue d'études palestiniennes* (1981–2008); and the work of the Palestine Film Unit, the PLO's filmic arm, which was active from 1968 to 1982.[19] These interventions ranged across cultural, intellectual and organizational activism, demonstrating what Dina Matar has described as 'the PLO's investment in and attention to diverse communicative platforms and cultural genres to mobilise a Palestinian-centric revolutionary aesthetic in language and image, mediate a new visibility for the Palestinian people, and help transform the organization into the most potent contemporary social and political movement in the Arab world'.[20] Matar is referring primarily to the PLO's Arabic-language outputs aimed at Palestinian and other Arab audiences, but the same can be said of the organization's outreach to non-Arab audiences, which similarly sought to 'resignify what it means to be Palestinian within the discursive frames and images of revolution, resistance, political mobilization, and armed struggle rather than through existential frames of dispossession and statelessness'.[21]

Cuban journalists' representation of Palestinian voices in the *Tricontinental* was also part of the PLO's cultural front, albeit indirectly, in part because of the strong political and diplomatic links between the Cuban government and the PLO in the 1970s.[22] However, OSPAAAL's ambition to facilitate revolution across the entire world meant that the *Tricontinental*'s intended readership and routes of circulation were not confined to Cuba and Latin America, nor indeed to the three continents. On the contrary, the publications sought to address a broad constellation of readers across the global South *and* North, in keeping with a 'deterritorialized vision of imperial power' that included exploited and dispossessed groups in the core capitalist countries, as Anne Garland Mahler has argued.[23] The *Tricontinental*'s implied readers were connected by their political commitments, which were often signalled through markers of geography or race but could not be reduced to these categories. Mahler calls this relationship between political belief and national/racial identity a 'metonymic color politics'. By this she means that although *Tricontinental* iconography often represented the struggle against capitalist imperialism as a clash between a white policeman and Black protestor or fighter, its abstract figuration of these combatants transforms 'color' into 'an umbrella for a resistant politics that does not necessarily denote the race of the peoples who are included' under it.[24]

While there are no subscription or production records for the *Tricontinental* before 1995, the extent of its reach can be seen in the letters from around the globe published in its early issues and from the complete or near-complete collections that today are held in libraries across the world.[25] It makes a notable appearance in Angela Davis' 1974 autobiography, when a Guadeloupean official confiscates boxes of the magazines and posters that Davis and her comrades are carrying from Cuba to Puerto Rico; the official is especially horrified by posters that 'depict Jesus Christ, with haloed head, wielding a carbine on his shoulder'.[26] Such references demonstrate not only the *Tricontinental*'s importance for Black liberation struggles in the United States but also its function as 'an official mouthpiece' for ideas that 'supersede[d] the Cuban state'.[27] Chief among these was a broad definition of imperialism that combined the categories of settler colonialism, exploitation colonialism and Lenin's definition of imperialism as the highest stage of capitalism, with a particular emphasis on the United States as the 'quintessential representative of imperialist aggression'.[28]

This chapter does not try to settle the Question of whether Palestine was central to the *Tricontinental*'s definition of imperialism and its support for armed resistance, as George and Camacho Padilla and Stites Mor argue,[29] or just one of a range of sites it covered, as Mahler's contrasting focus on its representation of the US-Black liberation struggle suggests. Instead, in keeping with the aims of this volume, I seek to challenge the 'persistent exceptionalism' that has 'pervaded and hindered' Palestine scholarship and some historical and contemporary Palestine solidarity activism.[30] The texts I discuss continually negotiate the specificity of Palestinian claims alongside the broader rhetoric of internationalist anti-imperialism. This can be seen in the tension between articulations of collective resistance and individual heroism (the latter often emerging in editorial commentary); the use of the interview form to privilege Palestinians' own political analysis, while also framing it through the perspective of the non-Palestinian interviewer; and the use of the *testimonio* form to lend authority to fighters' narratives. Thus, the Palestinian revolution of the *Tricontinental* is never depicted in isolation, but always in relation to a political project and an audience that is both regional and global.³¹

Heroes and geniuses: Interviews with Palestinian revolutionaries

The interview is probably the most common form in which Palestinian voices are represented in the *Tricontinental*. The origins of the print interview genre have been traced to the rise of penny dailies in the United States and England in the 1830s, a period that was marked by increasing commercial pressures on print journalism as well as rising class consciousness among workers. The form responded to the appetite for human interest stories among the dailies' growing readership, and it borrowed from criminal trials an emphasis on verbatim testimony and question and answer formats, which give the reader a sense of having been present at the scene.³² The rise of television in the 1960s and 1970s gave the interview new prominence as a tool of mass communication that was also 'a form of interpersonal communication between interviewer and interviewee … constituted through mundane practices of talk and interaction'.³³ These 'direct and essentially unscripted encounters between journalists and a wide range of public figures' – particularly elected public officials – rely on the journalist's 'practices of questioning and interrogation' to hold their subjects to account.³⁴ The contemporary news interview in English and in other news settings influenced by this tradition is thus typically characterized by an adversarial relationship between the interviewer and the interviewee.

By contrast, the print interviews in the *Tricontinental* take a much more deferential approach to their subjects. They present the interviewer and the interviewee as a united front, each playing different parts in the effort to inform and inspire the reader. This technique characterizes the contributions of both Osvaldo Ortega and Moises Saab, journalists for the Cuban state news agency Prensa Latina who also wrote for the *Tricontinental*, as well as pieces in which the journalist is not named. The interviews with military leaders are particularly striking for their adulatory tone and their emphasis on their subjects' achievements and insights. For instance, the preface to an unattributed interview with Abu Musa (Said Musa Maragha), the commander of Fatah forces in South Lebanon, describes him as a 'living legend' and a 'war genius'.³⁵ Similarly, another preface in the same issue to an interview with PFLP leader Taysir Kyba calls him 'intransigent, resolute and always striving to learn more in the school of revolutionary daring'.[36] In the text of the interviews that follow, the unnamed interviewer's questions are generally brief and open-ended: 'What is the situation in South Lebanon?'[37] 'What do you think of the "Camp David Accords?"'[38] and 'Who is, according to the Popular Front, the principal enemy of the Palestinian people?'[39] Each of these questions privileges the interviewee's expertise and authority, while also encouraging them to frame the response in a way that will be both relevant and informative for the non-Palestinian reader. Kyba's response to the final question above highlights this approach by succinctly emphasizing the struggle's global relevance: '[Our enemy is] North American imperialism, which is also the enemy of all oppressed peoples. But at the same time we fight its allies, Israel and the Zionist movement, the reactionary Arab forces and the bourgeois forces in the Arab countries.'[40] Like Abu Nidal, Kyba makes an explicit appeal for the reader's solidarity with the Palestinian revolution by insisting that they share a wider struggle.

Yasser Arafat was the most common Palestinian interviewee in the *Tricontinental*, in keeping with its centralization of Arafat and lack of attention to factional divisions within the PLO.[41] In Ortega's 1972 interview with Arafat, conducted at a meeting of the Palestinian National Council in Cairo, the journalist eschews a laudatory preface but maintains the format of open-ended questions that privilege Arafat's own analysis. Ortega asks Arafat for his thoughts on the constitution of Palestinian unity, military strategy on the Israeli and Jordanian battlefronts, the relationship of the Palestinian revolution to other liberation struggles and the Palestinian Jordanian victory at Karameh in 1968, which inflicted heavy casualties on the Israeli forces and led to a significant boost in the PLO's recruitment of soldiers and its material support from Arab states.[42] Ortega defers throughout to Arafat; indeed, he foregrounds this deference, noting at one point that Arafat interrupted Ortega's question 'with a smile' to correct his use of the term 'Jordanian' to 'Jordanian-imperialist'.[43] Arafat's replies repeatedly affirm Palestinian military strength and political consensus: he lists examples of victories in Lebanon and Jordan and minimizes any suggestion of disagreement among Palestinian organizations, which he says are of a tactical nature.[44] An adversarial approach to the interview form – like that frequently directed at Palestinian interviewees in contemporary Euro-North American mainstream news outlets – might challenge Arafat's claims about the significance of these victories and the unanimity of the PLO. Ortega, however, appears to take Arafat at his word by moving on to the next question. Meanwhile, the visual iconography of the piece – which includes a close-up photograph of Arafat, silhouettes of armed fighters and the seals of various Palestinian organizations – reinforces Arafat's assertions by celebrating the figure of the Palestinian *fedayee* and affirming the PLO's internal unity.

An interview with Arafat that appears in the same 1979 issue as Abu Nidal's appeal for internationalist solidarity endorses Arafat's analysis still more explicitly. The interview, conducted by Saab, begins with a lyrical two-page preface describing the neighbourhood in western Beirut where Arafat's office was located. Saab makes his own standpoint clear from the outset: he castigates Israel and the Lebanese 'rightist militias' for their 'continual attacks' on the Palestinian civilian refugee population and laments the Palestinian 'normal way of life [that] was so rudely interrupted by the Israeli occupation'.[45] But it is not until he introduces the figure of Arafat that Saab becomes truly effusive. Arafat is, he says, 'the living symbol of the war that the Palestinian people have been waging in an organized way for nearly 15 years against the fanatical hegemonism of Zionism'.[46] He describes Arafat's manner and physical presence in highly flattering terms: 'Passionate, emphatic, Arafat speaks unequivocally. He gesticulates and gives added force to his statements with his facial expressions and intonation. It is characteristic of him to stress the word horiya [freedom].'[47] Although this emphasis on Arafat's individual heroism and charisma might seem at odds with Saab's earlier praise for Palestinians' collective resistance, these claims are instead presented as complementary. This is achieved by Saab's reliance on a first-person narrative voice, which privileges his own response to the encounter and invites the reader to share his sense of awe at being in Arafat's presence, and by his reiteration of the idea that Arafat and the revolution are interchangeable. At the end of the preface, he juxtaposes an image of the 'Palestinian people stood firm, loyal to the cause of liberation' with Arafat's 'confidence that, no matter how long it might take, the Palestinian people would win'.[48] The images used in the piece also elevate Arafat more obviously than those of the Ortega interview. In addition to half a dozen photographs of Arafat taken during Saab's interview, the piece includes an image and English translation of a handwritten note in Arabic from Arafat to the readers of the *Tricontinental*, which asserts their shared cause – 'We fight together in the same trench' – and concludes with the phrase 'Revolution until victory!'[49] Here, the link between the Palestinian leader and the reader is cemented through the personal artefact of the handwritten note. Arafat's direct address to the reader bypasses the figure of the journalist, who has now completed his role as intermediary.

The praise bestowed on these Palestinian speakers indicates what Laleh Khalili calls the 'extraordinary coherence of the heroic liberationist narrative' across the various sites of anticolonial struggle from the 1950s to the 1980s.[50] This transnational narrative was characterized by an insistence that armed struggle is 'the only possible path to liberation' and by an emphasis on 'hyper-masculine heroism' exemplified by the figure of Ernesto 'Che' Guevara.[51] The admiring language used to portray the words and deeds of Arafat, Abu Musa, Kyba and other Palestinian fighters would thus have been familiar to the *Tricontinental*'s readers. The weaknesses of the heroic narrative included its unequal gender politics, it's glossing over of divisions within revolutionary movements and a teleological understanding of history that insisted on the inevitable victory of the present struggle, sometimes to the detriment of the movements' strategic decision-making.[52] However, it also made the aims of different anticolonial liberation struggles intelligible to one another and fortified the participants' will to continue the fight. Moreover, in the case of the Palestinian revolution, it helped negate the association of Palestinian statelessness with passivity or victimhood, instead positioning Palestinians as a source of inspiration and leadership for anti-imperial struggles across the world.

An explicit refusal of what Khalili calls the 'trauma drama' of humanitarian representation can be seen in Ortega's profile of the Naher el Bared (Cold River) refugee camp outside Tripoli in Lebanon, which appeared in the *Tricontinental Bulletin* no. 62 in 1971.[53] The title of the article, 'From a Palestinian Ghetto', invites a comparison between the camp and Black-US neighbourhoods as well as the Black liberation and Palestinian struggles, though the analogy is not pursued. In contrast to Ortega's interview with Arafat, this piece takes the form of a narrative: Ortega describes the landscape, the layout of the camp and the conditions in which the residents live, integrating his conversation with members of his PFLP escort into his account. These speakers summarize their party's political platform and describe their work in the camp: 'Tea arrives as Abu [Mustafa] goes on enumerating on his fingers, the enemies and friends of the Resistance.'[54] Throughout the piece, Ortega moves repeatedly from observations of the hardships of camp life to his interlocutors' political ideas and activities, making it clear that the latter is a considered response to the former. To further emphasize this point, the illustrations intersperse photographs of the camp's residents with silhouettes and ink drawings of fighters. Another of the PFLP representatives, Mayed, makes it clear that the party considers military training, political education and community organization to be interconnected parts of the struggle:

In the present stage, it is necessary for our combatants to know how to handle the rifle with their hands and the broadest concepts of Marxism-Leninism with their heads ... There's no water in the camp? The Front must be there to aid and resolve this problem. The same thing with education, illiteracy, social, medical and communal services. And we can go beyond that. Our aid and collaboration are not limited to the refugee camps but take place among peasants and neighboring Lebanese villages. Our party works not only for the Palestinian people but for all Arab peoples.[55]

By foregrounding Mayed and the other speakers' positions and tactics, Ortega refuses the conventional representation of the refugee camp as a site of suffering and stasis.[56] The article does not include any interviews with other members of the camp, and it does not address the speakers' own life experiences. Instead, it privileges his interlocutors' expertise, optimism and determination. Ortega's succinct yet emotive conclusion connects this recognition of the strength of the Palestinian organization to the future of the struggle: 'Farewells, good wishes, smiling, gesticulating children surrounding the car. The new Palestinian generation. The return to dignity or immolation. Then Cold River will be no more than that, and never again the name of a refugee camp.'[57] Here, Ortega looks forward to a Palestinian victory in a more reflective and wistful way than Khalili's characterization of the heroic liberationist discourse allows. He admits that the revolution's victory is not assured, but affirms its necessity, returning the reader's attention to the urgency and integrity of the struggle.

'My life's commitment': Palestinian revolutionary testimony

A different kind of interview, titled 'Testimony of a [female] guerrilla fighter: Words of rage and pain' ('Testimonio de una guerrillera: Palabras de ira y de dolor'), appeared in a 1978 issue of the *Tricontinental* magazine. The piece, again written by Saab, is a profile of Randa Nablusi, a PLO fighter from Nablus who joined the armed struggle as a teenager after Israel's defeat of the Arab armies in June 1967. In 1969, Nablusi was captured and held alongside other women comrades in an Israeli prison; she was released in 1970 following a Red Cross campaign for her release, on the grounds that she was seventeen at the time of her capture. Nablusi then went to fight in Jordan but immediately was caught up in the counterrevolutionary violence of Black September, when, she says, 'the Jordanian authorities had me condemned to death'.[58] The story ends there with an ellipsis: we are not told what happened in the intervening years, nor how Nablusi made her way to Havana, where the interview was conducted.

The piece is narrated in the first person, in the tradition of the Latin American *testimonio*. This form has its roots in the guerrilla narratives (*narraciones guerrilleras*) of the Latin American revolutionary movements of the mid-to-late twentieth century, the most famous example being Che Guevara's memoir of the Cuban revolution, *Pasajes de la guerra revolucionaria* (1963). Juan Duchesne Winter describes Guevara's narrative as a 'programmatic piece of writing with a clear ideological function and propaganda describing an executable project'.[59] In other words, Guevara's testimony has an organizational purpose: his account of the revolution provides an 'executable' model for current and future movements, from the vantage point of someone who fought it. This distinguishes it from the humanitarian equation of testimony with victim narratives: the *testimonio* is an account of a collective struggle, narrated by one of its participants on behalf of the movement.

As presented by Saab (and as indicated by the tension in his subtitle, 'Words of rage and pain'), Nablusi's testimony straddles both conceptions of the form. Unlike Guevara's narrative or other classic *testimonios* like that of the Sandinista leader Omar Cabezas, Nablusi's account offers only brief and vague references to armed combat, though this is potentially to protect the interviewee. Instead, the narrative is concerned mainly with Nablusi's story of her imprisonment, in keeping with the kinds of testimonies circulated by human rights organizations like Amnesty International that focus on the experiences of political prisoners. Nablusi reports a wide range of Israeli atrocities, both in and beyond the prison: the physical and mental torture of Palestinian prisoners, the detention and abuse of their family members, the use of napalm during the June 1967 war and home demolitions. Nablusi is eloquent on this last topic: 'This politics of the demolition of homes, perhaps the most intimate thing a civilized human being has, the most personal, is still a constant, as UN documents prove.'[60] The appeal to a common humanity shared by the narrator and the reader draws on a language of humanitarian feeling that is heightened by the language of intimacy and privacy that characterizes her representation of the home. It also makes direct reference to the international legal authority of the UN, in line with the conventions of humanitarian testimony.

However, Nablusi's narrative is notably not focused on her individual experience but on shared experiences of suffering and, more prominently, acts of collective organization and resistance. Her account of the Israeli state's attempt to demolish her family home to punish her family for her militancy centres the collective act of resistance that thwarted it: 'Dozens of men and women from the town gathered in the house and said that they'd have to blow it up with them inside'.⁶¹ Her narrative of her time in prison describes diverse practices of torture but offers few details of her own ordeal: she speaks either in the first-person plural or relates acts of violence inflicted on other people. She gives equal attention to a successful ten-day hunger strike that she organized with her comrades, which demanded that as political prisoners they be housed separately from criminals. She also notes their organization of a programme of political and literacy education for detained relatives of combatants, 'in order to incorporate them into the active Resistance'.⁶² In this way, the piece foregrounds a common Palestinian heroism and a collective programme of resistance. It emphasizes Nablusi's commitment to the national liberation struggle, which it depicts as representative of that of all Palestinians, and invites the reader to admire and learn from her actions.

Saab's profile also highlights Nablusi's political analysis, although the use of the testimony form integrates these insights into her life story rather than offering them as the main thrust of the piece, in contrast to the interviews discussed above. Yet Nablusi in fact has more to say about the Israeli state's strategies and tactics than the other interviewees I have discussed, on the basis of her authority as a former political prisoner. For instance, in a brief account of her trial in the Israeli military courts, she observes that the process is 'very superficial and paradoxically hands down higher sentences than those established by the Zionists' own laws. There no prisoner has a case: all are guilty and the defence's arguments fall on deaf ears ["son palabras muertas", lit. "are dead words"]'.⁶³ Here Nablusi also praises the work of her lawyer, the celebrated German Israeli defender Felicia Langer, who was a member of the Israeli Communist Party (Rakah) and represented hundreds of Palestinians in the Israeli courts from the mid-1960s to the 1980s. Nablusi cites Langer's 1974 book *With My Own Eyes* (circulated internationally in English, German and Japanese as well as Hebrew and Arabic) in support of her account, gesturing towards the *Tricontinental*'s international readership while also suggesting that the courts can be seen as another site of battle complementing the armed struggle. Nablusi also says that she was eventually released because of international protests against 'the crimes of the genocidal Israelis' in the occupied Palestinian territories, signalling the measurable impact of international solidarity activism.⁶⁴

However, the visual framing of the piece undermines this foregrounding of Nablusi's insights by linking her gender identity to the humanitarian representation of Palestinian suffering. An accompanying photograph of

Nablusi smoking a cigarette in a chair next to a bookcase presents the face of the fighter as calm and resolute, ready to continue the struggle that she calls 'my life's commitment' ('el compromiso de mi vida').[65] The portrait stands out in the *Tricontinental*'s coverage of the Palestinian struggle, which did not often feature images of women.[66] Yet Nablusi is not wearing a *kufiyya*, as Arafat and Abu Musa do in the portraits accompanying their interviews, and as the PFLP fighter and international icon Leila Khaled did in her famous portraits. There are also no photographs or drawings of fighters with guns used as illustration, as in the other pieces I have discussed. Instead, the reader is presented with photographs of a bandaged child and of the faces of unidentified corpses, as well as a drawing of a woman breastfeeding a baby next to a drawing of Nablusi's face. The choice of these images resonates with Nablusi's broader emphasis on Israeli atrocities – though not the specific crimes that she mentions – but it also connects her identity as a woman to Khalili's observation that the 'protagonist' of the 'trauma drama' is a 'suffering woman carrying a limp child.'[67] From the illustrations alone, the reader would not be able to recognize the profile as the testimony of an armed combatant.

Saab's editorial commentary mitigates this effect by emphasizing Nablusi's status as a fighter who is both personally heroic and representative of the heroism of the wider struggle. In a brief preface, he identifies her as a 'Palestinian combatant' who spoke to him of 'rebellion and her people's struggle; of her action, which is also a reflection of other actions that multiply in the face of repression and death.'[68] As in Saab's profile of Arafat, here the story of the individual Palestinian fighter stands in for the story of the Palestinian revolution, without reference to her gender. However, in the conclusion, he notes the softness of Nablusi's voice and lyrically describes her face as decorated with the colours of the Palestinian flag: 'The green of its usurped fields; the black of the mourning sown by the Zionists; the red of the blood spilled in the fight against the occupation and the white of the peace that this people will one day win.'[69] These lines layer together multiple forms of appeal: elegy, celebration of armed struggle and invocation of a coming victory. However, they also uncomfortably equate the body of the woman with the body of the nation and thus risk turning Nablusi from the active subject of the revolution into its object. It is hard to imagine Saab describing Arafat in such terms, as a canvas for the inscription of the revolution rather than the engine of its future triumph.

The problematic framing of Nablusi's testimony upholds Khalili's criticism of the masculinist assumptions of the heroic liberationist discourse, which struggles to accept women as revolutionary actors and thinkers despite women's extensive participation in the Palestinian national liberation movement (both then and now) and in many other revolutionary struggles.[70] Still, the record of Nablusi's speech remains: as Saab puts it at the end of his opening paragraph, '*these were her words* of rage and pain' (emphasis added).[71] As in my discussion of the interviews above, I am less interested in the question of whether Saab's presentation accurately transcribes what Nablusi said than in the editorial decision to present her account as if it were being spoken directly to the reader. The use of the *testimonio* form asks the reader to understand her narrative as a document of revolutionary strategy as well as revolutionary experience, and to see the Palestinian struggle as part of the same fight as contemporaneous liberation movements in the Americas. As if to emphasize this point, the piece is followed directly by a special section on poetry by 'poet-combatants or combatant poets' ('poetas combatientes o combatientes poetas'), which showcases poems written by participants in struggles in Guatemala, El Salvador, Uruguay, Peru, Nicaragua, Cuba, Argentina, Bolivia and Chile.[72] The juxtaposition of the explicitly literary genre of the poem with Nablusi's testimony invites the reader to see her words as an equally important commemoration of the Palestinian struggle and to welcome her as a fellow comrade in arms.

Conclusion

Mahler writes of the *Tricontinental* and its legacy that 'Tricontinentalist writers beg Tricontinentalist readers who are as internationalist in their thinking and understanding of oppression and resistance as they are'.[73] She thus identifies the *Tricontinental* as a point of origin for a much larger body of revolutionary internationalist and anti-imperialist thought that came after it instead of approaching it only or even primarily as a document of Cuban internationalism. This is a useful way of thinking about what the representation of Palestinian voices in the *Tricontinental* might mean today, particularly for non-Palestinians seeking to act in effective solidarity with the ongoing Palestinian struggle. This archive begs readers who are equally internationalist in their thinking, even though the conditions in which that internationalism can be conceived and practised are now markedly different.

A central tenet of the idea of solidarity is that the solidarity activist responds to a call for action from the main actors in a particular local or national struggle rather than imposing their own agenda on those actors. A key question raised by the *Tricontinental* archive is 'How do we respond to a call from the past?'

I contend that this archive's emphasis on the communication of Palestinians' political beliefs, its efforts to further the reader's political education and its foregrounding of Palestinian heroism and collective endeavour remain relevant even after the defeat of the phase of the armed struggle it champions. To a contemporary reader, the revolutionary optimism of these pieces might seem naïve or voluntarist, their register and vocabulary insufficiently critical and their imagery uncomfortably martial and masculinist. But they present a sharp contrast with later calls for solidarity with Palestine that only ask for recognition of their suffering.

The international platforms from which Palestinians speak today reach a much wider audience than the *Tricontinental* ever did. Where an issue of the *Bulletin* or magazine might have reached fifty thousand international readers at best, now a video of a Palestinian poet performing their work on YouTube can reach over a million.[74] Yet it is still relatively rare for members of the contemporary Palestinian resistance to have the chance to speak to an audience that shares their political convictions without having to try to make their commitments palatable to readers and listeners with very different beliefs. There are signs that the situation is changing. The recent appointment of Mohammed El-Kurd as the Palestine correspondent at the US magazine *The Nation* and, with his sister Mona, as one of *Time* magazine's People of the Year – neither of which are radical publications – suggests that Palestinians who 'Call things as they are', as El-Kurd puts it, by using terms of analysis like 'Settler colonialism and occupation', now have increased their share of what Edward Said famously called 'permission to narrate'.[75] This is part of a larger turn to anticapitalist and anti-imperialist commitments among a broader metropolitan audience than has been seen at any time since the era of the *Tricontinental*. The *Tricontinental* archive is a testament to the lasting power of a solidarity built on these principles.

Notes

1 'To the reader', *Tricontinental Bulletin*, 117, 1979, 2.
2 Abu Nidal, N. 'The Reason for Internationalist Solidarity with the Palestinian Revolution', *Tricontinental Bulletin*, 117, 1979, 5.
3 Ibid.
4 These are the dates of publication cited in Robert Young, 'Disseminating the Tricontinental', in *The Routledge Handbook of the Global Sixties: Between Protest and Nation-Building*, ed. Chen Jian, Martin Klimke, Masha Qirasirova, Mary Nolan,

Marlyn Young, and Joanna Waley-Cohen, 530–2 (Abingdon: Routledge, 2018). In what follows, I use the title *Tricontinental* to refer generically to both the *Bulletin* and the magazine. Citations are taken from Spanish, French and English-language issues, depending on availability. All translations from Spanish and French are my own.
5 *Tricontinental Bulletin*, no. 97, 1975.
6 See Roger Faligot, *Tricontinentale. Quand Che Guevara, Ben Barki, Cabral, Castro et Hô Chi Minh préparent la revolution mondiale (1964–1968)* (Paris: La Découverte, 2013); Nate George '"In the Hour of Arab Revolution": *Tricontinental* and the Question of Palestine', 2014 and 'Traveling Theorist: Mehdi Ben Barka and Morocco from Anti-Colonial Nationalism to the Tricontinental', in *The Arab Lefts: Histories and Legacies, 1950s–1970s*, ed. Laure Guirguis (Edinburgh: Edinburgh University Press, 2020); Anne Garland Mahler, *From the Tricontinental to the Global South: Race, Radicalism, and Transnational Solidarity* (Durham: Duke University Press, 2018); Isaac Saney, 'Dreaming Revolution: Tricontinentalism, Anti-Imperialism and Third World Rebellion', in *The Routledge Handbook of South-South Relations*, ed. Elena Fiddian-Qasmiyeh and Patricia Daley (Abingdon: Routledge, 2018); Robert Young, *Postcolonialism: An Historical Introduction* (Oxford: Wiley-Blackwell, 2001)and 'Disseminating the Tricontinental'.
7 Adom Getachew, *Worldmaking After Empire: The Rise and Fall of Self-Determination* (Princeton: Princeton University Press, 2019).
8 Fernando Camacho Padilla and Eugenia Palieraki, 'Hasta Siempre, OSPAAAL!' *NACLA Report on the Americas* 51, no. 4 (2019): 410.
9 Ibid., 410. For a discussion on the significance of the *Tricontinental* posters, see Camacho Padilla and Stites Mor, this volume; Richard Frick and Ulises Estrada, *The Tricontinental Solidarity Poster* (Bern: Commedia- Verlag, 2003); Lani Hanna, 'Tricontinental's International Solidarity: Emotion in OSPAAAL as Tactic to Catalyze Support of Revolution', *Radical History Review* 136 (2020): 169–84; Jessica Stites Mor, 'Rendering Armed Struggle: OSPAAAL, Cuban Poster Art, and South-South Solidarity at the United Nations', *Jahrbuch für Geschichte Lateinamerikas / Anuario de Historia de América Latina* 56 (2019): 42–65 and *South-South Solidarity and the Latin American Left* (Madison: University of Wisconsin Press, 2022); Young, 'Disseminating the Tricontinental', 525–7. A partial digital archive is available online: http://www.ospaaal.com/ (accessed 9 September 2022).
10 Young, 'Disseminating the Tricontinental', 523.
11 See George, '"In the Hour of Arab Revolution"'; Sorcha Thomson, 'A Cosmovisión of Solidarity: Anticolonial Worldmaking in Havana, Palestine and the Politics of Possibility', *Borderlines*, 6 June 2021; Padilla and Mor, this volume.
12 For a monumental effort to document and catalogue Palestine's literary history (including but not limited to the literary history of Palestine solidarity), see the work of the PalREAD project (Abu-Remaileh).

13 George, '"In the Hour of Arab Revolution"', 9.
14 I discuss the literary history of international solidarity at greater length and with particular attention to the role of fiction, poetry and memoir in previous publications: Anna Bernard, 'Cultural Activism as Resource: Pedagogies of Resistance and Solidarity', *Journal of Postcolonial Writing* 53, no. 3 (2017): 367–79; 'They Are in the Right Because I Love Them': Literature and Palestine Solidarity in the 1980s', in *The Edinburgh Companion to the Postcolonial Middle East*, 275–92, ed. Anna Ball and Karim Mattar (Edinburgh: Edinburgh University Press, 2018); 'You Start Where You Are: Literary Spaces of Palestine Solidarity', *Human Geography* 14, no. 3 (2021): 322–32; as well as my forthcoming book *International Solidarity and Culture: Nicaragua, South Africa, Palestine, 1975–1990*.
15 Jennifer Poncé de Leon, *Another Aesthetics Is Possible: Arts of Rebellion in the Fourth World War* (Durham: Duke University Press, 2020), 4.
16 See Michael Denning, *The Cultural Front: The Laboring of American Culture in the Twentieth Century* (London: Verso, 1996) and Barbara Harlow, *Resistance Literature* (London: Methuen, 1987).
17 See John Beverley, *Testimonio: On the Politics of Truth* (Minneapolis: University of Minnesota Press, 2004) and Georg M. Gugelberger, ed., *The Real Thing: Testimonial Discourse and Latin America* (Durham: Duke University Press, 1996).
18 At the time of writing, some issues of the *PFLP Bulletin* are available for download online: http://pflp-documents.org/tag/pflp-bulletin/ (accessed 15 January 2022).
19 For a comprehensive list of movement publications available in English, Arabic and other languages in 1971, see 'Periodicals in Review: Periodicals and Pamphlets Published by the Palestinian Commando Organizations', *Journal of Palestine Studies* 1, no. 1 (1971): 136–51. For an overview and analysis of the Palestine Film Unit's work, see Nadia Yaqub, *Palestinian Cinema in the Days of Revolution* (Austin: University of Texas Press, 2018).
20 Dina Matar, 'PLO Cultural Activism: Mediating Liberation Aesthetics in Revolutionary Contexts', *Comparative Studies of South Asia, Africa and the Middle East* 38, no. 2 (2018): 354.
21 Ibid., 358–9.
22 See Padilla and Mor, this volume.
23 Mahler, *From the Tricontinental to the Global South*, 195.
24 Ibid., 210.
25 Ibid., 215. In addition to library archives, a number of English-language editions are available in digital format on the website of the San Francisco–based Freedom Archives available online: https://freedomarchives.org/ (accessed 9 September 2022).
26 Angela Davis, *An Autobiography* (New York: Random House, 1974). Kindle edition. loc. 3429.

27 Mahler, *From the Tricontinental to the Global South*, 436, 33.
28 Ibid., 1999–2018.
29 George, '"In the Hour of Arab Revolution"'; Padilla and Mor, this volume.
30 George, '"In the Hour of Arab Revolution"', 7.
31 Ibid., 37.
32 Nils Gunnar Nilsson, 'The Origins of the Interview', *Journalism Quarterly* 48, no. 4 (1971): 707–13.
33 Steven Clayman and Heritage J., *The News Interview: Journalists and Public Figures on the Air* (Cambridge: Cambridge University Press, 2009), 12.
34 Ibid., 2.
35 Abu Musa, 'Au Moyen Orient, la solution est militaire', *Bulletin Tricontinental*, 113 (1978): 17.
36 Taysir Kyba, 'La révolution palestinienne est indestructible', *Bulletin Tricontinental* 113 (1978): 22.
37 Abu Musa, 'Au Moyen Orient', 18.
38 Abu Musa, 'Au Moyen Orient',19; Kyba, 'La révolution palestinienne est indestructible', 28.
39 Kyba, 'La révolution palestinienne est indestructible', 24.
40 Ibid., 24.
41 Padilla and Mor, this volume.
42 Yezid Sayigh, *Armed Struggle and the Search for State: The Palestinian National Movement, 1949–1993* (Oxford: Clarendon, 1997): 177–82.
43 Osvaldo Ortega, 'Palestine: People's Revolution: Interview with Yasser Arafat', *Tricontinental Bulletin* 66 (1972): 31.
44 Ibid., 32.
45 Moises Saab, 'Nobody Lives Twice to See the Glory', *Tricontinental Bulletin* 117 (1979): 6–7.
46 Ibid., 7.
47 Ibid., 7.
48 Ibid., 7.
49 Ibid., 14.
50 Laleh Khalili, *Heroes and Martyrs of Palestine: The Politics of National Commemoration* (Cambridge: Cambridge University Press, 2007), 21.
51 Ibid., 12, 18–20.
52 Ibid., 93. For a discussion of the misogyny and homophobia promoted by some articulations of 'Tricontinental brotherhood', see John Gronbeck-Tedesco, *Cuba, the United States, and Cultures of the Transnational Left, 1930–1975* (Cambridge: Cambridge University Press, 2015), chapter 6.
53 Khalili, *Heroes and Martyrs of Palestine*, 37.

54 Osvaldo Ortega, 'From A Palestinian Ghetto' / 'Desde Un Ghetto Palestino', *Tricontinental Bulletin*, 62 (1971): 18.
55 Ibid., 18–19.
56 This mode of representing the Palestinian camps was well established by the early 1970s: *Sands of Sorrow*, the first international documentary on camp life in Gaza, was produced by the US-based Council for the Relief of Palestinian Refugees in 1950.
57 Ortega, 'From A Palestinian Ghetto', 20.
58 Moises Saab, 'Testimonio de una guerrillera: Palabras de ira y de dolor', *Revista Tricontinental* 57 (1978): 75.
59 Juan Duchesne Winter, *La guerrilla narrada: Acción, acontecimiento, sujeto* (San Juan: Ediciones Callejón, 2010), 38.
60 Saab, 'Testimonio', 70.
61 Ibid., 70.
62 Ibid., 75.
63 Ibid., 72.
64 Ibid., 75.
65 Ibid., 75.
66 Padilla and Mor, this volume.
67 Khalili, *Heroes and Martyrs of Palestine*, 37.
68 Saab, 'Testimonio', 70.
69 Ibid., 75.
70 For a related argument about the masculinism of mid-twentieth-century thought that focuses on the Americas, see María Josefina Saldaña-Portillo, *The Revolutionary Imagination in the Americas and the Age of Development* (Durham: Duke University Press, 2003). On the role of women in the Palestinian revolution from the 1960s to the 1990s, see Amal Kawar, *Daughters of Palestine: Leading Women of the Palestinian National Movement* (Albany: SUNY Press, 1996).
71 Saab, 'Testimonio', 70.
72 'Los que supieron de la poesía y de la Guerra', *Revista Tricontinental* 57 (1978): 77–102.
73 Mahler, *From the Tricontinental to the Global South*, 546.
74 See e. g. 'We Teach Life, Sir' by Rafeef Ziadah, available at https://www.youtube.com/watch?v=aKucPh9xHtM (accessed 20 January 2022). (See also Bernard, 'You Start Where You Are').
75 Metras Editorial Board, ' "Simply put, I call things as they are": Mohammed El-Kurd on Shifting the Western Discourse on Palestine', *Mondoweiss*, 9 September 2021. Available online: https://mondoweiss.net/2021/09/simply-put-i-call-things-as-they-are-mohammed-el-kurd-on-shifting-the-western-discourse-on-palestine/ (accessed 5 October 2021). Originally published in *Metras*, 16 July

(Arabic); Edward Said, 'Permission to Narrate', *Journal of Palestine Studies*, 13, 3 (1984): 27–48.

Bibliography

Abu Musa. 'Au Moyen Orient, la solution est militaire'. *Bulletin Tricontinental* 113 (1978): 17–21.
Abu Nidal, N. 'The Reason for Internationalist Solidarity with the Palestinian Revolution'. *Tricontinental Bulletin* 117 (1979: 3–5.
Abu-Remaileh, Refqa. 'Country of Words: Palestinian Literature in the Digital Age of the Refugee'. *Journal of Arabic Literature* 52, no. 1–2 (2021): 68–96.
Bernard, Anna. 'Cultural Activism as Resource: Pedagogies of Resistance and Solidarity'. *Journal of Postcolonial Writing* 53, no. 3 (2017): 367–79.
Bernard, Anna. 'They Are in the Right Because I Love Them': Literature and Palestine Solidarity in the 1980s', in *The Edinburgh Companion to the Postcolonial Middle East*, edited by Anna Ball and Karim Mattar, 275–92, Edinburgh: Edinburgh University Press, 2018.
Bernard, Anna. 'You Start Where You Are: Literary Spaces of Palestine Solidarity'. *Human Geography* 14, no. 3 (2021): 322–32.
Beverley, John. *Testimonio: On the Politics of Truth.* Minneapolis: University of Minnesota Press, 2004.
Camacho Padilla, Fernando, and Eugenia Palieraki. 'Hasta Siempre, OSPAAAL!' *NACLA Report on the Americas* 51, no. 4 (2019): 410–21.
Clayman, Steven, and John Heritage. *The News Interview: Journalists and Public Figures on the Air.* Cambridge: Cambridge University Press, 2009.
Davis, Angela. *An Autobiography.* New York: Random House, 1974. Kindle edition.
Denning, Michael. *The Cultural Front: The Laboring of American Culture in the Twentieth Century*, London: Verso, 1996.
Duchesne Winter, Juan. *La guerrilla narrada: Acción, acontecimiento, sujeto.* San Juan: Ediciones Callejón, 2010.
Faligot, Roger. *Tricontinentale. Quand Che Guevara, Ben Barki, Cabral, Castro et Hô Chi Minh préparent la revolution mondiale (1964–1968).* Paris: La Découverte, 2013.
Frick, Richard, and Ulises Estrada. *The Tricontinental Solidarity Poster.* Bern: Commedia- Verlag, 2003.
George, Nate. '"In the Hour of Arab Revolution": *Tricontinental* and the Question of Palestine'. 2014. Available online: https://scholarship.rice.edu/bitstream/handle/1911/81430/George_Project.pdf (accessed 28 September 2021).
George, Nate. 'Traveling Theorist: Mehdi Ben Barka and Morocco from Anti-Colonial Nationalism to the Tricontinental', in *The Arab Lefts: Histories and*

Legacies, 1950s–1970s, edited by Laure Guirguis. Edinburgh: Edinburgh University Press, 2020.

Getachew, Adom. *Worldmaking after Empire: The Rise and Fall of Self-Determination*. Princeton: Princeton University Press, 2019.

Gronbeck-Tedesco, John. *Cuba, the United States, and Cultures of the Transnational Left, 1930–1975*. Cambridge: Cambridge University Press, 2015.

Guevara, Ernesto. *Pasajes de la guerra revolucionaria*. Havana: Ediciones Unión, 1963.

Gugelberger, Georg M., ed. *The Real Thing: Testimonial Discourse and Latin America*. Durham: Duke University Press, 1996.

Hanna, Lani. 'Tricontinental's International Solidarity: Emotion in OSPAAAL as Tactic to Catalyze Support of Revolution'. *Radical History Review* 136 (2020): 169–84.

Harlow, Barbara. *Resistance Literature*. London: Methuen, 1987.

Kawar, Amal. *Daughters of Palestine: Leading Women of the Palestinian National Movement*. Albany, New York: SUNY Press, 1996.

Khalili, Laleh. *Heroes and Martyrs of Palestine: The Politics of National Commemoration*. Cambridge: Cambridge University Press, 2007.

Kyba, Taysir. 'La révolution palestinienne est indestructible'. *Bulletin Tricontinental* 113 (1978): 22–9.

Langer, Felicia. *With My Own Eyes: Israel and the Occupied Territories, 1967–1973*, London: Ithaca Press, [1974] 1975.

'Los que supieron de la poesía y de la Guerra'. *Revista Tricontinental* 57 (1978): 77–102.

Mahler, Anne Garland. *From the Tricontinental to the Global South: Race, Radicalism, and Transnational Solidarity*, Durham: Duke University Press, 2018. Kindle edition.

Matar, Dina. 'PLO Cultural Activism: Mediating Liberation Aesthetics in Revolutionary Contexts'. *Comparative Studies of South Asia, Africa and the Middle East* 38, no. 2 (2018): 354–64.

Metras Editorial Board. ' "Simply put, I call things as they are": Mohammed El-Kurd on Shifting the Western Discourse on Palestine', *Mondoweiss*, 9 September 2021. Available online: https://mondoweiss.net/2021/09/simply-put-i-call-thi ngs-as-they-are-mohammed-el-kurd-on-shifting-the-western-discourse-on-palest ine/ (accessed 5 October 2021). Originally published in *Metras*, 16 July (Arabic).

Nilsson, Nils Gunnar. 'The Origins of the Interview'. *Journalism Quarterly* 48, no. 4 (1971): 707–13.

Ortega, Osvaldo. 'From A Palestinian Ghetto' / 'Desde Un Ghetto Palestino'. *Tricontinental Bulletin* 62 (1971): 14–20.

Ortega, Osvaldo. 'Palestine: People's Revolution: Interview with Yasser Arafat'. *Tricontinental Bulletin* 66 (1972): 27–35.

'Periodicals in Review: Periodicals and Pamphlets Published by the Palestinian Commando Organizations'. *Journal of Palestine Studies* 1, no. 1 (1971): 136–51.

Poncé de Leon, Jennifer. *Another Aesthetics Is Possible: Arts of Rebellion in the Fourth World War*, Durham: Duke University Press, 2020.

Saab, Moises. 'Nobody Lives Twice to See the Glory'. *Tricontinental Bulletin* 117 (1979): 6–15.

Saab, Moises. 'Testimonio de una guerrillera: Palabras de ira y de dolor'. *Revista Tricontinental* 57 (1978): 69–75.

Said, Edward. 'Permission to Narrate'. *Journal of Palestine Studies* 13, no. 3 (1984): 27–48.

Saldaña-Portillo, María Josefina. *The Revolutionary Imagination in the Americas and the Age of Development.* Durham: Duke University Press, 2003.

Saney, Isaac. 'Dreaming Revolution: Tricontinentalism, Anti-Imperialism and Third World Rebellion', in *The Routledge Handbook of South-South Relations*, edited by Elena Fiddian-Qasmiyeh and Patricia Daley. Abingdon: Routledge, 2018.

Sayigh, Yezid. *Armed Struggle and the Search for State: The Palestinian National Movement, 1949–1993.* Oxford: Clarendon, 1997.

Stites Mor, Jessica. 'Rendering Armed Struggle: OSPAAAL, Cuban Poster Art, and South-South Solidarity at the United Nations'. *Jahrbuch für Geschichte Lateinamerikas / Anuario de Historia de América Latina* 56 (2019): 42–65.

Stites Mor, Jessica. *South-South Solidarity and the Latin American Left*, Madison, WI: University of Wisconsin Press, 2022.

'To the reader'. *Tricontinental Bulletin* 117 (1979): 2.

Yaqub, Nadia. *Palestinian Cinema in the Days of Revolution.* Austin: University of Texas Press, 2018.

Young, Robert. 'Disseminating the Tricontinental', in *The Routledge Handbook of the Global Sixties: Between Protest and Nation-Building*, edited by Chen Jian, Martin Klimke, Masha Qirasirova, Mary Nolan, Marlyn Young, and Joanna Waley-Cohen, 517–47. Abingdon: Routledge, 2018.

Young, Robert. *Postcolonialism: An Historical Introduction.* Oxford: Wiley-Blackwell, 2001.

9

Black Panther Party: 'Intercommunalism' and global Palestine

Elizabeth Bishop

As much as Alex Lubin's *Geographies of Liberation* (2014) reveals vital connections between African American political thought and our concept of 'global Palestine', Lubin uses a vocabulary from the African American freedom struggle for his own purposes. For him, 'intercommunalism' means an 'anti-imperialist, trans-community politics',[1] and as far as he's concerned, this is 'a political imaginary that recognized the shared conditions of racial capitalism and possibilities for anti-imperialism among local communities around the world'[2] inextricably linked with Egypt's capital, Cairo, where David Graham Du Bois (son of Shirley Graham Du Bois and stepson of W. E. B. Du Bois) lived among five million Cairenes. Lubin locates Du Bois's novel ... *And Bid Him Sing* (1975) 'within the historical context of Malcolm X's famous 1964 visit to Cairo and address to the Organization of African Unity, as well as the tumultuous history—especially for Egypt—of the Six Day War in June 1967'. According to Lubin, 'intercommunalism' was specific to Egypt's capital, which was where Du Bois contributed to 'a community of African American expats in Egypt, some of whom [were] former Nation of Islam members, while others [were] drawn to Egypt due to its location at the intersection of the Afro-Arab world'.[3]

At the centre of the era's global politics, the French writer Jean Genet placed puzzles. As Genet wrote, 'The page which was blank to begin with is now crossed from top to bottom with tiny black characters—letters, words, commas, exclamation marks—and it's because of them the page is said to be legible.' He acknowledges 'a kind of uneasiness, a feeling close to nausea, an irresolution stays my hand—these make me wonder: do these black marks add up to reality?'[4] Lubin's is one of several different narratives which account for Fatah's origins and serves as an example of one way in which black marks on a page can add up to some kind of reality. Mistakes, queries and puzzles are all helpful in thinking through the contingency of past events. How did the Black Panthers contribute to the puzzle of bilateral relations between the United States and the People's Republic of China (PRC) and to what extent was Peking's foreign policy with regard to the United States based on its prior support of the Palestinian national movement?

With a series of observations about a global communication network which grew in support of the Palestinian national struggle and the Black Panther Party (BPP), this chapter tests the 'intercommunalism' concept, querying Lubin's timeline and geography. Considering parallel histories for the largest party in the Palestine Liberation Organization (PLO) and the Black Panther movement, 'intercommunalism' is analyzed in a series of cities at the intersection of Afro-Arab worlds: Gaza; Monroe, North Carolina; New York; Havana; Algiers; and Oakland, California. Across these cities, 'global Palestine' as a political movement overlapped with critical developments in journalism's expansion from print into radio, as well as China's political emergence. The concept of 'intercommunalism', then, extends the Black Panthers' historical narrative by a decade, expanding it to include Bandung and the communist government in Beijing, as well as drawing attention to a praxis of international politics which the Black Panthers appear to have shared with 'global Palestine'.

Cairo

Lubin's PLO 'was officially formed ... at the Arab League Cairo Summit convened by Gamal Abdel Nasser [and] the PLO's initial statement articulated its liberation agenda, "the right of the Palestinian Arab people to its sacred homeland Palestine and affirming the inevitability of the battle to liberate the usurped part from it, and its determination to bring out its effective revolutionary entity and the mobilization of the capabilities and potentialities of its material, military, and spiritual forces".[5] For him, the PLO was founded in Cairo, during 1964. From *ḥarakat al-taḥrīr al-waṭanī al-Filasṭīnī*, meaning the 'Palestinian National Liberation Movement', the Palestinian students in Egypt crafted the reverse acronym Fatah, meaning 'conquest', 'opening' or 'victory'.[6]

While Lubin considers Fatah equivalent to PLO, others distinguish between the two. Illegal in most Arab states (including Egypt, which supported the PLO), Fatah's monthly journal *Filastinuna* (Our Palestine) was published in Beirut.[7] This secret military wing enjoyed its own diplomatic and public relations complementing the PLO's public activities.[8] If members of the Palestinian diaspora (including Yasser Arafat, then head of Cairo University's General Union of Palestinian Students; Salah Khalaf, Khalil al-Wazir at an equivalent student organization in Gaza and Khaled Yashruti in Beirut) are invested with agency, then the foundation for the PLO shifts back, five years before the Arab League's Cairo Summit, to 1959. Furthermore, while Egypt was a member of the League of Arab States, the history of Cairo's al-Azhar mosque, its recent union with Syria in a 'United Arab Republic', its border with Gaza and relations with other Nile jurisdictions distinguish Egypt from other members of the Arab League.

The present narrative builds 'several conflicting stories' about the geographic scope of the party behind the black-coated leopard, and these conflicting stories bring us to the imbricated geographies of Black Panthers and global Palestine. While it is generally accepted that the BPP was founded in Alabama's Lowndes County after the November 1966 US general election, Hasan Kwame Jeffries acknowledges 'several conflicting stories about the origins of the [BPP] symbol, including one that has [Student Nonviolent Coordinating Committee (SNCC)] activists choosing it because it reminded them of a fiercely determined local activist; in truth, the logo was the brainchild of SNCC field secretary Ruth Howard, who patterned it after the panther mascot of Clark College in Atlanta GA' [Georgia]. Jeffries credits a high rate of adult literacy, permitting the organization previously known as the Lowndes County Freedom Organization to select 'a snarling black panther as their ballot symbol to meet the state requirement that every political party have a logo'.[9] This chapter complements these contributions, by addressing connections between a 'global Palestine' and the BPP in a series of locations.

Gaza

Khalil al-Wazir was born in Ramla during 1935. Zionist militias forced him and his family to leave (in 1948); al-Wazir's family made their way to Ramallah, then Hebron and finally Gaza, where al-Wazir attended a United Nations Relief and Works Agency for Palestine Refugees in the Near East (UNRWA) school. The UN General Assembly passed Resolution 212 (III) and established the UN Relief for Palestine Refugees (UNRPR) for emergency relief on 19 November 1948. In collaboration with the UNRPR, the General Assembly adopted Resolution 194, creating the UN Conciliation Commission for Palestine (UNCCP), to facilitate 'repatriation, resettlement and economic and social rehabilitation of the refugees'. The UNCCP recommended creation of an 'agency designed to continue relief activities and initiate job-creation projects'; in support of these, the General Assembly adopted Resolution 302 (IV), which established UNWRA to succeed the UNRPR with a broader mandate. This direct connection with the global community of the UN brings the concept of 'intercommunalism' to Gaza. With an initial scope of its work to 'direct relief and works programs' to Palestine refugees, in order to 'prevent conditions of starvation and distress ... and to further conditions of peace and stability', Resolution 393 (V) (2 December 1950), expanded UNRWA's mandate to 'establish a reintegration fund which shall be utilized ... for the permanent re-establishment of refugees and their removal from relief'. A subsequent resolution allocated four times as much funding on reintegration, requesting UNRWA to otherwise continue providing programs for health care, education and general welfare (26 January 1952).

As Elaine Mokhtefi recalls, 'Every Algerian home equipped with a radio was tuned to Radio Tunis or Radio Cairo nightly for news.'[10] At this time, al-Wazir joined the local branch of the Muslim Brotherhood, serving as secretary for its student wing. When local leadership refused to endorse a proposal regarding armed struggle, al-Wazir left the Muslim Brotherhood and enrolled in Alexandria University's Department of Journalism. Until 1955, Gaza was home to Egyptian military intelligence's 'voice of Free Iraq', which beamed news embarrassing to the Hashemite monarchy into Iraq.[11] The choice to locate Egypt's clandestine radio transmitter outside Egypt's borders, in Gaza (yet under the military control of Egypt), brought Gaza-based journalists to the forefront of broadcasting innovation in the Arab world. While al-Wazir was a journalism student, Egypt's 'Free Officers' coup controlled all radio; devoting 'considerable financial resources to the expansion of public broadcasting', the 'Radio Cairo' to which Mokhtefi referred (in particular its 'Voice of the Arabs', *Sawt al-Arab*) first aired on 4 July 1953 as a half-hour radio program. Such early programming conveyed news from Gaza;[12] where the UN maintained a communications centre.[13] In addition to local news in local dialects, programming at *Sawt al-Arab* included Qur'anic recitation and recorded music.[14] A year after its initial broadcast, the service's transmission time tripled, making Egypt the dominant broadcaster in the Middle East as well as internationally.

Accessing international networks through the UN, and regional networks through Egyptian radio, a model for governance identified with 'global Palestine' came into being. During April 1955, the Bandung Conference initiated China's foray into Arab politics. At Bandung, the delegation representing the PRC voted for the return of the Palestine refugees to their homes.[15] Mokhtefi insists 'the Asian Communist countries—North Vietnam, North Korea, and China, an early purveyor of arms—recognized [Algeria's provisional government] *de jure* in its first month of existence',[16] and Chinese premier Zhou Enlai's statement at the closing session placed Beijing in 'full sympathy and support to the struggle of the people of Algeria, Morocco, and Tunisia for self-determination and independence'.[17] The same autumn, Egypt extended diplomatic recognition to the PRC (1956), expanding these international networks. A first delegation from Beijing arrived in Cairo,[18] where 'Palestinian Arabs were asking for a survey of their appalling conditions',[19] which Nasser blamed on 'the imperialists'.[20] Eventually, members received army cadet training from Eastern Bloc member nation-states including North Korea, Vietnam and Yugoslavia; for historian Tareq Ismael, though, China remained 'alone' in the significance it placed on Palestine's national liberation movement.[21] The concept of 'intercommunalism', then, unites the Palestinian national movement, Egypt's 'Free Officers' coup and the communist leaders of China through highly contingent moments of connection.

Monroe, North Carolina

Named for James Monroe, this city serves as the county seat of Union County, North Carolina, an hour's drive from the secondary city Charlotte. Senator from North Carolina (1973–2003) and chair of the Senate Foreign Relations Committee (1995–2001), Jesse Helms described this, the community into which he was born, as 'surrounded by farmland and with a population of about three thousand where "you knew just about everybody and just about everybody knew you"'.[22] Like Helms, Robert Williams was an American journalist, media executive and politician. As a child in Monroe, Williams listened to Cuban radio broadcasts in English.[23]

Before returning to Monroe, Williams was recruited into the Marine Corps with promises of college-level training in journalism.[24] On his return, Williams joined the local chapter of the National Association for the Advancement of Colored People (NAACP), a chapter which had not been very active and was declining in numbers; Williams registered a Black Armed Guard as the Monroe Chapter of the National Rifle Association. At the same time as Williams was emerging as a leader in Monroe, a first major expansion in Radio Beijing's target audiences coincided with the first large-scale Asian African or Afro-Asian Conference—the Bandung Conference (1955).[25] At Bandung, Hocine Aït Ahmed and Abdelkader Chanderli represented Algeria; these men travelled to

New York to develop connections with local journalists and serve as the Algerian national liberation front's (FLN's) representative at the UN General Assembly (news which was broadcast to North America in English).[26]

As head of Monroe's NAACP chapter, Williams defended two boys (aged seven and nine) placed indefinitely in a reform school (1958). Thanks to Williams's publicity campaign, press coverage of the 'Kissing Case' shamed responsible officials involved; so the governor of North Carolina eventually pardoned the boys, who were released. The same news networks circulated the case of the two boys and news of France's war in North Africa.[27] As local officials in Monroe felt the sting of international attention, Chanderli encouraged free elections in order to end France's war in North Africa.[28] Seeking political allies, Algeria's delegation provided reporters with finely grained analysis of local developments.[29] At the UN, Chanderli organized nine African states' representations seeking official action condemning torture at eighty-two prison camps and internment centres;[30] contributed to a panel discussion with faculty from Harvard's Government Department, Law School, and Boston University's School of African Studies;[31] and publicized open letters to the US president.[32] Through highly contingent moments of connection, the concept of 'intercommunalism' then unites those who followed news from Monroe, NC, with those who followed news of Algeria's national liberation struggle.

New York, New York

'Intercommunalism' encompassed the politically active communities in New York, where regularly African American newspapers turned to the 'Voice of the Arabs' for news.[33] Hitherto neglected is the question of the Cairo-based network's technical influence on Radio Havana, as well as dissemination of Monroe NC's news from Cuba. To do so, let us consider New York after David du Bois left the city. UNRWA maintained an office at 43rd Street and 1st Avenue. Nearby, at the Hotel Tudor (304 East 42nd St), the FLN's delegation produced forty-six brochures on different aspects of the struggle during 1960 alone.[34] Balancing the extraordinary efforts which characterized the Algerian delegation with the Arab League in Cairo (essentially, a provisional government), the Algerian delegation in New York extended its organizing efforts to encompass thirty-one African and Asian nations to call for debate on 'the right of Algeria's people to independence' among the General Assembly.[35]

During the Algerians' campaign,[36] the African American press reported on Prime Minister of Cuba Fidel Castro's visit to the UN General Assembly (as did

Radio Havana, Radio Moscow and Radio Beijing).[37] In New York, for the same purpose, President of the United Arab Republic Gamal Abdel Nasser visited Castro who experienced difficulties with Shelbourne Hotel management (303 Lexington Ave). In a highly publicized move to Harlem's Hotel Theresa (125th St and 7th Ave), the foreign delegations drew upon 'the friendship of the Afro-American community while using the opportunity to tell them [as the *New York Times* reported] "he understood United States Negroes were not as 'brainwashed' as whites by official propaganda about Cuba, and had more sympathy for his government, which he added, had wiped out race discrimination"'.[38]

Allegedly, Robert Williams approached Castro with a proposal for a radio program in New York,[39] bringing the international communications model we've already identified with 'global Palestine' to African American journalists during the late 1950s. After 'the New York summit', the 'Voice of the Arabs' radio service became a principal medium through which the Egyptian government spread information about Arab affairs to this new audience. The summer after Castro's meeting with Nasser in Harlem, the Federal Bureau of Investigation (FBI) claimed Williams was wanted on kidnapping charges, 'reported to be heavily armed and … "extremely dangerous"',[40] prompting Williams and his wife to leave for Cuba.[41]

Havana

Amal Jamal emphasizes the fluidity of the Palestinian national movement's political positions. For Jamal, 'the concept of *kiyan* ("entity") reveals [the movement's] pragmatic character; Fatah supported this policy from the end of the 1950s until 1964, but abandoned the idea when the [League of Arab States] established the PLO as the Palestinian entity' during 1964.[42] This marked the ascendance of a tendency 'to overstep the barrier of national unity in order to promote a certain political program, while retaining rhetoric about the importance of this unity for the achievement of the national goals'.[43] Havana is our next opportunity to query the concept of 'intercommunalism'. As commander-in-chief, Fidel Castro appointed an organizing commission for an Independent Front of Free Broadcasters (*Frente Independiente de Emisoras Libres, FIEL*; colloquially, 'Radio Mambi') to be based at radio station Cadena Oriental de Radio (18 January 1960). During the year leading up to Castro's UN visit during September 1960, the African American press reported boxer Joe Louis's visit to the capital of revolutionary Cuba.[44] 'Voice of the Arabs' had become known for targeting news to audiences (which included hiring local journalists, broadcasting in the vernacular and broadcasting local musical forms).[45] Similarly, Radio Havana's 'Cadena Latinoamericana' reported on violations of African American's human rights,[46] while in Spanish Radio Mambi called for a revolution in the United States,[47] and Radio Beijing reassured listeners that Cuba remained free of racial discrimination.[48]

'Radio Free Dixie' was an English-language radio program broadcast from Radio Havana after 1962; African American print media reported 'Radio Free Dixie' before the service had gone on the air.[49] With Beijing, Cairo and Prague, Williams's 'Dixie' service reported on Willie Mae Mallory (one of the 'Harlem Nine' who filed a suit against the New York City Board of Education seeking implementation of Brown v. Board), who was held in Cuyahoga County Jail in Cleveland, Ohio, on the same allegations regarding kidnapping that instigated Williams's flight.[50] Arguably, 'Radio Free Dixie' (which reached the continental United States at 11pm Eastern time) replicated elements of 'Voice of the Arabs' success, which were crucial to the 'global Palestine' model of communications and recognition.[51] While Radio Havana had neglected the Palestinian cause before Cuba's revolution, after the revolution government radio came to follow the sister service in Cairo closely. Before the Harlem meeting, the national radio services exchanged invitations for head of state visits;[52] from Cairo, Cuba's ministry of foreign affairs clarified the nation's policy on Congo's national liberation struggle;[53] and to Cairo, came Cuba's leading journalists.[54]

As Williams broadcast, 'Freedom is not an easy goal to accomplish; time alone is not an agent of liberation,'[55] and 'the Afro-Americans must wake up now, this is no time for foot dragging,'[56] referencing 'the case of Mrs Willa May Mallory, now fighting extradition from a Cleveland, Ohio jail to keep from being delivered up to lynch law justice in Monroe, North Carolina, the little Angola of the Americas'.[57] It was 'Radio Free Dixie' which reported on the Baptist Street church bombing, 15 September 1963, from Havana for audiences in the United States.[58] In addition to news, musical recordings were a key element of the program's success.[59] Broadcasting news from the African American community back to the United States, 'Radio Free Dixie' programming included jazz and blues recordings as well.[60]

Algiers, one

Radio Beijing had a strong record of support for Algeria's national liberation movement, which built on three key elements of 'global Palestine' (i.e. the UN, Egypt and the PRC).⁶¹ Mere weeks after the signature of the Evian Accords in March 1962, which recognized Algeria's independence, Radio Cairo's domestic service reported President Ahmed Ben Bella's statement, 'While today entering a new stage in their struggle against imperialism, [as a people we] are well aware the revolution continues and it is their duty to continue their struggle to shoulder their responsibilities in the Arab and African fields, *especially in the battle of Palestine*.'⁶² Helena Cobban reported, 'A heavyweight delegation of *al-Fateh* leaders including Arafat, al-Wazir, and Farouq Qaddumi at the invitation of Ben Balla, hero of the newly victorious FLN.'⁶³ When al-Wazir began his activities, there were only fourteen Palestinians in Algeria as teachers.⁶⁴ Cobban adds, 'The Algerian President did not want to act openly against the wishes of his more important ally, Egypt's President Nasser, who still feared concerted guerrilla action against Israel would provoke retaliations extremely damaging for Egypt and the other Arab states.'⁶⁵ For this reason, Ben Bella limited military assistance to Gaza; while visiting Egypt, he held 'the plots of colonialism and the ambition of the renegades of the Arab ranks' responsible for the current situation in Palestine.⁶⁶ Fatah was invited to attend Algeria's independence celebration, in the course of which Arafat obtained President Ben Bella's approval to establish an official presence. After its formal inauguration on 23 September 1963, al-Wazir left Beirut and *Filastinuna*'s editorship, to run the Palestine Office in Algiers (where he began recruiting 400 Palestinian teachers for Algeria's schools and 150 bursaries for Palestinian students in Algerian universities).⁶⁷

In independent Algeria, public broadcasting connected the local revolution, semantically, with 'independence, dignity, and Arabism ... an active and positive factor in the battle of liberating the Arab homeland, especially Palestine'.⁶⁸ Algiers' 'Palestine Office' was established in the midst of a major policy shift in support of the Palestinian national cause. Houari Boumedienne, as deputy premier, clarified the responsibility of the Zionist entity, 'established on the debris of Arab Palestine ... nothing more than a form of imperialism'.⁶⁹ Abdulaziz Bouteflika, as foreign minister, stated, 'The Palestine question should be solved objectively, and not through bargaining or dealings ..."we are preparing to train our Palestinian brothers in Algeria and to provide them with all necessary funds and arms to restore Palestine." '⁷⁰ In Algiers, Ernesto 'Che' Guevara met Fatah's staff (and pledged Cuba's support), the staff received an invitation to visit China for talks with the Afro-Asian Solidarity Committee (after which a Palestine Office opened in Beijing).⁷¹ From Algiers, al-Wazir also organized military training for 100 to 200 Palestinian volunteers in guerrilla warfare and edited periodicals including *Akhbar Filastin* (*News of Palestine*). Benoit Faucon observes, 'It is with Mao's China, the cooperation got the closest; in Algiers [during] 1962, Abu Jihad got in touch with the Chinese embassy and travelled to Beijing with Arafat; there, he met Prime Minister Chou En-Lai who told him "I hope I can live to see this revolution."' Soon, Chinese military academies accepted Palestinian guerrillas, and a plane loaded with Chinese weapons landed at Damascus airport.[72] From Radio Beijing's broadcasts, a foreign policy emerged supporting Algeria's goals.[73] From Algiers, al-Wazir was able to include himself in an official Algerian delegation to Beijing in early 1964.[74]

On the eve of the founding of a BPP in Oakland, the capital city of revolutionary Algeria was already an important element in the 'global Palestine' communications network. In Algiers, al-Wazir and Ahmad Shuqayri were introduced. A member of the Syrian delegation to the UN (1949–51), Shuqayri then served as assistant Secretary General for the Arab League (1950–6), and Saudi ambassador to the UN (1957–62), before the Arab League Summit in Cairo gave him a mandate to initiate establishing a Palestinian entity (1964). Perhaps alarmed by Fatah's ties with Algeria's provisional government's Minister of Information Mohammad Khider in Cairo, perhaps conscious of Shuqayri's ties with the 'useless and colonized' jurisdictions, authorities in Algiers ordered the movement to hand its 'Palestine Office' to Shuqayri.[75] Algeria became central to intercommunalism shortly before the Black Panthers emerged as a political organization.

Oakland, one

County seat of Alameda County, California, Oakland's population had declined to 367,548 by the 1960 census. While in a seven-part series in the *Oakland Tribune*, reporter Ernie Cox painted a picture of Merritt College as a 'racially tense' and 'chaotic' campus in the 'flatlands ghetto', where 'blackboard jungle bullies' were held captive by the Faculty Senate, it is worth considering Oakland as a comparable space of 'intercommunality'.[76] The term 'intercommunality', is associated with Huey Newton, who specified four phases for a 'Black Panther Society for Self Defense'; the four phases were Black nationalism, revolutionary socialism, internationalism and intercommunalism.[77] These four phases map against the Marxist concepts ('between the capitalist and the communist society lies the period of the revolutionary transformation of the one' in the 'Critique of the Gotha Program'), as well as Leninist vocabulary ('the latest phase of capitalism, i.e. imperialism' in *State and Revolution*), which – through Gaza, Havana and Algiers – Oakland connected with Beijing.

The Black Panthers followed Malcolm X's success in establishing a security team, 'Fruit of Islam' (as Kathleen Cleaver writes of them, 'To their credit, they had perfected a method of recruiting, organizing, and training [although little training was provided] that was unparalleled').[78] Faced with attempts on the part of the FBI to 'expose, disrupt, misdirect, discredit, or otherwise neutralize the activities of the Black nationalists',[79] Oakland's BPP provided an alternative to 'the perceived unwavering nonviolence of the civil rights movement'.[80] In the name of these Black Panthers, Bobby Seale (1936–) and Newton (1942– 89) adopted Malcolm X's slogan 'freedom by any means necessary' as their own. Few observers disagree with Matthew Holden Jr. rendering the issue of foreign technical assistance as secondary (questioning Black people's technical capabilities to wage a successful military campaign).[81] While Williams's 1962 book, *Negroes with Guns*, is credited for its influence on the strategic approach of Newton,[82] military struggle was problematic among US-based Panthers for ideological reasons. Jones adds, 'Holden is also correct twenty-five years later the Black people should be hesitant to depend on Third World countries for political support.'[83] In a number of ways, these debates within the African American community replicated discussions among proponents of the Palestinian national movement. Furthermore, Richard Masato Aoki emerged as a problematic character who appeared to unite the Panthers with a Third World Liberation Front in California. Aoki

> had been recruited as an informer in the late 1950s by Burney Threadgill, one of the agents who worked ... at the Bureau's Berkeley office; Threadgill approached Aoki after [a] FBI wiretap on the home phone of Saul and Billie Wachter, local members of the Communist Party, picked up his conversation with his fellow Berkeley High classmate Doug Wachter, who in a few years would be subpoenaed to testify before HUAC at San Francisco City Hall.

Threadgill reported that Aoki (at the Bureau's direction, under threat of harassment) began to attend meetings of the political organizations.[84]

Aoki's subsequent undercover activities 'followed a pattern similar to other FBI informers, in which they established credentials in a left wing organization and used them as entrée into other groups'.[85] Released from prison during December 1966, Eldridge Cleaver joined the Oakland-based Panthers as spokesperson (later serving the organization as Minister of Information). Newton's contributions from this period include a position paper, 'The Correct Handling of a Revolution' (1968).[86] In a 'Functional Definition of Politics' (1967), the equation 'politics is war without bloodshed/war is politics with bloodshed'[87] came to offer strategic direction for a party with more female members than male and active health care and school breakfast programs. Historian Curtis Austin adds, 'Acquiring guns turned out to be easy; the familiar story of Newton and Seale buying their first weapons with proceeds from peddling Mao Tse-Tung's *Little Red Book* to University of California Berkeley students, told by Seale in his autobiography and by dozens of other Panthers is interesting, even colorful, but not necessarily where their first guns came from.'[88]

At the time, Cuba was known for giving sanctuary to American radicals wanted for violent crimes;[89] and Cleaver was familiar with Williams's exile.[90] Newton ordered Cleaver to leave for Cuba, from where Williams continued to broadcast 'Radio Free Dixie';[91] from Williams's experience, Cleaver expected 'to be hailed and supported as the head of a liberation movement, with privileges like a radio program'.[92] In Havana, Cleaver lived under guard for seven months, waiting for authorities to fulfill promises to bring over his wife and other members of the Party.[93] The Reuters wire service exposed Eldridge Cleaver's presence in Havana.[94] Cleaver received an invitation from the Algerian Government to attend a Pan-African Cultural Festival being held in Algiers.[95] Lee Lockwood, who happened to be in Havana at the time, intercepted Kathleen in Paris and rerouted her from a Havana-bound flight to Algeria.[96]

Algiers, two

The imbrication of a 'global Palestine' was evident in this city which celebrated its independence by means of something very similar to 'intercommunalism'.[97] One example is the invitation of the BPP to the Pan-African Festival, which was scheduled to coincide with the Apollo II mission to the moon. Invited to the festival were hundreds of delegates from thirty-one independent African countries and 'representatives from six movements for … liberation, from Palestine, to Angola-Mozambique, and the Congo-Brazzaville'; as Mokhtefi recalled, 'Every country on the continent of Africa, as well as the African diaspora, was sending artists.'[98] President of an independent Algeria, Houari Boumediene opened the festival by saying, 'Culture is a weapon in our struggle for liberation.'[99]

Kathleen Cleaver recalled this as a counter-event, 'While America celebrated the triumph of science and technology the moon landing symbolized, African culture was the focus of celebration in Algeria … the colorful crowds thronged under the festive banners and lights spread above the streets of Algiers [representing] hundreds of nationalities and ethnic groups from the huge continent, but only a fragment of the staggering diversity of Africa's peoples and cultures';[100] at the Festival, Cleaver (as Minister of Information for the BPP told an American reporter, 'I don't see what benefit mankind will have from two astronauts landing on the moon while people are being murdered in Vietnam and suffering from hunger even in the United States.'[101] According to a subsequent issue of *The Black Panther*, Fatah held a press conference on the second day of the Cultural Festival. The BPP's newspaper reported,

> The room was filled to maximum capacity. Attending the press conference were: Algerian workers, students, and government officials, representatives from the African liberation movements (SWAPO, FRELIMO, MPLA, ZAFU), members of the domestic and foreign press, two embassy representatives from the Peoples Republic of China, and four members of the Black Panther Party Central Committee – Eldridge Cleaver, David Hilliard, Emory Douglas, and Kathleen Cleaver. (23 August 1969)

According to the same issue of *The Black Panther*, the hosting delegation was queried, 'What is your attitude toward the Black Panther Party?' Fatah reportedly answered, 'We support them. Absolutely! And revolutionaries all over the world. We see our battle as one and the same – a fight against imperialism and capitalism – and a fight can't be divided' (23 August 1969).

The Algerian national film board (*l'Office national pour le commerce et l'industrie cinématographique*, ONCIC) retained William Klein to film the Pan-African Cultural Festival. While in Algiers, Klein took the opportunity to film 'Eldridge Cleaver, Black Panther' for himself. Within Klein's film, an unidentified man (presumably Algerian, wearing a distinctive red shirt) asks Cleaver questions – initially through a female interpreter, then increasingly without interpretation. These begin with the fragmentary '*aussi quelles sont les moyens quelles les peoples … pour parvenir la lutte?*', which she translated as 'What are the means you are going to reach your [goals]?' Cleaver replies, 'Guns, guns.' Without requiring interpretation, the man in the red shirt understood the response in French, '*la force*', with the translator off camera providing further clarification, '*les fusils*'. The man in the red shirt countered both the translator and Cleaver, inquiring, '*les fusils, uniquement les fusils?*' Then, the female translator asked the BPP's Minister of Information, 'He asks if it's only guns.'

Seale is credited with instructing, 'To be a member of the Black Panther Party, every member must have two weapons and a thousand rounds of ammunition.'[102] In Klein's film, Cleaver interrupted the translator to answer, 'And bombs. Guns. Just like you had to do it here. The way you did it here, with understanding of the problem, with the ideology for liberation, and with fighting men who put the ideology into practice.' The man in the red shirt who asked the initial question responded by raising his eyebrows, '*c'est beau, que puis-je dire*' ('Great, what can I say?'), then he laughed as an expression of futility.

Remaining in Algiers after the Pan-African festival, Cleaver established an International Office and made contact with Fatah's delegation in Algiers. He announced that his movement backed the Palestinian liberation struggle because they both had a common enemy—'American capitalist imperialism', and he and Arafat embraced one another at the First International Conference of the Committees for Solidarity with the Palestinian People in December 1969, appearing to pledge mutual support.[103] Subsequently, the English-language newspaper *Fateh* quoted one of the Panthers as acknowledging 'a great similarity between the status of the Palestinian people and the status of the Blacks.'[104] As if responding to Cleaver's 'guns and bombs', journalist Richard Hottelet of CBS television reported that Palestinian spokesman 'Abu Bassam' in Algiers acknowledged 'combat training [for] a number of American Black Panthers'. From Algiers, CBS television reported Black Panthers training in North Vietnam, North Korea and Cuba 'in combat, sabotage, the use of time bombs, and other tactics'.[105] Cleaver himself later acknowledged, while in Algeria, that 'the FLN was … willing to enable the Black Panthers to display their presence publicly, which had symbolic importance in a nation where the United States government was denied formal representation … the military training facility Cleaver had envisioned never materialized'.[106]

Beijing

Peking's NCNA International Service in English reported, 'Leaders of the Black Panther Party of the United States Huey Newton, Elaine Brown, and Robert Bay arrived by air this afternoon for a friendly visit at the invitation of the Chinese People's Association for Friendship with Foreign Countries.'[107] The delegation was received during a grand reception in the Great Hall of the People, celebrating the twenty-second anniversary of the founding of the People's Republic.[108] A week later, the *Baltimore Afro-American* reported the same news, adding that the Panthers crossed from Hong Kong into the People's Republic, and providing details of Newton's ongoing trial in California on voluntary manslaughter charges.[109] Since 1955, Chou En-Lai had been responsible for the Question of Palestine, which (as historian Muhamad S. Olimat observes) 'was addressed as a human rights issue, rather than a question of self-determination … China maintained its fundamental perspective on the conflict, which were Arabs and Israelis could resolve the conflict, live in peace together if they were not deterred by external intervention'. It was Chou En-Lai's negotiations with Ahmad Shuqayri during which the PRC pledged and delivered light arms to the PLO.[110]

In addition to the Panther delegation, they included Pablo Y. Guzmán of the Young Lords, sixteen 'young people led by Mrs Carmelita Hinton' as well as American communists, diplomats, journalists, one of the founders of Physicians for Social Responsibility and members of the Southern Christian Leadership Conference.[111] With regard to the foreign policy of the PRC during this era, historians H. C. Ling and Yuan-li Wu pose two questions: 'First, how soon does Peking think an armed insurgency in the United States can be successful, and does Peking think the insurgency can succeed without Chinese aid? Or does Peking really believe an armed revolution in the United States can be sufficiently effective in helping Communist China without its being able to overthrow the U.S. government?'[112] The story of 'global Palestine' suggests the answer to the first was 'soon, and the insurgency would succeed without Chinese aid', and the answer to the second might be 'yes'.

Oakland, two

Abu Bassam's statement of Fatah's support for the Panthers' armed struggle found its way from CBS Television into local newspapers and the pages of campus newspapers, bringing this discussion of 'global Palestine', the Black Panthers and Newton's idea of 'intercommunalism' back to Oakland. Of Newton, Kathleen Cleaver writes, '[He] was uncomfortable with the military development of the [Black Panther Party].'[113] Fujino notes, 'Ground in dialectical materialism … Cleaver's emphasis on armed action, once useful to promote organized, disciplined self-defense, was by the early 1970s alienating the party from the majority of the Black community;… by contrast, Aoki's political analysis, promoting Newton's Marxist-influence theory of intercommunalism over what he saw as Cleaver's anachronism, complicated [a] well-trod dichotomy between community service and militaristic strategies.'[114] Even as the Oakland organization supported its members' Second Amendment rights, Oakland Panthers condemned terrorist actions of a so-called Symbionese Liberation Army in the United States, with both constituting a 'failure to adopt an offensive military strategy'.[115] A Fatah spokesperson in Amman told CBS Radio's Michael O. Sullivan, 'I firmly deny we are training Black Panthers in terrorism or sabotage.'[116]

Allegedly, Newton and Seale received an M-1 and a 9mm from Richard Aoki.[117] Similarly, news circulated regarding the Panthers' Chinese support, as when the *Stanford Daily* reported Newton, Elaine Brown and Robert Bay paid a 'recent visit to China', which 'enabled them to experience many specifics of socialist transformation and establish strong, direct ties between the Chinese people and the Black Panther Party'.[118] The International Office, which had promised the Black Panther organization so many opportunities, proved crucial to the unwinding of its leadership. Richard Aoki recalled, 'We called Eldridge in Algeria from my apartment. ... Alex [Haley] had the number and dialed. Let me tell you, we got through faster to Eldridge in Algeria from the phone in my Berkeley apartment than I would have calling my mama in Berkeley.'[119]

Conclusion

Lubin's concept of 'intercommunalism' serves as an example of one way that black marks on a page add up to some kind of reality. While more recently Michael R. Fischbach's *Black Power and Palestine* asks why Martin Luther King Jr., Malcolm X and Muhammad Ali acknowledged the justice underlying the Palestinian national cause,[120] Elaine Mokhtefi's memoir expresses her reservations (e.g that Malcolm X's 'Americanized brand of Islam' had limited knowledge of Algeria). This contribution argues that Fatah represented 'global Palestine' as a political movement at the same time as the growth of local radio in Egypt (then spread into regional use), overlapping critical developments in diplomacy in Algeria and coinciding with the PRC's political emergence.

Like the Palestinians' communication strategy, the BPP's communications strategy also grew from Egyptian military intelligence's use of clandestine radio stations and the resources of third parties. Providing local news in local dialects made Cuba (like Egypt) the 'dominant broadcaster in the Middle East and a major international broadcaster'.[121] When Chinese premier Zhou Enlai closed the Bandung conference in 'full sympathy and support to the struggle of the people of Algeria, Morocco, and Tunisia for self-determination and independence',[122] expanding international networks through diplomatic relations with Egypt, the BPP's reliance on Fatah's model gained a new dimension. Just as members of Fatah received army cadet training from Eastern Bloc member nation-states, including North Korea, Vietnam, and Yugoslavia, Algeria's national liberation movement helped the BPP seek similar training in the PRC. The concept of 'intercommunalism', then, unites the Palestinian national movement, Egypt's 'Free Officers' coup, the National Liberation Front in Algiers and China's communist leaders through highly contingent moments of connection.

Notes

1 Alex Lubin, *Geographies of Liberation: The Making of an Afro-Arab Political Imaginary* (Raleigh: University of North Carolina Press, 2014).
2 Ibid., 113.
3 Ibid., 111.
4 Jenet Gean, *Prisoner of Love* (New York: New York Review of Books, 2003), 5.
5 Lubin, *Geographies of Liberation*, 111.
6 Moshe Shemesh, *The Palestinian Entity 1959–1974: Arab Politics and the PLO* (London: Frank Cass, 1988), 34.
7 Helena Cobban, *The Palestinian Liberation Organisation: People, Power and Politics* (Cambridge: Cambridge University Press, 1984), 27.
8 John K. Cooley, *Green March Black September: The Story of the Palestinian Arabs* (London: Routledge, 2015), 95.
9 Hasan Kwame Jeffries, *Bloody Lowndes: Civil Rights and Black Power in Alabama's Black Belt* (New York: New York University Press, 2010), 152.
10 Elaine Mokhtefi, *Algiers, Third World Capital: Freedom Fighters, Revolutionaries, Black Panthers* (London: Verso, 2018), 60.
11 Reem Abou-El-Fadl, *Foreign Policy as Nation Making: Turkey and Egypt in the Cold War* (Cambridge: Cambridge University Press, 2019).
12 'Israel Panic-Stricken Over Canal Pact', *Voice of the Arabs*, 12 August 1954; 'Israeli Aggression Motivated by Fear', *Voice of the Arabs*, 17 August 1954; 'U.N. Warned to Act on Refugee Issue', *Voice of the Arabs*, 20 March 1955.
13 Avaialable online: https://www.unmultimedia.org/avlibrary/uploads/filefield_paths/015-171.pdf (accessed 2 March 2022).
14 Laura M. James, 'Whose Voice? Nasser, the Arabs, and "Sawt al-Arab" Radio', *Transnational Broadcasting Studies* 16 (2006). Available online: https://www.arabm

ediasociety.com/whose-voice-nasser-the-arabs-and-sawt-al-arab-radio/ (accessed 9 September 2022).
15 Cooley, *Green March Black September*, 173.
16 Mokhtefi, *Algiers*, 63.
17 Donovan C. Chau, *Exploiting Africa: The Influence of Maoist China in Algeria* (Annapolis: Naval Institute Press, 2014), 38.
18 'Nasser Receives Chinese … Delegation', Beijing, NCNA, 17 April 1957.
19 'Coverage of Cairo Conference Drops', *Communist China International Affairs*, 2 January 1958.
20 'Gheorghiu-Dej, Nasser Speeches', Beijing, NCNA, Radioteletype, 2 September 1960.
21 Tareq Y. Ismael, *International Relations of the Contemporary Middle East: A Study in World Politics* (Syracuse: Syracuse University Press, 1986), 210.
22 Jesse Helms, *Here's Where I Stand: A Memoir* (New York: Random House, 2005), 3.
23 'Radio Programs: WSB', *Atlanta Daily World*, 25 February 1938; 'Radio Programs: WGST', *Atlanta Daily World*, 15 November 1937; 'Radio Programs: WAGA', *Atlanta Daily World*, 15 July 1938; Joe Street, *The Culture War in the Civil Rights Movement* (Gainesville: University Press of Florida, 2017), 67.
24 Timothy Tyson, *Radio Free Dixie: Robert F. Williams and the Roots of Black Power* (Chapel Hill: University of North Carolina Press, 1999), 63.
25 Çağdaş Üngör, 'China Reaches Turkey? Radio Beijing's Turkish Language Broadcasts During the Cold War', *All Azimuth* 1, no. 2 (2012): 19–33.
26 'Political Resolution Adopted', Beijing, NCNA, 10 April 1955; 'Text of Written Speech', Beijing, NCNA, 19 April 1955; 'Bandung Conference Proceedings Reported', Beijing, NCNA, 20 April 1955.
27 James R. Lawson, 'Algiers Notes', *Atlanta Daily World*, 19 January 1955; 'Algeria Rebels Get Reprieves', *Chicago Defender*, 15 January 1959; Chas. P. Howard, Sr, 'Deadline Nears for France in Algeria', *Baltimore Afro-American*, 12 September 1959.
28 Rudolf V. Ganz, Jr, 'Algeria Before the United Nations Nationalists Ask U.N. For Wartime Aid', *Harvard Crimson*, 18 October 1960.
29 'French Army Invades Tunisia in Rebel Hunt', *Daily Boston Globe*, 28 May 1959.
30 'U.N. Action on Captives Urged', *New York Times*, 15 January 1960.
31 'Harvard Forum to Hear Algerian Rebel Speaker', *Christian Science Monitor*, 2 February 1960.
32 'Algerian Asks Ike to Halt Aid to France', *Chicago Daily Tribune*, 21 April 1960; 'Algerians in Bid to Eisenhower', *New York Times*, 10 September 1960.
33 'Survey Shows Anti-British Propaganda', *Atlanta Daily World*, 18 April 1956; 'Anti-West Forces Win in Jordan', *Chicago Defender*, 23 October 1956; Zaki Salama, 'All Africans, Arabs Too, Seek Inspiration in Cairo', *Chicago Defender*, 5 July 1958.
34 Martin Evans, *Algeria: France's Undeclared War* (Oxford: Oxford University Press, 2011).

35 Sam Pope Brewer, 'Algerian Liberty Is Pressed in U.N.', *New York Times*, 16 December, 1961.
36 'Castro to Attend U.N. Assembly', *Chicago Defender*, 14 September 1960; James L. Hicks, 'Our Achilles Heel', *New York Amsterdam News*, 24 September 1960; 'Nasser Visits Castro in Harlem', *Chicago Defender*, 26 September 1960.
37 'Fidel Finds Welcome with Harlem Negroes', Havana, *Radio Progreso*, 20 September 1960; 'Report on Khrushchev-Castro Meeting', Moscow *TASS*, Radioteletype, 20 September 1960; 'U.S. Plots Rude Treatment for Castro', Beijing, *NCNA*, Radioteletype, 20 September 1960.
38 'President Won't Meet Khrushchev Or Castro', *Atlanta Daily World*, 22 September 1960; 'Nasser Visits Castro In Harlem', *Chicago Defender*, 26 September 1960; 'Khrushchev, Castro Visit in Harlem: Greeting, Is Mixed for "K", Castro', *Baltimore Afro-American*, 1 October 1960; Federico Vélez, *Latin American Revolutionaries and the Arab World: From the Suez Canal to the Arab Spring* (Cambridge: Cambridge University Press, 2017), 39.
39 Tyson, *Radio Free Dixie*, 172.
40 'I Am Not Guilty—Robert Williams', *The Militant* 25, no. 34 (1961).
41 Ayesha Hardison, 'Stalled in the Movement; The Black Panther Party in Night Catches Us', in *The Strange Careers of the Jim Crow North: Segregation and Struggle outside of the South*, ed. Brian Purnell, Jeanne Theoharis, and Komozi Woodard (New York: New York University Press, 2020).
42 Amal Jamal, *The Palestinian National Movement: Politics of Contention, 1967–2005* (Bloomington: Indiana University Press, 2005), 18.
43 Ibid., 61.
44 'Castro, Joe Louis Confer in Havana', *Chicago Defender*, 4 January 1960.
45 David A. McDonald, *My Voice Is My Weapon: Music, Nationalism and the Poetics of Palestinian Resistance* (Durham: Duke University Press, 2013).
46 'FBI in Alleged Kidnapping of Negroes', Havana, *Cadena Latinoamericana*, 17 December 1959.
47 'Need for a U.S. Revolution Reiterated', Havana, *Radio Mambi*, 18 January 1960.
48 'Castro: No Racial Discrimination in Cuba', Beijing, *NCNA*, Radioteletype, 26 March 1960.
49 'Robert Williams Begins Cuban Radio Broadcasts', *Baltimore Afro-American*, 28 July 1962.
50 'Woman Prefers Ohio Jail to North Carolina Cell', *Atlanta Daily World*, 12 September 1962.
51 'Radio Free Dixie Broadcasts to USA', Havana, *Radio Progreso*, 13 October 1962; 'Robert Williams Commentary', Havana, *Radio Progreso*, 13 October 1962; 'No Freedom in U.S. For Afro-Americans', Havana, *Radio Progreso*, 17 October 1962.
52 'Nasser Visit', Havana, *COCQ*, 13 January 1960.

53 'Cuban Government Receives World Support', Havana, *Radio Progreso*, 15 July 1960.
54 'Pardo Llada, Kuchilan Arrive in Cairo', Havana, *Cadena Oriental de Radio*, 27 July 1960.
55 'Robert Williams Commentary', Havana, *Radio Progreso*, 13 October 1962.
56 'No Freedom in U.S. for Afro-Americans', Havana, *Radio Progreso*, 17 November 1962.
57 Williams Attacks Kennedy and Johnson', Havana, Radio Progreso, 19 January 1963.
58 Avaiable online: https://online.ucpress.edu/res/article/1/4/344/116086/The-Radio-Free-Dixie-Playlists (accessed 4 March 2022).
59 'Robt. Williams on 'Radio Free Dixie', *Baltimore Afro-American*, 20 October 1962.
60 Available online: https://deepblue.lib.umich.edu/handle/2027.42/122073 (accessed 4 March 2022).
61 'CPR Statement on Massacre of Algerians', Beijing, *NCNA*, Radioteletype, 14 December 1960; 'French Atrocities in Algeria Denounced', Beijing, *NCNA*, Radioteletype, 1 January 1961.
62 'Cairo Radio Carries Statement by Bella', *Cairo Domestic Service*, 4 April 1962.
63 Cobban, *Palestinian Liberation Organisation*, 31.
64 Shemesh, *The Palestinian Entity*, 139.
65 Ibid., 32.
66 'Algerian-UAR Communique of 8 May', *Algiers Domestic Service*, 8 May 1963.
67 Yezid Sayigh, *Armed Struggle and the Search for State: The Palestinian National Movement, 1949–1993* (Oxford: Oxford University Press, 1997), 102.
68 'Algerian-Syrian Joint Communique', *Algiers Domestic Service*, 23 June 1962.
69 'Boumedienne Reports on Army Moderation', *Voice of the Arab Nation* (Clandestine), 21 July 1963.
70 'Bouteflika Says Palestine Must be Liberated', *Baghdad Domestic Service*, 28 September 1963.
71 Sayigh, *Armed Struggle*, 103.
72 Benoit Faucon, *West Bankers* (Beirut: Masreq Publishers, 2010), 42.
73 'CPR *Charge d'Affaires* Arrives in Algiers', Beijing NCNA, 11 September 1962.
74 Faucon, *West Bankers*, 32.
75 Sayigh, *Armed Struggle*, 100; Hana Sleiman, 'The Paper Trail of a Liberation Movement', *Arab Studies Journal* 24, no. 1 (2016): 42–67.
76 Diane Carol Fujino, *Samurai among Panthers: Richard Aoki on Race, Resistance, and a Paradoxical Life* (Minneapolis: University of Minnesota Press, 2012), 381.
77 Judson L. Jeffries, *Huey P. Newton: The Radical Theorist* (Jackson: University of Mississippi Press, 2006), 77.
78 Kathleen Cleaver and George Katsiaficas, *Liberation, Imagination, and the Black Panther Party: A New Look at the Panthers and Their Legacy* (London: Routledge, 2014), 129.

79 Frederica Newton, *Revolutionary Suicide* (London: Penguin Classics, 2009), xii.
80 Curtis, *Up Against the Wall*, 46.
81 Charles E. Jones, 'Revisiting Black Nationalist Politics: An Assessment of Essay III: 'Politics as a Collective Psychiatry: A Critique of Withdrawal', in *The Politics of the Black Nation*, ed. Georgia Persons, 30–6 (London: Routledge, 2021).
82 Mina Khanlarzadeh, 'Dreaming Political Concepts in *Iran* and the United States: Huey Newton and Ali Shariati, through the Movie Black Panther', *Jadaliyya*, 17 October, (2018).
83 Persons, *Politics of the Black Nation*, 35.
84 Fujno, *Samurai among Panthers*, xxviii.
85 Seth Rosenfeld, *Subversives: The FBI's War on Student Radicals, and Reagan's Rise to Power* (London: Picador, 2012), 421.
86 Curtis, *Up Against the Wall*, 40.
87 Waldo E. Martin and Joshua Bloom, *Black against Empire: The History and Politics of the Black Panther Party* (Berkeley: University of California Press, 2016), 68.
88 Curtis, *Up Against the Wall*, 57.
89 Reese Erlich, Stephen Kinzer, *Dateline Havana: The Real Story of US Policy and the Future of Cuba* (London: Routledge, 2016).
90 Rafael Rojas, *Fighting over Fidel: The New York Intellectuals and the Cuban Revolution* (Princeton: Princeton University Press, 2015), 177.
91 Justin Gifford, *Revolution or Death: The Life of Eldridge Cleaver* (Chicago: Lawrence Hills Books, 2020).
92 Mokhtefi, *Algiers*, 170.
93 Jessie Carney Smith and Shirelle Phelps, *Notable Black American Women* (Ann Arbor: Gale Research, 1992), bk 2, 102.
94 Eldridge Cleaver, *Target Zero: A Life in Writing* (London: Macmillan, 2015), xx.
95 Richard M. Juang and Noelle Morrissette, *Africa and the Americas: Culture, Politics, and History* (Santa Barbara: ABC-CLIO, 2008), 173.
96 Kathleen Rout, *Eldridge Cleaver* (New York: Macmillan, 1991), 104.
97 P. Schoner, 'Palestine Guerillas vs Israeli Pigs', *Black Panther*, 4 January 1969.
98 Mokhtefi, *Algiers*, 179.
99 Keith Feldman, *Shadow over Palestine: The Imperial Life of Race in America* (Minneapolis: University of Minnesota Press, 2015), 83.
100 Kathleen Neal Cleaver, 'Back to Africa: The Evolution of the International Section of the Black Panther Party', in *The Black Panther Party (Reconsidered)*, ed. Charles E. Jones, 211–56 (Baltimore: Black Classics, 1998)
101 'Eldridge Warmly Received by the People of Algiers', *Black Panther*, 9 August 1969.
102 Aaron Dixon, *My People are Rising: Memoir of a Black Panther Party Captain* (Chicago: Haymarket Books, 2012), 81.
103 US Congress, *Black Panther Party* (1979), 4183.

104 Cooley, *Green March Black September*, 185
105 '*Fatah* Eyes Aid to Blacks', *Austin Statesman*, 3 February 1970.
106 Cleaver, 'Back to Africa', 231.
107 'Black Panther Leaders', Peking *NCNA International Service*, 29 September 1971.
108 'State Council, Friendship Group Reception for Foreign Friends', Peking *NCNA International Service*, 2 October 1971.
109 'Huey Newton Visits China', *Baltimore Afro-American*, 9 October 1971.
110 Muhamad S. Olimat, *China and the Middle East since World War II: A Bilateral Approach* (London: Rowman, 2019), 176.
111 'Chou En-Lai, Kuo Mo-Jo, Others Meet American Friends', Peking *NCNA International Service*, 6 October 1971.
112 H. C. Ling, Yuan-li Wu, *As Peking Sees Us: 'People's War' In the United States and Communist China's America Policy* (Palo Alto: Hoover Institution Press, 1969), 47.
113 Cleaver and Katsiaficas, *Liberation*, 8.
114 Ibid., 166.
115 Charles E. Jones and Judson L. Jeffires, ' "Don't Believe the Hype"; Debunking the Panther Mythology', in *The Black Panther Party (Reconsidered)*, ed. Charles Earl Jones, 40. Baltimore, MD: Black Classic, 1998.
116 'Train Black Panthers, Arab Commandos Say', *Los Angeles Times*, 1 February 1970.
117 Curtis, *Up Against the Wall*, 56.
118 Miriam Cherry, 'Peace and Freedom: Black Panthers Visit China', *Stanford Daily*, 25 October 1971.
119 Fujino, *Samurai among Panthers*, 158.
120 Michael R. Fischbach, *Black Power and Palestine: Transnational Countries of Color* (Palo Alto: Stanford University Press, 2020).
121 Zahlan, *Palestine and the Gulf States*, 45.
122 Chau, *Exploiting Africa*, 38.

Bibliography

Abou-El-Fadl, Reem. *Foreign Policy as Nation Making: Turkey and Egypt in the Cold War*. Cambridge: Cambridge University Press, 2019.

Berg, Jerome S. *On the Short Waves, 1923–1945: Broadcast Listening in the Pioneer Days of Radio*. Jefferson, NC: McFarland Publishing, 1999.

Chau, Donovan C. *Exploiting Africa: The Influence of Maoist China in Algeria*. Annapolis, MD: Naval Institute Press, 2014.

Cleaver, Eldridge. *Target Zero: A Life in Writing*. London: Macmillan, 2015.

Cleaver, Kathleen Neal. 'Back to Africa: The Evolution of the International Section of the Black Panther Party', in *The Black Panther Party (Reconsidered)*, edited by Charles E. Jones, 211–56. Baltimore, MD: Black Classic, 1998.

Cleaver, Kathleen, and George Katsiaficas. *Liberation, Imagination, and the Black Panther Party: A New Look at the Panthers and Their Legacy*. London: Routledge, 2014.

Cobban, Helena. *The Palestinian Liberation Organisation: People, Power and Politics*. Cambridge: Cambridge University Press, 1984.

Cooley, John K. *Green March Black September: The Story of the Palestinian Arabs*. London: Routledge, 2015.

Curtis, J. Austin. *Up Against the Wall: Violence in the Making and Unmaking of the Black Panther Party*. Fayetteville: University of Arkansas Press, 2006.

Dixon, Aaron. *My People are Rising: Memoir of a Black Panther Party Captain*. Chicago: Haymarket Books, 2012.

Erlich, Reese, Stephen Kinzer. *Dateline Havana: The Real Story of Us Policy and the Future of Cuba*. London: Routledge, 2016.

Evans, Martin. *Algeria: France's Undeclared War*. Oxford: Oxford University Press, 2012.

Faucon, Benoit. *West Bankers*. Beirut, Lebanon: Mashreq Publishing, 2010.

Feldman, Keith. *Shadow over Palestine: The Imperial Life of Race in America*. Minneapolis: University of Minnesota Press, 2015.

Fischbach, Michael R. *Black Power and Palestine: Transnational Countries of Color*. Palo Alto: Stanford University Press, 2020.

Fujino, Diane Carol. *Samurai among Panthers: Richard Aoki on Race, Resistance, and a Paradoxical Life*. Minneapolis: University of Minnesota, 2012.

Genet, Jean. *Prisoner of Love*. New York: New York Review of Books, 2013.

Gifford, Justin. *Revolution or Death: The Life of Eldridge Cleaver*. Chicago: Lawrence Hill Books, 2020.

Guridy, Frank. *Forging Diaspora: Afro-Cubans and African Americans in a World of Empire and Jim Crow*. Chapel Hill: The University of North Carolina Press, 2010.

Hardison, Ayesha. 'Stalled in the Movement; The Black Panther Party in Night Catches Us', in *The Strange Careers of the Jim Crow North: Segregation and Struggle outside of the South*, edited by Brian Purnell, Jeanne Theoharis, and Komozi Woodard, 307–32. New York: New York University Press, 2020.

Helms, Jesse. *Here's Where I Stand: A Memoir*. New York: Random House, 2005.

Ismael, Tareq Y. *International Relations of the Contemporary Middle East: A Study in World Politics*. Syracuse, NY: Syracuse University Press, 1986.

Jamal, Amal. *The Palestinian National Movement: Politics of Contention, 1967–2005*. Bloomington: Indiana University Press, 2005.

James, Laura M. 'Whose Voice? Nasser, the Arabs, and "Sawt al-Arab" Radio', *Transnational Broadcasting Studies* 16 (2006). Available online: https://www.arabmediasociety.com/whose-voice-nasser-the-arabs-and-sawt-al-arab-radio/ (accessed 9 September 2022).

Jeffries, Hasan Kwame. *Bloody Lowndes: Civil Rights and Black Power in Alabama's Black Belt*. New York: New York University Press, 2010.

Jeffries, Judson L. *Huey P. Newton: The Radical Theorist*. Jackson: University Press of Mississippi, 2006.

Jones, Charles E. 'Revisiting Black Nationalist Politics: An Assessment of Essay III: 'Politics As a Collective Psychiatry: A Critique of Withdrawal', in *The Politics of the Black Nation*, edited by Georgia Persons, 30–6. Abingdon, UK: Taylor & Francis, 2017.

Jones, Charles E., and Judson L. Jeffries. ' "Don't Believe the Hype"; Debunking the Panther Mythology', in *The Black Panther Party (Reconsidered)*, edited by Charles Earl Jones, 25–56. Baltimore, MD: Black Classic, 1998.

Juang, Richard M., and Noelle Morrissette. *Africa and the Americas: Culture, Politics, and History*. Santa Barbara, CA: ABC-CLIO, 2008.

Ling, H. C., and Yuan-li Wu. *As Peking Sees Us: 'People's War' in the United States and Communist China's America Policy*. Palo Alto: Hoover Institution Press, 1969.

Lubin, Alex. *Geographies of Liberation: The Making of an Afro-Arab Political Imaginary*. Raleigh: University of North Carolina Press, 2014.

Martin, Waldo E., and Joshua Bloom. *Black against Empire: The History and Politics of the Black Panther Party*. Berkeley: University of California Press, 2016.

McDonald, David A. *My Voice Is My Weapon: Music, Nationalism and the Poetics of Palestinian Resistance*. Durham, NC: Duke University Press, 2013.

Mokhtefi, Elaine. *Algiers, Third World Capital: Freedom Fighters, Revolutionaries, Black Panthers*. London: Verso, 2018, 60.

Newton, Frederica, and J. Herman Blake. *Revolutionary Suicide*. London: Penguin Classics, 2009.

Olimat, Muhamad S. *China and the Middle East since World War II: A Bilateral Approach*. London: Rowman, 2014.

Rojas, Rafael. *Fighting over Fidel: The New York Intellectuals and the Cuban Revolution*, trans. Carl Good. Princeton, NJ: Princeton University Press, 2015.

Rosenfeld, Seth. *Subversives: The FBI's War on Student Radicals, and Reagan's Rise to Power*. London: Picador, 2012.

Rout, Kathleen. *Eldridge Cleaver*. New York: Macmillan Publishing Company, 1991.

Sayigh, Yezid. *Armed Struggle and the Search for State: The National Movement, 1949–1993*. Oxford: Oxford University Press, 1997.

Shemesh, Moshe. *The Palestinian Entity 1959–1974: Arab Politics and the PLO*. London: Frank Cass, 1988.

Sleiman, Hana. 'The Paper Trail of a Liberation Movement'. *Arab Studies Journal* 24, no. 1 (Spring 2016): 42–67.

Smith, Jessie Carney, and Shirelle Phelps. *Notable Black American Women*. Ann Arbor, MI: Gale Research, 1992.

Street, Joe. *The Culture War in the Civil Rights Movement*. Gainesville: University Press of Florida, 2017.

Tyson, Timothy. *Radio Free Dixie: Robert F. Williams and the Roots of Black Power*. Chapel Hill: University of North Carolina Press, 1999.

Üngör, Çağdaş. 'China Reaches Turkey? Radio Beijing's Turkish Language Broadcasts during the Cold War'. *All Azimuth* 1, no. 2 (2012): 19–33.

Vélez, Federico. *Latin American Revolutionaries and the Arab World: From the Suez Canal to the Arab Spring*. Cambridge: Cambridge University Press, 2017.

Zahlan, Rosemarie Said. *Palestine and the Gulf States: The Presence at the Table*. London: Routledge, 2009.

Epilogue

By Mezna Qato

What to the world is Palestine? What in the world is Palestine?

We've learned that it is a cause, it is an inconvenience, it is guilt and redemption, it is survival and it is freedom. Palestine is adventure; Palestine is an escape hatch. Palestine is a mirror and reminder. It haunts political programmes and mocks ideological hypocrisies. It is a muse and an experiment. It produces rebellion, and it demands testimony, by voice, by pen, by brush and by frame.

Past is present as the writers before you reassembled an archive, closely read text and film and image, and sat in communion with sets of ideas and people. They conjured a Palestine of the postwar world back to us.

Palestine is an offering. It gave the young in Kuwait the ground upon which to imagine a better future for themselves and those around them. It charted the French migrant's demand to claim home. It was a sanctuary for the Black Panthers, and for Matzpen, it was an embrace.

Every offering to the cause of Palestine – Masao Adachi's films, OSPAAAL's posters, the various *Ittihad*s – was also at the same time an offering from Palestine back. It was a node in an internationalism wrought not only through current and network, ideas and figures but also in waves of everyday resolutions: to embrace that which was shunned and to struggle against imperial behemoths. And it is to do so together, with others, in literary productions, in organization of protest and conventions, at lecterns and in suites at the St. Georges.

Palestine arrests malaise, flooding artists and writers, filmmakers and poets, and organizers and ideologues, with urgency: we must remake this world ourselves.

Palestine is a commitment. But it isn't an easy one. It troubles. It makes for awkward silence. Lest we fall into nostalgia, these chapters map the whispers of discontent and raucous fractures before ideological conformities and filial binds crack open. And it is often Palestinians who prompt it. Always there to startle, and prod and question: where are you? Where were you? Join us!

So Paul Robeson's trepidations become the Black Panther Party's intercommunalism. Palestine as not irrelevant to the world but at the very core of making the world.

And as these essays show, it is solidarity that acts as the bulwark against devastation, dissolution and despair. To be able to tell one's story in the *Tricontinental*, and to know you will be read on your terms, remains as fresh a practice and politics now as it was then. Solidarity is, we learn, a commitment, first and above all, to listen. And through our bonds to each other, we pull away from the precipice of alienation and defeat and advance together towards a just world.

Index

Note: Figures are indicated by page number followed by "f". Endnotes are indicated by the page number followed by "n" and the endnote number e.g., 20 n.1 refers to endnote 1 on page 20.

Abdel Nasser, G. 39, 40, 170, 222, 227
Abourahme, N. 15
Abu Nidal. A. 197, 199, 204, 205
Acosta, T. 184
activism, processes of 4
Adachi, M. 9, 73
   films 7
   landscape theory 80
   life of 69
   with Palestinian revolution 76, 81–4
   solidarity, idea of 80
   and student activism 74–6
Afro-Asian Bandung Conference 72
A.K.A Serial Killer (film) 79, 80
al-Ayyubi, H. 126
al-Fattal, R. K. 52
Algeria 4, 6, 58, 59, 61, 72, 99, 123, 131, 150–2, 155, 170, 179, 184, 225, 229, 230, 232, 234, 236, 237
Algerian National Liberation Front (FLN) 170
Algerian national liberation movement (1954–62) 2
Algiers 4, 11, 12, 49, 58, 60, 61, 167, 170–2, 228–30, 232, 235–6
al-'Ikri, A. A. 118, 131
Ali, M. 50, 106, 236
al-Ittihad (The Union) (magazine) 117, 119, 122, 124–35
al-Ruba'i, A. 129
al-Thawra al-Filastiniyya (Palestinian revolution) 2
al-Wazir, K. 223, 224, 229, 230
American Crusade against Lynching (ACAL) 29, 33
American New Left 50–2
Amman 1, 2, 52–4, 59–61, 71, 127, 128, 147, 236

The Anabsis of May and Fusako Shigenobu, Masao Adachi and 27 Years without Images (film) 70, 76, 77
anticoloniality 174–82
anticolonial struggle 2–5, 8, 12, 15, 37, 119, 145, 148, 150, 152, 155, 156, 206
antiracist activism
   emergence of 10
   forms of 156
   'transcolonial' forms of 144
antiracist protest *147*
Aoki, R. M. 231, 236
Arab Information Office (AIO) 51, 52
Arab Israeli war (1967) 3, 143, 149, 151
Arab League 51, 105, 226, 233
Arab League Cairo Summit 222, 223, 226, 230
Arab nationalism
   anticolonial 124
   language of 124
   radicalization of 125
Arab Nationalist Movement (ANM) 172
Arab nation, issue of 122–8
Arafat, Y. 50, 52, 53, 109, 127, 172–4, 179, 182, 204–6, 210, 229, 230, 234
Argüello, P. 50, 57
armed struggle 42, 50, 79, 97, 98, 104, 123, 124, 129, 130, 168, 200, 201, 206, 209, 210, 212, 224, 235
Ashkenazim 97

Baltimore African-American, The (newspaper) 53
Bandung 39–41, 222, 225
Bandung conference (1955) 95, 198, 224, 225, 236
Bashkin, O. 9, 12
Baudelaire, E. 70

Beckett, S. 78
Beijing 222, 225, 228, 230, 234–5
Beirut 2, 4, 6, 9, 12, 50, 53, 54, 56, 58–61, 83, 119, 120, 126, 132, 172, 173, 175, 182, 201, 222, 229
  Israeli invasion of 69
Bernard, A. 11
Beur movement 150
Biladi (film) 146
Bishop, E. 11
Black civil rights 29, 32
Black Lives Matter 62
Black Panthers/Black Panther Party (BPP) 11, 12, 49, 51, 52, 57–9, 61, 103, 222, 223, 230–4, 236, 237
  and Matzpen 101–5
Black Power activists 8, 29, 49, 50
Black Power and Palestine (Fischbach) 236
Black September (1970) 1, 50, 55, 61, 72, 96, 105, 126, 144, 147–50, 149, 152 n.19, 172
  al-Ittihad issue 130
  violence of 207
Bober, A. 102, 107
Boutelle, P. 52
Bouziri, H. 152
Bouziri, S. 152
Boycott, Divestment and Sanction (BDS) movement 14, 15
Brecht, B. 78

Cairo 4, 49, 58, 61, 71, 119, 120, 122, 132, 170–2, 204, 221–3, 225, 226, 228–30
capitalism 3, 9, 30, 31, 93, 97, 99, 108, 125, 197, 202, 221
Carmichael, S. 49
Castro, F. 169–74, 179, 184, 226, 227
Central Intelligence Agency (CIA) 54–6, 59, 100
Chamberlin, P. T. 2, 3
Che Guevara, E. 4, 11, 170–2, 176, 179, 184, 206, 208, 229
China 37, 117, 224, 225, 229, 235
cinema/film
  Cannes Film Festival 75
  underground cinema 75
Cleaver, E. 49, 58–61, 231–5
Cleaver, K. 232–3
Cobban, H. 229
Cold War 3, 30, 75, 168, 187

colonialism 3, 27, 72, 95, 100, 122, 150, 155, 168, 229
  multidirectional critique of 148
Committee on New Alternatives in the Middle East (CONAME) 107
Committees in Support of the Palestinian Revolution (CSRP) 10, 144–153, 155, 156
communism 169
Communist Party of Czechoslovakia 38
Communist Party of the USA (CPUSA) 27, 30, 35–8, 40, 51
Compter sur ses propres forces (film) 146, *147*
conferences 1, 8, 49, 134
Cuba 11, 167, 169, 181, 182, 186–8, 200–3, 227–9, 232, 234, 236
  Palestinian relations 169–74
  Tricontinental Conference in 132
Cuban Communist Party 167, 175
Cuban foreign policy
  reorientations and repositionings of 187
  solidarity cause of 11

Daily Worker (*DW*) (newspaper) 27
Damascus 55, 60, 119, 127, 201, 230
Darwish, M. 187
Davis, A. 202
Davis, B. J. 40, 41
decolonisation
  influence of 29
  period of 3
  process of 39
Democratic Front for the Liberation of Palestine (DFLP) 97, 131, 173, 174, 186
Dhofar 117–20, 128–32, 135
Di-Capua, Y. 72, 75
diplomacy 2, 3, 11, 42, 236
Du Bois, W. E. B. 29, 37

Egypt 9, 31, 40–2, 58, 121, 131, 170, 171, 174, 179, 181, 184, 221–5, 229, 236
Egyptian Gazette (newspaper) 49
En-Lai, C. 230

Farjoun, E. 109
Fatah 2, 11, 12, 49–52, 57–61, 235–7
  centrality of 128
  emergence of 120

medical clinic 54
military camp 53
military operations 71
training camps 182
Faucon, B. 229
Featherstone, D. 13, 14
Fedaï :Journal de soutien a la r e volution palestinienne 148, 149, 153–6
fedayeen 125, 144–50
Federal Bureau of Investigation (FBI) 30, 55
Fifth Estate (newspaper) 53
Fischbach, M. R. 8, 29, 236
Fleischmann, E. 135
France 6, 10, 40, 41, 99, 100, 109, 110, 143–53, 155–7
friendship 106, 227

Gaza 4, 11, 12, 40, 49, 50, 96, 101, 170, 175, 184, 222–5, 229, 230
Gaza Strip 40, 101
General Union of Palestinian Students (GUPS) 53, 121, 123, 124, 127, 128, 143, 153 n.19
    Amman conference 1, 53, 54, 61, 127
Genet, J. 10
Geographies of Liberation (Lubin) 221
George, N. 199
Getino, O. 78
Ghubeish, R. 124, 128
global sixties 4, 5, 12
Godard, J.-L. 10, 72, 73, 144
Gorin, J.-P. 72
Gramsci, A. 14
Great Speckled Bird, The (newspaper) 53
Guerrero, G. 55

Hajjat, A. 150
Halevi, I. 99–101, 109, 110, 111
Hameed, K. 10
Hanegbi, H. 98–100, 102, 109
Harap, L. 38
Harootunian, H. 77
Harrison, O. C. 10
Havana 12, 72, 168, 170, 171, 173, 174, 181, 198, 208, 222, 227–8, 230, 232
Hawatmeh, N. 97, 131, 173, 186
Hebrew 32
Here and Elsewhere (Ici et Ailleurs) (film) 73

Hernández, M. 175
Hitler, A. 33, 39
Hô Chi Minh 179
Holocaust 35, 36, 143
House Un-American Activities Committee (HUAC) 28

imperialism 3, 30, 31, 36, 40, 57, 72, 73, 94, 125, 127, 130, 167, 171, 173, 174, 197, 229
    Lenin's definition of 202
    Tricontinental's definition of 202
Inner City Voice (newspaper) 53
intercommunalism, concept of 12, 221, 222, 224–7, 230, 232, 235–7
international solidarity, *see also* solidarity activism 209
    era of 14
    history of 199, 214 n.14
    movements of 199
    practice of 13
    strengths of 14
Intifada 109, 144, 156–7
Iraq 100, 105, 123, 131, 179, 184
Ismael, T. 124
Israel 6, 8, 9, 14, 35, 50, 54, 55, 62, 81, 175, 184–7, 204, 229
    Black struggle 29
    diplomatic recognition of 36
    establishment of 28
    Jewish ethnicity 93
Israeli Black Panthers Movement 101
Israeli Socialist Organization (ISO) 94

Jabra, N. 95, 97
James, C. L. R. 37
Japan 6, 77, 80, 83
    student activism in 74–6
Japanese Red Army (JRA) 73, 76, 77, 81, 83
Jericho (film) 31
Jerusalem 33, 34, 98, 101–3
Jewish Anti-Fascist Committee 32
Jewish Life (magazine) 38
Jews 31–7, 39, 41, 51, 62, 94–101, 104, 108, 169
    history of 106
Jibril, A. 54

Jordan 1, 50, 52–8, 60, 61, 69, 72, 75, 76, 83, 95, 96, 121, 123, 127, 130, 143, 172, 184, 204, 207
journalism 109, 199, 209, 224

Kanafani, G. 76, 78, 172
Khaled, L. 50, 57, 76, 78, 96, 210, 223
Khalili, L. 206
Khamsin (magazine) 96, 105, 106
Klein, W. 233
Kohso, S. 77
Kuwait 6, 10
  British colonial authorities in 119
  institutions in 117
  NUKS fifth annual conference in *123*
  political movements in 117
  social movements of 120
  student movement in 117
Kuwait Airways 131
Kuwait Oil Company 120
Kuwait Red Crescent 121

Leary, T. 9, 50, 57–61
Lebanese Civil War (1975–90) 172
Lebanon 2, 9, 52–5, 58, 60, 61, 69, 70, 72, 75, 76, 79, 81, 83, 105, 117, 131, 150, 169, 172, 174, 179, 181, 182, 184, 187, 204, 206
  invasion of 2, 172, 192 n.48
  refugee camps in 50
  visions of 135
Les Temps Modernes (magazine) 99
Lev, T. 93
Liberated Guardian (newspaper) 53, 54
Liberation News Service (newspaper) 53, 54, 99
Liberation of Palestine-General Command (PFLP-GC) 54, 55
literature 3, 7, 11, 118, 199
Little Red Book (Tse-Tung) 232
Lubin, A. 221, 222, 236

Maasri, Z. 71, 119, 135, 175
Machover, M. 94, 95, 97, 104
Mahler, A. G. 201
Maira, S. 14
Malcolm X 49, 99, 101, 221, 231, 236
Maoism 96, 148
Maoist 129, 146, 149

Marxism-Leninism 207
Matar, D. 3, 201
Matsuda, M. 79
Mattison, G. 55
Matzpen
  assessment of 95
  founders 94
  history 93
  members of 95
  and Panthers 101–5
Medvecky, N. 53–5
Meir, G. 101, 107
Metro, The (newspaper) 53
Middle East Research and Information Project (MERIP) 55, 62
Miéville, A.-M. 73
Mizrahi 93
  Arab Jew 97–101
  nativist 97–101
  question 105–8
Mizrahim joined the Israeli Communist Party (MAKI) 94, 95
Mokhtefi, E. 224, 232, 236
Monroe, North Carolina 222, 225–6, 228
Monthly Review (magazine) 94
Morgen Freiheit (newspaper) 36
Mor, J. S. 11
Movement of Arab Nationalists (MAN) 121
Muhammad Speaks (newspaper) 53
munadil 118
Munich Olympics 73

Nablusi, R. 207–11
Nabulsi, K. 4
Nakba (1947/8) 2, 71, 119, 125
National Association for the Advancement of Colored People (NAACP) 225, 226
national liberation 2, 209
  anticolonial movements 2
  politics 14
  prioritization of 181
National Union of Kuwaiti Students (NUKS) 117, 118
  fifth annual conference *123*
  liberatory framework 128
  radical students 119–22
  regional connections 119–22

Negroes with Guns (Williams) 231
Neoconservative Movement 62
Newton, H. P. 57, 101, 230–2, 234, 236
New York 27, 31, 36, 51, 52, 57, 61, 225–8
New York Times, The (newspaper) 52
Nicola, J. 97
Non-Aligned Movement (NAM) 72, 172, 173, 179, 187

Oakland 12, 56, 101, 222, 230–2, 235–6
Organization of Lebanese Socialists (*Munadhamma al-Ishtirakiyyin al-Lubnaniyyin*) 126
Organization of Solidarity with the Peoples of Asia, Africa, and Latin America (OSPAAAL) 11, 198, 201
  cultural production 174–82
  visual materials 169
Orr, A. 94, 95, 97, 104
Ortega, O. 200, 203, 206, 207
Oslo Accords 69, 109
The Other Israel: Th e Radical Case against Zionism (Bober) 107

Padilla, F. C. 11
Palestine 32–5, 118–21, 167, 173, 199, 212
  anticoloniality 174–82
  Arab nation, issue of 122–8
  culture 77–9
  and Dhofar revolutions 128–32
  fedayeen 146–8
  and immigrant cause 148–56
  politics 77–9
  question 35–8
  solidarity 13–16
  visibility of 174–82
  Zionist colonization 95
Palestine: Crisis and Liberation (Rostgaard) 175, *180*
Palestine Film Unit (PFU) 71–2
Palestine Liberation Organization (PLO) 1, 14, 39, 69, 83, 95, 96, 101, 105, 110, 120, 127, 128, 170–4, 181, 186, 188, 201, 204, 207, 222, 235
  guerrilla organizations 52
Palestine vaincra (film) 146
Palestinian Cinema Institute (PCI) 71
Palestinian guerrilla groups 51–2, 54, 57, 61, 175, 230

Palestinian refugee camps 49, 53, 56, 75, 101
Paris 4, 12, 75, 81, 95, 144, 152, 153, 156, 170, 232
People's Voice (newspaper)
Philadelphia Free Press, The (newspaper) 54
photography 10, 71, 109, 168, 186
Pilavsky, O. 94
pink films, genre of 74
Polley, G. 8
Popular Democratic Front for the Liberation of Palestine (PDFLP) 56, 57, 61, 131
Popular Front for the Liberation of Palestine (PFLP) 51, 57, 73, 76, 83, 127, 131, 173, 174, 201, 204, 206, 210
Popular Revolutionary Movement (*al-Haraka al-Thawriyya al-Sha'biyya*) 122
posters 71, 102, 149, 174, 175, 177, 179, 181, 198, 202
poverty 37
PRC's political emergence 236
Prisoner/Terrorist (film) 83
Progressive Labor Party 51
protest 54, 103, 146
  antiracist 147

Qato, M. 7

racism 30, 33, 37, 108, 147–51, 153, 155–7, 181
Rashoud, T. 119
Rat:Subterranean News (newspaper) 53
Red Army/PFLP: Declaration of World War (film) 69–70, 73, 76, 77–80, 83
Red Cross campaign 207
refugee camps 1, 4, 81, 83
  in Jordan 69
  in southern Lebanon 50
  women militants from 134
revolutionary participation, concepts of 70
Rice Bowl (film) 74
Robeson, P. 8, 27–30, 29–42, 32–42
Rostgaard, A. *180*
Ryan, P. J. A. 57

Saab, M. 200, 203, 205, 207–11

Said, E. 76, 96, 212
Samour, N. 40
Sandinista National Liberation Front (FSLN) 57
Saqfalhait, D. 9
Sartre, P. 99
Sayegh, F. 51, 52
Schleifer, M. 54, 56, 60
Seale, B. 57, 231, 232, 234, 236
Second World War 27, 32, 36
Sephardim 97
settler colonialism 27
Shegenobu, F. 76
Shemesh, K 103–5, 109
Shenhav, Y. 93
Shuqayri, A. 49, 101, 170, 230, 235
Six Day War (1967) 42, 167, 171, 221
Sleiman, H. 6, 82
Socialist Workers Party (SWP) 51–3
Solanas, F. 78
solidarity 31, 33, 39
  with African Muslims 99
  American New Left and 50–2
  Arab Jewish 93
  Black Power 61
  coalitions of 42
  concept of 83
  idea of 80
  life in 29–31
  Palestinian Mizrahi, vision of 105
  presence, relationships and images of 182–7
  sign of 41
  transcolonial 143–5
  typologies of 7–13
Soviet Union 30, 36, 38, 39, 41, 83, 108, 176
Spanish Civil War 28, 33
Stanford Daily (newspaper) 236
Student Nonviolent Coordinating Committee (SNCC) 49, 51, 52, 223
students
  activism 74–6
  activists 2
  conference 125
  groups in Egypt 9
  movements 72
  organizations 121
  role of 118
  union 123
Students for a Democratic Society (SDS) 51
Suez Crisis (1956) 4, 8, 38–41
Sun-Dance (newspaper) 53
Syria 49, 50, 52–5, 59, 60, 76, 105, 131, 150, 172, 179, 181, 182, 184, 223

Takriti, A. R. 15, 130
Third Worldism 15, 157 n.5
Townes, J. 54
training
  Black Panthers 236
  delegations 9
  diplomatic missions 9
  Fatah camps 182
  guerrilla camp 174
  programs 9
  refugee camp 56
transcolonial solidarity 143–5
transnationalism 3, 4
travel 7, 9, 30, 35, 41, 53, 54, 60, 62, 83, 172
Tricontinental (magazine) 11, 168, 173, 175, 177–9, 181, 182–6, 198, 200–7, 209–12
Tricontinental Conference (1966) 72, 132, 168, 171, 198
tricontinentalism 12
Tritsibidas, Y. 146
Trotskyism 96
Tse-Tung, M. 232
Tu'ama, K. 96

UN Conciliation Commission for Palestine (UNCCP) 223
United Kingdom (UK) 120
United Nations (UN) 27, 28, 39, 130, 167, 223
United States (US) 3, 4, 6, 8, 29–32, 35, 37, 39, 49–58, 60, 74, 83, 99, 101, 102, 106, 107, 120, 124, 127, 129, 168, 175, 176, 179, 188, 202, 203, 222, 227, 228, 233–6
United Nations Relief and Works Agency for Palestine Refugees in the Near East (UNRWA), 223, 224, 226

United Nations Relief for Palestine
  Refugees (UNRPR) 223, 224
Until Victory (film) 72

Vertov, D. 72
Vietnam 4, 62, 72, 76, 96, 100, 117, 126,
  129, 132, 179, 186, 198, 233, 237
Vietnam War 62, 76, 106

Wakamatsu, K. 73, 76
Weather Underground Organization
  (WUO) 58
West Bank 50, 94, 96, 105, 121
Williams, R. 225, 227, 228, 231
Winter, J. D. 208
With My Own Eyes (Nablusi) 209
women
  movements 135
  right to vote 134
  role of 13
  social position 134
  unions of 2
  with weapons 182
Workers World Party 51
World Zionist Organization 32

Yaqub, N. 70, 73, 80
Young, R. 198
YouTube 146, 147, 212

Zionism 27, 28, 32, 35, 94, 96, 98, 106,
  125, 173, 197
  acceptance of 36
  Black support of 33
  historical analysis of 94
  labour 99
  victory of 34
Zionist colonization 95, 106
Zionist movement 27, 31, 34–6
Zog Nit Kaynmal (song) 39

www.ingramcontent.com/pod-product-compliance
Lightning Source LLC
Chambersburg PA
CBHW062129300426
44115CB00012BA/1865